W9-COJ-034

CHRISTIAN
WOMEN
AT WORK

CHRISTIAN
WOMEN
AT WORK

Patricia A. Ward and Martha G. Stout

ZONDERVAN
PUBLISHING HOUSE
OF THE ZONDERVAN CORPORATION
GRAND RAPIDS, MICHIGAN 49506

331.4
W 262

192386

CHRISTIAN WOMEN AT WORK
Copyright © 1981 by The Zondervan Corporation
Grand Rapids, Michigan

This printing, October 1981

Library of Congress Cataloging in Publication Data

Ward, Patricia A.
  Christian women at work.

  Includes bibliographical references.
  1. Women—Employment—United States. 2. Women—Conduct of life. 3. Women—
Religious life. 4. Women in church work—United States. I. Stout, Martha, II. Title.
HD6095.W197   331.4'0973   81-13021
ISBN 0-310-43700-8   AACR2

Unless indicated otherwise, all Scripture is from the New International Version, copyright © 1978 by New York International Bible Society.

All rights reserved. No part of this publication may be reproduced, stored in an electronic system, or transmitted in any form or by any means, electronic, mechanical, photocopy, recording or otherwise, without the prior permission of the copyright owner. Brief quotations may be used in literary reviews.

Designed and edited by Judith E. Markham

Printed in the United States of America

For

Alice Fowler Girling

and

Edwinna Wilson Ward (1907–1963)

CONTENTS

ACKNOWLEDGMENTS

This book depends on interviews we conducted with women in various parts of the United States. We thank them for their willingness to share their lives and for their permission to use the recorded material from those interviews. The actual names of people and places have been used, except for a few instances where first names have been changed. Transcribed quotations have been edited slightly for purposes of readability. The information given in this book about women and their work reflects their situations at the time they were interviewed; in most cases, we have not indicated subsequent changes in their lives. We have tried to be as accurate as possible in our reporting; any errors or misrepresentations are accidental, and we take full responsibility for them.

In our travels a number of people assisted by housing and transporting us and by offering Christian hospitality. The project could not have been completed without the help of Evelyn Bence, Ruth and James Cameron, the Covenant Community (Evanston, Illinois), Alice and Gordon Girling, June Hagen, Barbara Howard, Diane Jepsen, Martha and Robert Jones, Sara Ann and Frank Kocher, Patricia Mortenson, Nita and James Newing, Peggie and Clark Robinson, Ruth Schmidt, Marcia and Richard Schoolmaster, Noel Sipple, Helen and Harold Stout, and Charles Ward.

We wish to acknowledge with thanks the support and prayers of many friends in Grove City and State College, Pennsylvania, and the encouragement of Judy Markham, our editor. We are also indebted to Mary Jane Knudson, Director of Cooperative Education and Career Development at Gordon College, for her sensitive and knowledgeable critique of our manuscript, and to Barbara and Wayne Wallace for their expert typing and proofreading.

Above all, we owe much to Richard Stout for his thoughtfulness and love toward us both during the long months of travel and writing.

INTRODUCTION

In the 1970s more women began to work or reentered the work force than at any other time during this century. Great numbers of Christian women were among them. If the church will listen, their voices can be heard: shouting their exhilaration and excitement at the possibilities offered by their new roles within society, calling for role models as they forge new ways of life, questioning and doubting as they try to find their way as Christians in a changing world, seeking emotional support as they struggle as wage earners for their families.

The changes of the 1970s were so rapid that the Women's Bureau of the Federal Department of Labor published a fact-sheet entitled "The Myth and the Reality." The first "myth" cited was the adage "a woman's place is in the home." This was contradicted by the reality that the majority of adult women were working outside the home and that nine out of ten women would work outside the home at some time in their lives. Even women with small children were no longer staying at home. By 1978, 5.8 million working women had children under the age of six.

The Urban Institute calls the entry of so many women into the labor market "a revolution." The forecast is that by 1990, 55 percent of American women over the age of sixteen will be working, including half of the mothers of young children.

The myth of the ideal woman (and of the ideal Christian woman)—the full-time housewife and mother—never was universal, even among Christians. Today the myth lies shattered, for 51 percent of all women over sixteen (about forty-three million) were in the work force by mid-1979, and a great many Christian women were among them.

In this book we portray the experiences of about one hundred Christian women and examine the issues which concern them. Their stories are also the stories of all Christian women, and their voices are asking the same questions and expressing the same feelings as most of their Christian sisters. We hope the church will truly listen, understand, and act to meet the needs of working women. A glimpse of the varied roles of contemporary Christian women highlights the issues which we will examine in more detail in subsequent chapters.

First, there are an increasing number of homemakers who are taking part-time jobs in order to help their families survive economically in a period of severe inflation. Joanne is in her thirties and has returned to work after ten years because her family needs the income. She was trained as a legal stenographer, but now works in a pizza parlor. One day she happened to see a help-wanted sign in the shop window. She walked in and asked if she could work during the lunch hour so that she could be at home when her son returned from school. "I had to find something between 8:30 and 2:30 when my son is at school. I go in at 8:30 and prepare the pizza sauces." In her geographical area where the cost of living is among the highest in the country, many of Joanne's friends have returned to work part-time as cafeteria helpers or teachers' aides in order to help make ends meet. "We had a wonderful Bible study, but it had to break up mainly because a lot of the girls got jobs. We had about thirty to forty in the group, and a majority of them have gone out to work in the last year or two."

Many women are employed because they are single parents; they, too, are often limited as to the type of job they can take. Leah is divorced, in her early thirties, and has two children in school. She works as a secretary. "I realize that I'm in the pink-collar ghetto. I'm not always content with that, but with the training and skills that I have I'm going to have to be content with that for a while. There is a pink-collar ghetto. We're secretaries, we're waitresses, we're teachers. We're janitors, beauticians. And all of those jobs pay less than semiskilled or unskilled jobs for men. That never really bothered me until I became head of a household."

Ruth, on the other hand, is a single "career woman" by choice. She has a satisfying, well-paid position as an educational administrator—but little free time. Of her relatively new job at a small women's college she says, "I believe this is where God called me to be." Yet she has a work load she calls "crushing." "I don't see how it would be possible to live the life I live and be responsible to a roommate, a mate, or anyone else really close in my life. We don't organize work in the United States the way we ought to. I really feel concerned about that for both men and women, no matter what their marital status. We must somehow learn to provide work in this country so that there are jobs in which you are considered a serious professional but which don't consume your whole life."

Denise is also single and is embarked on what appears to be an exciting career in a large city, but she has ambivalent feelings about her professional success. She has also found two sets of standards for single and married women. "Occasionally I get fits of panic when I just want to quit. I went to my parents' home recently and told them I was going to resign. They had a fit! 'What are you going to do? . . . You can't just quit without doing something else!' I'm twenty-seven and single, and I'm supposed to be climbing. My older sister, who is married and has children, went out to get a job, and my father's lecture to her was, 'What do you want to get a job for?' At the time I wanted to be a clerk in a bookstore so I could write. My father seemed to be telling me, 'You can't be a clerk in a bookstore. You'll be bored. It won't be fulfilling. You'll be doing nothing with your life.' My sister who wanted to get a job, any job, was told exactly the opposite."

A minority of women—those with exceptional energy—are able to combine marriage, family, and a career. Rosalie is in charge of the interior design department for several stores within a nationally known retailing concern. Her day begins at 5:30 in the morning so that she can spend time with her two children before they go to school at 7:00. She is in her office by 7:30. Of her job she says, "I love it. Within a year I hope to make it the only interior design department in the system that operates on a profit. If that happens, I would like to go a little further and get into the furniture field." Rosalie wants to try out some innovative ideas, not just to express her own creativity, but also to gain "respect for a woman in the field" because there are so few women executives in her area. Rosalie had worked with her husband in their own interior design business until it was established. She then decided to launch her new career, a decision her husband fully supports. Despite the long hours, she says, "It's really less work than I've done for a long, long time. I don't have the pressure to make ends meet that I had, and I feel that I'm producing better now that some of the pressure is off."

Other women, especially those with young children, find themselves frequently exhausted by work outside the home. Martha and her husband have two adopted children of preschool age and live in an extended household with four other adults as part of a Christian community. Martha works part-time as a nursery school teacher; she and her husband share child care. "My job does not pay well, so it's really for my own sense of fulfillment. I don't worry about what's happening at home, and I think that in itself is a sign of my involvement there. It's a real release to get so involved, and the fact that I'm working with other people and affecting at least some value-structure in their lives is important to me. Right now, however, I'm at a real burnt-out point." In the past year Martha had flown to Korea to pick up their second adopted daughter, whose health problems required considerable care. Martha's mother had broken her leg on a visit to her daughter, who then had to nurse her, too. Exhausted, Martha cut back her teaching hours and her responsibilities in the community. "I'm working on a more inward journey, a kind of renewal. It's been a rough year, and I need to step back and just reflect."

Barbara, who is a homemaker, belongs to the very large group of Christian women who believe that a mother's first commitment is to her family. In addition to her work at home, Barbara has a part-time job which she says, "makes me feel a little pride or accomplishment in myself." Her real fulfillment lies in caring for her two sons and her husband. "Fulfillment for a woman doesn't necessarily have to be out of the home bringing in money. The media and advertisements, and just society in general, have made a woman who is at home feel less important than somebody who is out 'where it's all happening.' I disagree with that. I feel it's all happening in the home. One concern I have is that we don't know the result of this working-mother syndrome yet, and I wonder if someday there might be a lot of regrets in the minds of mothers who did work. I would at least like to know that I tried my best and was at home when needed."

Finally, there are the retired women, many of whom look back on some difficult years. Fennie is a widow who worked thirty-five years as a waitress. Due to severe arthritis and other physical problems brought on by her years of hard physical work in a diner, she has been able to qualify for disability benefits. When her children were in school, she worked the night shift—from 7:00 P.M. to 7:00 A.M.—in order to be at home when they left in the morning and when they returned in the afternoon. (Her husband, who was chef at the diner, worked the day shift.) Looking back on her years of hard work, Fennie comments, "I did my best at all of my [activities], but I think the job got the most of me, and the children and the house were second and third. . . . Of course, I don't believe work hurts you. My grandmother lived to be ninety-six years old, and I don't think anyone worked harder than she did."

In listening to these women and the others who figure in this book, we discovered that Christian women experience the same economic worries, the same guilt, the same conflicts about priorities as non-Christian women. In fact, their beliefs may even increase their conflicts! We have interspersed anecdotes with the analysis of issues and have tried to develop a biblical context for understanding the nature of good work, the meaning of vocation, the relationship of work to creativity, and the liberation of the inner potential of women. Women are responsible for their own lives and for dealing with their worries and conflicts. This book uses biblical principles and the experience of women actually in the work force to develop ways of making choices, handling change, taking risks, coping, and dealing with discrimination.

In the wealth of material recently published about working

women, no one has paid much attention to the Christian. We wrote this book in response to the need for an approach to work which integrates Christian values, practical principles, and the experience of role-models.

A woman in her forties told us that she saw a need for such a book because of her experience in dealing with young women who have graduated from Christian colleges. "I sense a real ambivalence among young single women as to what their role is and a tremendous amount of guilt because they are working. Their parents sent them to Christian colleges, but even though they were prepared for careers, it seems that there was an unspoken feeling that the real aim of their going to college was that they should meet qualified men and be married by the time they graduated. These women have been given the benefits of an education, but they don't have the confidence or the sense of self to really feel good about themselves.

"This is a new wave among evangelical Christians—something I had been protected from because I was a 'fifties' girl, not a 'seventies' girl. I come from a Depression family, a totally different thing. Today young women . . . are getting almost schizophrenic if someone has not said, 'Will you be my wife?' by the time they graduate. They know they have to work, but they're ambivalent about it, and it's a very tough thing. A book like this could perhaps give young women mentors."

This book has been written to provide those mentors and to show Christian women as they are, not as they are "supposed to be." Our material is based on interviews conducted in various parts of the United States. We spoke with a variety of women in a wide range of jobs: the first woman to be named a vice-president of General Motors, a novelist, an actress, an ordained Presbyterian minister, a civil engineer, a housewife, a factory worker, a secretary, a teacher, a social worker, a nurse, a farm wife, and many others. The settings also varied—from the deck of a yacht to the examining room in the office of an elderly country doctor, from the library at the Cathedral of Saint John the Divine in New York City to a fellowship room in a Church of God in Detroit. The "mythic" Christian woman with a limited opportunity for service in a circumscribed world no longer exists.

A friend wrote us: "I hope your book deals with women other than 'Christian celebrities'! They seem very unreal and self-serving to me. So far, I have seen three types of women depicted either on TV or in books, and I trust your book will go deeper than these three caricatures: the 'super-Christian, super-mom, super-career-woman, isn't-God-wonderful' type; the harried and helpless wife and mother who feels guilty because her family exists on McDonald's and convenience foods, but is madly seeking her own identity at everyone's expense; and the bitter, anti-male, 'I-can-raise-my-children-alone-all-men-are-rotten-look-what-I-did-myself' type. As Americans we tend to love extremes . . . but I believe the time has come for a fair, balanced picture to be presented."

We have endeavored to give the balanced picture for which our friend asked. We have tried to find out how Christian women are coping in practical ways with their changing lifestyles. It is our hope that the personal stories shared here will speak to women who feel they are struggling alone, letting them know that others have gone ahead of them and have emerged from conflicts as stronger, more complete persons.

During our interviews, we tried to be good listeners, and as we wrote, we attempted to let the women speak for themselves as much as possible. Our interview sample, although large, was not scientific, but it was fairly representative. The majority of women who figure in this book are white, middle-class, evangelical Protestants. They are from a wide range of denominations, however, and some are Catholics. Our sample also includes minority groups—Blacks and Cubans and Mexican Americans. Not all the women would accept the label "evangelical," but all would describe themselves as Christians whose faith has practical implications in their lives.

Because of that faith their lives are characterized by a freshness, joy, and sense of service which set them apart. The stories they relate are straightforward, without the jargon about success and glamour of glossy magazines. This book celebrates their distinctive quality of life and their special accomplishments.

CHRISTIAN
WOMEN
AT WORK

STRUGGLE AND HOPE

By the mid-1970s, nearly half of all working women were working because of economic necessity. This group of women, fighting for survival, is made up of single women, widowed, divorced, and separated women, and women whose husbands' incomes are insufficient to maintain even a low standard of living. Contrary to the popular assumption that the salaries of most working women go for "the extras," the reality is that a great many women work for the same reason men work—to support themselves and their families. In many cases, for Christian women this struggle to make ends meet is complicated by the fact that they feel guilty for working, guilty for failing to conform to a traditional role. During our interviewing, we encountered a number of women who work out of sheer necessity. Five of these women are profiled in the following pages. Each one tells a story of struggle and hope.

Florence
There is "no way," says Florence, that her family could survive without her income as a spot welder on an automobile assembly line. Florence is about thirty and lives in Detroit with her children, aged nine and seven, and her husband who is a cook. He is partially incapacitated by a form of anxiety brought on by the pressures of city life.

21

When Florence was a girl happily growing up on a Mississippi farm, she had two dreams: to become a nurse and to build a house for her parents. But Florence's dreams clashed with reality when she migrated to Kansas City to find work. Although she had one year of training to be a key-punch operator, she was always turned down for jobs because she had "no experience." Instead, she did piecework, waitressing, housekeeping, cooking, and dishwashing. She married in Kansas City and has worked continuously, even when her children were small.

After moving to Detroit, Florence decided to try to get a job in an auto plant. That meant getting in line by 6:00 A.M. and waiting, waiting, waiting just to get inside the building. "Me and my sister-in-law got up every morning and went out there and stood in a long line. We'd get in there, and they'd say they weren't hiring. We'd go back the next day, and it would be the same thing." Finally she was hired, and she has held her job for six years, although there are frequent layoffs, often just before a holiday. (It was Thanksgiving eve when we talked with Florence, and she had just been laid off.) She explained that layoffs are particularly hard because there is always a lapse of about two weeks before she can obtain unemployment compensation and it is impossible to save anything from her income.

The hardest thing about Florence's job is "getting up and going out. But I know I got to go, so I get up and go." Another difficulty is that the union rules for seniority aren't always observed where she works. "They give us the run-around. They're supposed to go by seniority, but they don't. If the foreman likes you, he'll pick you for the job." And the union often can't do much to help someone like Florence. "Most of the time if you don't watch it, they'll get you fired. You pay your dues every month, but most of the time they don't do nothin' for you."

When Florence worked the day shift, her in-laws cared for her children; day-care was just too expensive. Now she works at night and enjoys being able to see her children off to school in the morning. "Now I can get up in the morning and get them ready for school and fix them a hot breakfast; before they was eating cornflakes."

During the August before our interview, Florence had had a

conversion experience while visiting relatives in Kansas City. "I said, 'When I go back home, I'm going to join the church.'" Florence is now a faithful member of the Church of God and is being trained to be a Sunday school teacher; she spends all week preparing her lessons. We got the impression that her new-found faith was keeping her going in rough times.

Asked about her dreams for her children, Florence answered, "I want them to do whatever they want to do. My little boy wants to be something that is dangerous like a policeman or a fireman. I tell him, 'If that's what you want to be, be good at it. Whatever you are, be good at it.' My little girl says she wants to be a teacher, and I tell her she has to study for that. And I tell her, 'Do your best. That's all anybody can ask you to do.'"

Florence is black, and the slightly wistful tone with which she spoke of her early dreams seemed to betray the disappointments encountered by many blacks who have migrated north. In describing her life and the values which she brings to her work and tries to instill in her children, she revealed an acceptance of life, a dignity, and a hope which characterized many of the women to whom we spoke. In their moving book, *Women of Crisis: Lives of Struggle and Hope*, Robert Coles and Jane Hallowell Coles speak of the angers and disappointments of women of different backgrounds, frustrations bound up with sex, class, and race, and of moments of transcendence when these women affirm their human potential. Florence expressed no anger to us, but she did not hide the fact that life was tough for her.

Nyra   Being the breadwinner can be physically and emotionally demanding; for many Christian women, faith alone sustains them in the midst of the tremendous drains made on their energy. Cast into a position of earning her own way in life, the individual who has little physical stamina survives only with difficulty. Even for a strong woman, the struggle to make ends meet can be exhausting.

Nyra is the mother of two teen-age boys. "Financially, it's me or nothing," she says, because her husband abandoned her when her younger son was eleven months old. "I was raised by very hard-working, very ethical, blue-collar parents. I was taught that you work hard, you're loyal to your employer, and you work at one job until you die or retire. My father was in construction all his life. My mother has always done factory or cafeteria work. She still works, and she's seventy." Nyra has worked since she was thirteen; as a teen-ager, she was a dietary aide, a dimestore clerk, and a factory worker.

"My parents only hoped we'd finish high school. They never finished grammar school. No one in my family had ever gone to college." But Nyra did, finishing two degrees in education, including a master's in counseling. "Like most people in my age group, I guess I assumed that when I got a degree in education I would teach the rest of my life." Then, about 1970, a radical change occurred in her life.

Nyra was teaching on the university level and had a Christian student on her tennis team. "She was a radiant Christian, and she would talk to me about the Lord. I thought she was a lovely, but very idealistic young woman." One summer the student lived at Nyra's home for a few weeks and gave her a Bible to read. "When I got through with Romans, I asked Christ into my heart."

Because she wanted to raise her sons in a Christian environment and to study and grow spiritually herself, Nyra made a risky decision. A year after her conversion experience, she resigned her teaching position and moved to Wheaton, Illinois, where Wheaton College is located. "In 1971, there simply were no teaching jobs available. In fact, I remember sending an application to a junior college, and they returned it saying that they had received 6,000 applications and they weren't even accepting any more. They weren't even opening the envelopes. I knew I needed to find a new profession to support my family." Since then she has held a variety of jobs—employment counselor, secretary, director of financial aid on the college level, and realtor. Because of the high cost of living in her area, she has never been able to make ends meet on a continuous basis. "I was the kind of person who was going to teach in a school and stay there until I retired. I just couldn't imagine myself jumping around. The more you do it, the easier it gets, but at first it's really traumatic."

Sometimes Nyra's life seems to be one of perpetual crisis, but that for her is the secret of real faith. "You have no choice. When you're in a state of need, you really have to depend on the Lord." On more than one occasion, she has experienced financial miracles. Just two weeks before our interview, she had sat down to write checks, knowing that she didn't have enough money to pay her bills. "My checkbook didn't balance, and it always balances. I went back and checked it again, and all my entries were exactly right. Then I went down and checked the deposit column and found that someone had deposited $1,000 anonymously."

Nyra has no regrets about her decision to give up her security in order to live in Wheaton. The Christian influence of the community has been "wonderful" for her sons who are both Christians. In her own life, Christ is "almost a touchable, tangible reality." Yet, she admitted to being worn-out. "God has always been faithful, and yet he doesn't ever rescue us until we're on the edge of the cliff. After all these years, I ought to be getting used to it, but I'm exhausted by it. It isn't that I distrust him. If anybody believes God is capable, I do because I've seen him prove it over and over and over again. I have no doubt that he has a way out of my dilemma right now. But I'm exhausted by the lifestyle that he's chosen for me." When we talked with her, Nyra was in real estate, but because the real estate market has been so depressed, she has been working part-time as the secretary to a lawyer. She had also just applied for a job at a warehouse but had been told that she could not be hired because she was over-qualified.

Coping with the reversals and disappointments which life brings and then learning from them are major signs of maturity. In addition, changing one's early job expectations and adapting one's skills to new circumstances require assertiveness, ingenuity, and courage. Nyra, who had worked as an employment counselor, told us that most people have a very limited view of job possibilities. For example, more and more women who almost automatically became teachers are finding that their personalities are not suited to the profession or that the limited number of openings in education is forcing them to look elsewhere for employment. They have few ideas, however, as to what their alternatives may be.

Ann   Ann comes from a Dutch background and grew up in the Reformed theological tradition. She attended church-run schools from the early grades through college. Her parents served as missionaries in the southwestern United States, and she has warm memories of the years she spent in New Mexico between the ages of ten and eighteen. "I loved it. I wouldn't have traded it. You just could be your own person. We had very innocent pastimes—roller-skating, group games, toboggan parties. It was a really nice place to grow up. Unfortunately, it wasn't much like the real world."

Ann always thought she would be a teacher, probably because her role-models were teachers. In college, however, her goals began to change when she met her future husband, Dan. "I pictured myself as a professor's wife." They both went to graduate school to study German literature, and after one year, they were married. Ann received a master's degree and spent two years teaching high school. Looking back, she said, "I don't think I was really cut out to be a teacher. I had a lot of trouble with discipline. I found it very difficult to teach and handle the discipline."

Her husband pursued his doctoral studies in German literature, and the two of them spent a year abroad while he did research for his dissertation. "When I got back, it was very difficult to find a job. I had previously worked for a company in the summer doing secretarial work, so I called the fellow I had worked for and said, 'Do you have any business contacts who need office help? If you do, could you let me know?'" He put Ann in contact with a bank where she began to work as a clerk-typist in the trust department. "They offered the most money, and at the time my husband wasn't working. He was writing his dissertation, so my salary supported us." When Ann and Dan were married, they had agreed that she would support them for three years before they had their family. Things didn't work out that way, however.

While they were in Germany, Dan discovered German folk art. As a consequence, his career interests began to shift to the area of crafts. Since the market for Ph.D.'s in German literature disappeared, he did not finish his dissertation but went into a partnership running a crafts shop. After bouts with illness, he is struggling to get the business firmly established and is working long hours, but his income is insufficient to support the family which now includes a small son. What was to be a temporary arrangement has become more or less permanent, and Ann has now made a commitment to pursue a career in banking. "My husband is doing the best he can, and it's important to me that he be happy. He will have to work his whole life, and what he's doing now is building for our future. Whenever I get down about it, I figure, 'Well, he's doing the best he can with circumstances, and it won't always be this way.'" Dan realizes that his wife has sacrificed some dreams to be supportive of him and to relieve him of some financial pressure. For example, Ann's health insurance from the bank has paid for three operations for Dan. In turn, Ann calls her husband "my rock."

Even though Ann did not expect to work at the bank on a long-term basis, she began to take initiatives at the end of her first year there. She asked for a promotion and was transferred to a more interesting department. After about five more years she became a supervisor and is now in management training. "About a year ago the bank's personnel department started a program to single out potential managers, and I was one of those selected. They told us they were putting us on a career path and wanted to know where we wished to work at the bank. The personnel department would be counseling us along the way.

"I went to school, and later I went to a career management seminar given by the National Association of Bank Women. This was enlightening because I found out there were other women like me. It made me aware that I could get somewhere if I really tried and pursued a career in some kind of organized fashion. We were advised to write down all our accomplishments and all our responsibilities and make sure that information got to the attention of the right people so we would be visible. I was doing that. Then the bank offered me the promotion to supervisor. They reopened the position just for me, I think partly because I had indicated an interest in the loan department." Ann would like to become a bank officer, but she realizes that this means taking more courses, transferring to the loan department, and taking on responsibilities other than those between 9:00 and 5:00. She feels hesitant to commit herself to a career path that would take her away from home for even longer periods of time.

Ann has adapted remarkably well to the unexpected and sometimes painful adjustments demanded of her as she has moved from a sheltered background and traditional female role expectations into a banking career. She can now say that the most fulfilling thing about her job is interacting with her colleagues. "It took a long time to get used to them, actually, because of my background. I never went to public school, and I just didn't run into some things. These people have done everything. They've experienced everything. They've been through everything. For example, most of them have been divorced at least once. I used to just sit there, not knowing whether I should associate with them or not. But I've learned they're basically warm and loving people. I guess we didn't hit it off right away because they thought I was square, and I pretty much looked to people from church for my social life."

Now Ann feels she belongs to her office world, and she and her husband are invited to more social events. At a crucial point she came to grips with the fact that the office was not a temporary stopping-place. She realized that her attitude was, "I was trained as a teacher, and this is only temporary. I'm really better than this." She set out to change. "When I finally came to grips with the fact that this was my life and I had to relate to these people with my whole person, it got better."

Ann had a three-year-old son and was expecting another child at the time of the interview. Although she is able to take a six-month maternity leave, returning to work and leaving her child with a baby-sitter has been painful. There were tears in her eyes as she spoke of her conflicts. "It's a first in my family. All of my sisters are home with their kids, and I have to take a lot of flack from everyone. Older people, of course, think that the place for a mother with young kids is at home. I'm from a traditional background, and the same thing holds true there, so it's been a little difficult." Ann believes that it was providential that she found her baby-sitter, an older woman who is like a grandmother to Lee, her son. The sitter watches Lee and one other little boy. "I worried that Lee would learn to call her mother instead of me. But the sitter said, 'It's probably a lot harder on you than it is on him.'" Ann leaves for work before her husband each morning, so Dan takes Lee to the sitter; then Ann picks him up on her way home from the bank. "Lee takes a long afternoon nap, so actually he's awake for only three or four of the hours he's away from us. He stays up longer in the evening so we can be together, so it's worked out real well."

In addition to the support of her husband and of small groups at the Presbyterian church they now attend, Ann has relied on a sister and a close friend. "My sister, who is eight years younger than I, is real supportive. She doesn't have children yet and is putting her husband through medical school. A couple of months ago, she said certain people could handle both work and a family, and she thought I was one of them." Her friend, although less pressured than Ann, has been supportive because she also has small children and works part-time.

Ann's struggles have brought her to the point where she has been able to turn her disappointments into a potentially rewarding career. Her marriage has also been strengthened by the mutual sacrifices both she and her husband are making. Personally, she has discovered the challenge and reward of responsibility and the true nature of her spiritual gifts. One of her gifts is patience. "I try to see the long term rather than the immediate."

From Passivity to Responsibility Learning to take responsibility for one's own life is a major theme in the lives of contemporary Christian women. And for many this theme is also connected with the search for individual authenticity and identity.

In some ways, responsibility and authenticity are the slogans of middle-class American life and social change. They might seem irrelevant to women in cultures where there is little leisure time, where there is an extended family and women are constantly bearing children, and where women are immersed in running a household and working in the fields. The sociologist Evelyne Sullerot has pointed out that an integrated set of elements (ideology, role in the family and society, economics, spheres of commonly accepted or forbidden activities) contribute to the position of women in a society. The fact that American women are dealing with such issues as responsibility and authenticity is itself a sign of the disruption of the integrated set of elements governing the middle-class image of the ideal wife and mother which dominated society after World War II.

Responsibility is frightening for many women. For Ann, becoming responsible meant giving up the myth of the ideal Christian wife and mother and brought her into conflict with the traditional values of her family and upbringing. Women who find themselves suddenly alone whether through widowhood, divorce, or some other unexpected circumstance are often totally unprepared for the responsibility thrust upon them. In many cultures where there are extended families, loss of a husband may be somewhat less traumatic because the widow and her children are taken under the wing of another male in the family. But there is no family buffer for women in nuclear families. They find themselves alone, weighed down by low self-esteem and grief and the necessity of earning a living. For instance, a young divorcee told us that she and her two children looked like waifs after the separation. "I had failed," she said. "It was devastating."

Responsibility is also frightening because girls usually grow up visualizing themselves as Sleeping Beauty who is rescued by Prince Charming. As adults, then, they subconsciously respond to life in passive, rather than active, terms. Carolyn Heilbrun has commented that "woman's fantasies have been trapped eternally in a romance where she is the passive figure, without control, awaiting her destiny in the person of the man who will provide her with a life."

Too often the church has fostered passivity, even with respect to personalizing the gospel. The wife of an elder within the

Plymouth Brethren denomination, where women usually do not speak during the meetings, admitted that passivity was a real spiritual danger. "If I have something on my mind, I want to express it. Particularly in a worship service, I'm often frustrated because I have to keep silent. The temptation is to become passive and not to be involved emotionally in worship." Another former missionary commented, "Often when women read the Scripture they don't apply it personally. When it talks about the farmer sowing the seed, the runner running the race, do we think it is speaking to men and not really make personal application of Scripture in our own lives for today?"

Theologian Tom Driver has described an experience which graphically illustrates the tendency of women to act out the role of Sleeping Beauty. Several years ago he and his wife were conducting a workshop and requested small groups of women to create stories in which the protagonist was a woman. Out of twelve groups, only one was able to invent such a story. "The others all fantasized romantic tragedies in which a woman started out as the central figure, only to end up as the wife, mistress, queen, slave, or victim of a male hero."

A female protagonist is the central actor, the heroine of her own actions. She assumes an identity in her own right; her role with respect to her husband, king, or whomever may be important, but she does not define herself ultimately by this role. Becoming the heroine of one's own life story is not easy because it means giving up many of the myths with which young girls grow up.

Helen   Helen, single and twenty-seven, is fully aware that the fairy tale of Prince Charming offers no realistic answer to her uncertainties about her life and work. "There are times when I would like to marry someone very, very rich so I would have the freedom to do exactly what I want. The problem with that is that I know it's not real. And given that much freedom, I probably would not have the discipline to make myself actually make something out of it."

When she talked to us, Helen had been working for three months as an assistant bookkeeper in a jewelry store which is part of a national chain. When she was hired, she was told, "We think you would be qualified as a management trainee, but we would like to hire a guy." (An inauspicious beginning to her career with a business concern Helen called "old-fashioned." She quit four months after her interview with us.) Helen's feelings about her work were very mixed. "I like it because I like the feeling of organizing things. I like the contact with people. It's interesting, and I enjoy it because practically speaking it's good experience. If I want to get a better job or go on to something else, this is probably one of the best things I can have on my résumé, in some cases, possibly even better than a college degree. In terms of what I really want, I still come home from work and dread having to get up the next morning."

Helen has completed three and three-quarters years of college; her interests have included literature, writing, psychology, and political science. Intense and articulate, she has gifts in counseling; she also thinks she might like to write. But she feels trapped without a college degree, and her course in life seems very unclear. If she had no limiting circumstances, her goals would be to find out if she can write, to be involved in a L'Abri-type community where she could counsel, and to have a home, possibly a husband. "I feel like I'm stuck in a little box. I feel I'm above average in terms of intelligence, maybe enough so that the whole college system as I was exposed to it didn't work, or hasn't been working. But I am nowhere near brilliant enough to do it without the system."

She admitted that her job appeared to be an ideal opportunity to get ahead in the business world, but she was not sure she believed in retailing. "There's a need for products. There's a need for selling. There's a need for the exchange of goods. But the way it's done bothers me: trying to get people to 'need' something they really don't need."

When she chatted with us, Helen saw no immediate alternative to her job. "I'm there because I have to make money. My parents have supported me for a long time. I've been in college for over nine years. I'm sick of it. They're sick of it. Mostly I'm sick of it. I have to make money. I want to be on my own. I want to be independent." Why has her college experience been so disappointing? "If I could say exactly why it's been lousy, I could probably go back tomorrow and finish my degree. Partly, I've never known what I really wanted to do. I've always been frustrated." Then, too, she could never please herself. "I could never do well enough. If I got a B, it should have been an A. If I got an A, it should have been good enough to get published. I would stay up the night before an exam or before a paper was due and drive myself to distraction. I knew it would never be good enough."

A tragedy struck when Helen was finally nearing the end of her college work. She was driving a car in which the steering mechanism failed. A close friend, recently married, was beside her, and her friend's husband was in the rear seat. Helen's friend was killed, and she herself was seriously injured. Helen was in no way responsible for the accident, but the trauma of the experience caused her to withdraw from college. Since then she has been sorting out her life, working first as a sales clerk in a women's clothing boutique and then in the jewelry store. (After her two stints in retailing, she decided, after our interview, to return to the university once again and to finish her degree as quickly as possible.)

"Does God have a plan for your life?" we asked.

"I think he has an ideal plan. I think there's a way you're supposed to live and by living in that way you're going to be the most fulfilled or the most true to who you were intended to be. In terms of specifics, I'm not sure I would agree there is a detailed plan. What we do is important as it ties into the character of God. What we do will reflect and make us who we are. It gets tricky for me because I keep thinking back to the accident and wondering how that figures into God's working in the lives of people. There has to be a working. If you say that events are out of the control of God, then something like that loses all meaning."

Dilys   Almost everyone has a friend who has suddenly become a widow or whose husband has experienced a catastrophic illness which has caused havoc in a family. Sometimes situations drag on for years and can take a tremendous toll. Dilys impressed us by her buoyant and optimistic attitude toward life in the presence of prolonged adversity. During the early years of her marriage, Dilys raised three daughters and did not work outside the home. After some time, her husband, who was an orphan himself, decided to become involved in a school for orphan boys. They moved and became houseparents to twenty-three boys in the fifth through the eighth grades. For Dilys, this meant overseeing the housekeeping and preparing breakfast for the boys when they got up at 6:00 in the morning.

"You have to be able to handle it," said Dilys about the stress of keeping discipline among the boys. The strain was too much for her husband, who also had a full-time job, and he suffered a stroke at the age of forty-six. At the time, her youngest daughter was eleven, and her oldest daughter was engaged. Her husband lived twelve years and recovered enough so that for a time he was able to do gardening, but he was never again able to support his family. Dilys wanted to be home when her daughter returned from school, so she took a job working in a school cafeteria. (In returning to work, many women use their most up-to-date skills—the cooking and cleaning of their homemaking experience.) The school job did not bring in enough money, and one day Dilys got the idea that she could clean both before and after her cafeteria job. "I was so excited when the idea came to me. You can get a lot of work doing that, an awful lot of work."

She cleaned a motel in the morning before she went to school; in the afternoon she cleaned doctors' offices. The exciting aspect to her second job was that Susie, her youngest daughter, could go with her on her late afternoon jobs. In the midst of the hard work, they sang as they cleaned, and Dilys said she praised the Lord for her physical strength and happiness. She liked her work in the cafeteria because she enjoyed being a servant, and an added bonus to the income from her cleaning was that she and Susie became good companions.

The low point in the twelve-year aftermath of the stroke came when her husband began to be violent and the possibility arose that he would have to be committed to a state hospital. "There are terrible stories about that place. It was a really bad time for me." Dilys usually never left her husband at night, but once she had to stay overnight at the home of her married daughter. The next day she started home, facing a two-hour drive. "On my way home I was looking at the sky, and I saw Jesus as a shepherd. And he said to me, 'Dilys, why are you worrying? Don't you know I'm your shepherd? I'll take care of you.' Well, when I came home from that experience everything worked out." Her husband was able to enter a home where his expenses were paid. About the time of her special encounter with Jesus as shepherd, Dilys also went through a radical change in attitude. "I'm a different person now. I used to be a fighter. No one ever trod on me." She had always felt sufficient, but now Dilys knelt and admitted that she needed God's help. That act made all the difference in her life.

Her husband's illness and death were not the only blows Dilys experienced. One day she was home alone when a telegram came with the news that one of her daughters had died unexpectedly of pneumonia while she was in Germany. "One thing I learned through all this is that no one can help you but the Lord. He's with you all the time. During the nights, he's there."

Dilys had intended to retire at the age of sixty-two, but she so wanted to do something different in life that she decided, after prayer, to retire at the age of sixty. Now she has an apartment in the basement of Susie's home. She sometimes watches her grandchildren, but often she is busy with her volunteer work. "Once you ask the Lord to take care of your life, you have to let it happen," she commented about the way things have worked out. She revels in the freedom of being able to volunteer. "I can just do whatever I want. I work at the hospital, and I work with Meals on Wheels, and the Catholic school, and the home for the elderly near here. Oh, I have learned to love so many people."

Asked for what advice she might give other women, Dilys replied, "I don't think a woman should ever get so that she isn't able to take care of herself. I wasn't expecting my husband's stroke at all. You have to learn to handle things and not think that just because you have a husband he's going to be there the rest of your life." A woman has to be self-sufficient, but she also has to lean on God. "You can't do anything other than give it all to the Lord."

Struggle and hope. . . . Economic struggle brings a vast number of women through the crucible of suffering to the unexpected discovery that they can assume responsibility for their own lives and those of their families. Changed circumstances often force them to dig deep within to find the dignity and strength which lie hidden in the self they have never really known. The women to whom we talked live lives of struggle and quiet courage; these are the heroines, not of a romance, but of a pilgrimage of faith.

BIBLICAL PERSPECTIVES ON WORK

The Mass Media and Secular Feminism

The mass media, always quick to profit from social change, have been paying considerable attention to the entry of great numbers of women into the work force. And through the media, the public has been receiving confusing messages about the reasons women are working and the expectations of working women. One of the most unfortunate impressions created by the popular press is that secular feminism has downgraded homemaking and that all feminists believe no woman can be fulfilled unless she has a career outside the home. Homemakers are often made to feel that they are second-class citizens. It is true that some feminists who feel they had no real choice when they married and became homemakers have overreacted and taken extreme positions, but the major thrust of feminism throughout the twentieth century has been social equality for women and freedom of choice for both men and women.

Since feminism had a tremendous impact on the American consciousness during the 1970s, the press picked up many of its themes, including the misleading idea that freedom equals a career; it created a new image for women, that of the stylish professional who can be a winner if she throws off her deferential behavior, puts off marriage, and plays her cards right. An enormous number of self-help books, some useful and some geared to the success syndrome, have appeared since 1970 when Caroline Bird published *Born Female: The High Cost of Keeping Women Down*. One of the most troubling for Christians is Betty Lehan Harragan's *Games Mother Never Taught You* in which the author views corporate life as a game where rules are determined by a male power structure. Women, unpracticed in team sports and military tactics, may enter corporations, but their power is nonexistent. (Affirmative action programs to seek out qualified women and the tendency to give new titles to women employees are mere window dressing.) The name of the corporate game is to get to the top of the company pyramid where the power lies. According to Harragan, if women want to be winners, they must play by the male rules and wrest power from the men. For example, they must learn that legal deception is admired in business. They must capitalize on the discomfort which they cause their male colleagues and use it to gain control of situations. Women have to learn the jargon, signs, and symbols of the game in order to make it work to their own advantage.

Harragan is correct in suggesting that American women have led sheltered lives which have not prepared them for the hurlyburly of the real world of work. Her descriptions of the all-male networks that control power in most organizations are also accurate. But she is dead wrong in her cynical advice which emphasizes the pragmatic manipulation of people and in her refusal to question the assumption that corporate power and success are worth having for selfish purposes.

Magazine publishers have also taken advantage of the new market of working women with periodicals that range from *Working Mother* to *Working Woman* to *Savvy* (for women executives). Traditional women's magazines now offer regular columns and feature articles for the working woman. Some typical titles, drawn from a random sampling of magazines, repeat the themes of professionalism, glamour, success, and manipulation:

"How to Act Like a Pro the First Time Out"
"First Jobs: 7 Big Successes Talk About Their Small Beginnings"
"Stress: The Signals, Symptoms, Cures"
"How to Turn Your Job Into a Career"
"How to Get Paid What You Think You're Worth"
"Surviving Ambition and Competition: On the Cutting Edge at the Harvard Business School, Dual Career Couples Worry About Pieces of Life on the Cutting Room Floor"

"Postponing Parenthood"
"Power! The Leadership Crisis: New Room at the Top for Women"
"Superwoman: Ways to Save Time and Money"
"How to Negotiate a Raise"
"The Perfect Outfit for 1980—To Get You a Job, a Raise, a Promotion"
"12 Career Mistakes"

Behind such shallow approaches to professionalism lie two truths: women will have many more options available to them in the 1980s, and they must learn to adopt assertive rather than passive patterns of behavior. Young women today think in quite different terms than did their counterparts in 1970. For instance, "fear of math" is rapidly becoming a thing of the past, and young women are being recruited by industry and professional schools in such fields as mining and engineering. One ten-year-old girl, whose father is the maintenance supervisor at an apartment complex, told us she would like to become either a rig-driver or an automobile mechanic.

Feminism has drawn the attention of the public to a number of issues that affect working women, particularly the questions of equal pay for equal work and fair working conditions. For example, the actress Linda Lavin, who has played the role of the waitress Alice in the CBS television series by that name, commented in an interview that she herself was moved by Alice's "courage, her having obstacles to overcome, her having a dream." Viewers have written letters to Alice, urging her on in her protests against unfair treatment of women on the job. (As a result of her concern, Lavin became a member of the National Commission on Working Women, an organization concerned with the problems of the "Eighty Percenters," the working women clustered in the pink-collar, nonunion female job ghettos.)

In our interviews, we found that the majority of Christian women feared the term "feminism" because to them it connoted a radical, unfeminine, aggressive stance, but all the women felt they should receive equal pay for equal work. Often those who rejected "women's liberation" most vigorously revealed subsequently that they agreed with many of the issues of the "movement" by the very nature of their personal choices, their marriage, and their work.

One woman said she was "very much opposed" to the secular women's movement, but then went on to explain her views more fully. "The pay part I can see, but I just really feel they're carrying it too far. I'm one that likes to have the door held for me. I like to wear slacks, but I have the feeling when I see a lot of women in slacks, they portray men. . . . In the job here I find that if I wear a dress—it sounds crazy, but it works this way—and I go to a meeting like Rotary, they treat me as a lady much more. And that's what I want to be treated as. That's what God put me here as—a lady. I don't think we have to be second-class citizens as women. I always felt marriage is fifty-fifty. You don't take a back seat to a man, nor do you try to be pushy."

A nurse with two daughters was able to see through the extremes of the feminist movement and to accept the possibility of quite new roles for her daughters in the future. "I grew up in a family where my mother was very liberated. She could roof a house, hammer a nail, do anything like that, and she was as liberated as anyone could be. I honestly feel that I should have as many rights as a man in order to carry out my interests. I like to think of it in relation to the fact that in Scripture we're told, 'there is no Greek or Jew or free man or slave'; you know, we're equal. That's how I view aspects of the women's movement.

"There are swings of the pendulum, and sometimes it swings too far," she added with respect to more radical feminism. Then she went on to discuss the proposed Equal Rights Amendment to the Constitution. "I don't think it means we're going to have to use the same bathrooms or all of those silly kinds of things. I think what the amendment is saying is 'equal pay for equal work' and 'equitable treatment is right for all people, regardless of sex, color, creed, or national origin.' I don't see these things as threatening to me at all."

Of her daughters she said that she and her husband did "not have anything patterned out that they must go to college or that they must marry handsome men or that they must go into any particular field of work. I think it's important that they find their own thing. Right now Amy's interested in archaeology, and a few years ago she was interested in being a rancher. I would see both of those as being nice things for her to do."

**Work
in
Industrial
Society**   The entry of Christian women into the work force is complicated not only by confusing messages from society about the role of women, but also by the problems surrounding work in an industrial age. For many, perhaps the majority, of those employed today, work is the curse of the human race. In our society many workers have no control over their own destinies and are doomed to carry out meaningless jobs in a new kind of servitude. Studs Terkel describes this side of work in the introduction to his book *Working,* a series of interviews with American workers. His book, he says, portrays "daily humiliations. To survive the day is triumph enough for the walking wounded among the great many of us." Despite the humiliations of work, Terkel sensed a search "for daily meaning as well as daily bread, for recognition as well as cash, for astonishment rather than torpor; in short, for a sort of life rather than a Monday through Friday sort of dying."

The reasons behind the despair of modern workers are explored further in E. F. Schumacher's critique of large-scale, technocratic and industrial society in *Good Work.* He says both manual and white-collar workers are engaged in activities which distort the true nature of work. "Mechanical, artificial, divorced from nature, utilizing only the smallest part of man's potential capabilities, it [industrialism] sentences the great majority of workers to spending their working lives in a way which contains no worthy challenge, no stimulus to self-perfection, no chance of development, no element of Beauty, Truth, or Goodness." Most corporations and industries are complex and hierarchical in structure, so often the individual worker feels that he or she has no say in the direction the company might be going. The personal element is lost in the ever-increasing division of labor into smaller and smaller parts. Fortunately, more and more companies are studying and implementing ways to humanize the workplace; and in an attempt to reverse declining productivity, many firms are experimenting with decentralized decision-making and lateral rather than hierarchical management.

Why Work? The problems of workers in a complex society are great; yet we need to work—not only for money but also for psychological well-being. The issue is the quality of our individual jobs and our perception of them. Psychologist Abraham Maslow has explained human motivation to work by distinguishing between our basic needs for survival (physiological needs) and an ascending order of higher needs: for security, love and belonging, self-esteem, and self-actualization. Work plays a role on a basic level in that it helps to take care of our needs for survival and security. The fight for bare survival is so consuming for some people that they are forced to live almost entirely at this basic level of existence. But we all long to get more out of life—to love, to feel significant, and to fulfill our potential. Studs Terkel's cross section of American workers spoke of such longings, often in vague and ill-expressed ways. Florence, the spot welder, whom we described in the preceding chapter, told us that she would have liked to do more fulfilling work. She commented that instead of challenging or stimulating her, her job required endless repetition of the same simple task.

Work which fulfills the higher needs of the individual, according to Maslow, is "simultaneously a seeking and fulfilling of the self *and* an achievement of the selflessness which is the ultimate expression of *real* self." Studies by social scientists bear out Maslow's theory that work ought to be worthy of the potential of the worker and permit self-expression. In a standard study of worker attitudes, *The Motivation to Work*, the two most frequent emotions which workers associate with job satisfaction are feelings that they have achieved and that they have been recognized.

Self-Expression and Self-Esteem These issues of motivation are directly linked to the feminist movement of the 1970s and the entry of women into the labor force. Some people ask why women are no longer content to remain at home and to volunteer their skills in their spare time. To some it appears that the feminist movement has placed "the self" above everything else. One woman whom we interviewed spoke with great pain in her voice about her younger sister, a non-Christian, who had become a part of the secular feminist movement. "I have one sister, and she's a militant and a feminist, I would say. She's into the self thing, seeking herself, finding herself—everything the feminists represent. She comes first; the children come second; her job comes third. . . . I grew up during the fifties. I think the five-year difference between my sister and myself is important. She grew up in the sixties and that was when they were blowing apart the family, and everybody was going their own way." She went on to say that women's liberation is "selfish and egotistical. They're just living for themselves. Each individual is for each individual. Even as a group they don't stand very strong."

On the other hand, this same person, whose primary responsibilities are as a wife and mother, finds that artistic activity is something she enjoys. She paints and creates with fabrics. If she could do anything she wanted, she would probably open a cooperative craft shop. "I kind of happened upon creating things with fabric a couple of years ago, and I really like it a lot. I've sold four or five hundred pieces in different little shops. I make mostly animals and mobiles." Financial profit is not her main motive in this work. "I enjoy doing it, and I don't care if it's successful, although it would be nice if it was."

Many, many women expressed similar satisfaction in their full or part-time jobs outside their homes, indicating a deep human need for varied work. One woman of forty-eight who has been a realtor for two years explained her intense personal involvement in selling homes. "I happened to get into it really as a result of encouragement by my husband as my children were getting older. He thinks it's a wonderful means of security when a woman can have a vocation of her own. I have found it to be a very lucrative business and one that I thoroughly enjoy. Money is only part of it. I love people; I love meeting them. I love trying to help them find a home which I think is a very important thing. It's a very personal thing for me. A particular joy to me are the young couples, especially those coming for their first home. There's a great deal of excitement and a great deal of appreciation. This last year I have placed several couples in their first homes, and it is a decided thrill for me."

Judith Bardwick, the author of a major study of the psychology of women, has made a useful distinction which helps sort out these statements about the motivation of women who work outside the home. Many women, particularly educated women, define their *femininity* in terms of marriage and motherhood; on the other hand, their *self-percept* or self-image requires independent achievement. Such independent achievement can come about in many ways— through a full-time or part-time job, volunteer work, or a hobby. Now, the single woman in particular realizes that her femininity does not depend upon being a wife and mother, if she is to come to grips with who she is as a person. But women are socialized to define being female in certain ways. When their children leave home and they are no longer able to bear children, many women discover they have not faced the larger issues of who they are as humans. That is a primary reason women often face a crisis in middle age.

Psychological theories and certain aspects of feminism have shed light on women's need for self-expression and self-esteem. For Christian women, however, an understanding of the biblical view of work can provide a deeper basis for dealing with our need for self-expression and self-esteem as Christians and as women. As Christians, our self-fulfillment is not merely an end in itself, but a means to serve God and others.

**Work and the
Genesis Account
of Creation**   The word "work" in Scripture has three principle meanings: God's work in creation, human work (all the types of productive activities that people do), and activity for the sake of the gospel. In Genesis, the first glimpse of the nature of God is in his work, and he viewed all that

he created as good, culminating in his supreme handiwork—humankind. "So God created man in his own image, in the image of God he created him; male and female he created them" (1:27). "When God created man, he made him in the likeness of God. He created them male and female; at the time they were created, he blessed them and called them 'man'" (5:1–2). God created humankind as male and female, each distinct but necessary to the other, both made in his image. They fulfill their true nature and reflect their Maker when they engage in fruitful labor. In fact, God's first injunction to man and woman was that they procreate and work: "fill the earth and subdue it" (1:28).

While the creation account of Genesis one stresses the relationship between God and man and woman, the story of Adam and Eve in chapter two emphasizes their mutual dependence in the marriage relationship and their relationship to the world into which they had been placed. "The Lord God took the man and put him in the Garden of Eden to work it and take care of it" (2:15). Adam was to cultivate the garden and be a steward of it, but he could not do the work alone. "The Lord God said, 'It is not good for the man to be alone. I will make a helper suitable for him'" (2:18). Eve's unity with Adam in marriage mirrors the completeness and love of God, and her relationship to Adam shows that meaningful work is accomplished as we work with and for others.

In verse eighteen, the Hebrew word *ezer* literally means "help." In the King James translation, the phrase is translated "an help meet for him" which means a "help suitable for him." The word "helpmate" is a corruption of this phrase. Instead of using the word "help," other translations have resorted to "helper fit for him" (RSV), "helper suitable for him" (NIV), "partner" (NEB), and "a suitable companion to help him" (TEV). Elsewhere in the Old Testament, the word *ezer* is used to describe the activity of God who helps and delivers his people (Gen. 49:25; Exod. 18:4; Deut. 33:26); it in no way suggests subservience or inferiority.

Before the Fall, Adam and Eve worked together, fulfilling God's injunction, participating in the proper rhythm of life, that of work and rest. The dignity of human work and the importance of a balance between work and rest are basic to the Hebrew tradition.

The fact that the six days of creation were followed by a seventh day of rest suggests this pattern for the created world. The Ten Commandments take for granted that work is part of life, but they state explicitly the need for rest (Exod. 20:8). In the Old Testament, creative work done with one's hands is seen to parallel God's work in creating the splendor of the universe. In the Psalms, God is portrayed metaphorically as working with his hands in the creation of the world; by implication, human labor is a cooperation with God in caring for his handiwork. "When I consider your heavens, the work of your fingers . . . what is man that you are mindful of him, the son of man that you care for him? . . . You made him ruler over the works of your hands; you put everything under his feet. . . . O Lord, our Lord, how majestic is your name in all the earth" (Ps. 8:3, 4, 6, 9).

The Fall changed everything. It disrupted the harmony of the world and distorted the balance in a number of relationships: between God and humankind, man and woman, the individual and the communal, humans and their environment. For Eve, childbirth (her part in the command to procreate) became painful, and for both Adam and Eve work became toil (Gen. 3:14–19). Ultimately, the Fall led to the conflict between Cain and Abel in which work (tilling the soil and herding) played a vital part, culminating in the murder of Abel.

The accounts of the Creation and the Fall give important clues to a balanced view of work and the changing role of women in the late twentieth century. Scripture describes woman first as human and second as female. She receives the same injunctions as the male—to fill the earth and to care for it. Thus work is equally as important to women as it is to men. Human work also images the work of God. Women and men should do the kind of work which allows them to be pleased with what they have produced as God was pleased with what he created. Good work is intended to benefit the community of creatures, not selfish interests, by using wisely the resources given to humans as a trust.

As fallen creatures, however, our lives are marked by conflict between our longing and capacity for good work and the demands of our sinful self and the secular world around us. As Dorothy L.

Sayers has put it, we forget that work is what one lives to do and think of it as what we do to live. We find ourselves toiling without thought of the product, earning so we can consume, struggling to survive and succeed. We feel pressured to compete. The writer of Ecclesiastes captures these ambivalent feelings toward work. On the one hand, he realizes it is a gift from God; on the other, he questions the lasting quality of its results: "A man may do his work with wisdom, knowledge and skill, and then he must leave all he owns to someone who has not worked for it. This too is meaningless and a great misfortune. What does a man get for all the toil and anxious striving with which he labors under the sun? All his days his work is pain and grief; even at night his mind does not rest. This too is meaningless. A man can do nothing better than to eat and drink and find satisfaction in his work. This too, I see, is from the hand of God, for without him, who can eat or find enjoyment?" (Eccl. 2:21–25).

Despite such conflicts, the general thrust of Scripture is that we are not to capitulate to the values of the nonbelieving world, but to present an alternative way of living. When Paul tells the Roman Christians, "Do not conform any longer to the pattern of this world, but be transformed by the renewing of your mind" (Rom. 12:2), the injunction is so general that it includes both the individual's attitudes and values and their expression in activity. The transformation of work in a fallen world, bringing glory to God, was a logical extension of the gospel for the early church.

The Example of Christ   Hebrew society accepted daily work as part of human existence and attached no stigma to working with one's hands. The rabbis taught that the father who did not teach his son a trade or craft was training him to be a thief. In New Testament times, rabbis themselves did not receive payment for their religious teaching; each earned his own living by means of a trade. Similarly, the apostle Paul supported himself as a tentmaker. In Mark 6:3, when the people of Nazareth were amazed at Jesus' teaching in the synagogue, they called him a *techton*, a craftsman. Matthew reports their question as "Isn't this the carpenter's son?" (Matt. 13:55). Jesus apparently had worked at a trade in the Hebrew tradition, and he set an example for us of the dignity of manual labor.

The examples Jesus uses in his parables reveal his recognition of the toil at the heart of daily existence. Furthermore, his compassion for those burdened by this toil is obvious. "Come to me, all who labor and are heavy laden, and I will give you rest. Take my yoke upon you, and learn from me; for I am gentle and lowly of heart, and you will find rest for your souls. For my yoke is easy, and my burden is light" (Matt. 11:28–30 RSV).

The early church interpreted the life and work of Christ to be redemptive. One analogy used to teach believers the theology of the incarnation and redemption was that Christ was like a slave or servant *(doulos)*. In New Testament times, the *doulos* was still a bond-servant, and bond-servants constituted the primary work force. There were degrees of servitude in the Roman Empire, ranging from respected household workers, to field laborers, to criminal slaves, but in any case, the *doulos* had none of the rights of the citizen.

In Philippians 2:1–11, the analogy of the bond-servant is used in two important interpretations of Christ's redemptive work. First, Paul admonishes early Christians not to act out of ambition or self-interest, but to take into account the interests of others. "Do nothing out of selfish ambition or vain conceit, but in humility consider others better than yourselves. Each of you should look not only to your own interests, but also to the interests of others" (vv. 3–4). Unfortunately, sometimes readers have skipped over the second sentence and have misinterpreted this passage to mean that they must be doormats and deny their own self-worth. The second sentence is a key to a balanced approach to life, an approach which takes into account both the needs of the self and of others. Second, believers are to follow the example of Christ who "made himself nothing, taking the very nature of a servant, being made in human likeness" (v. 7). As Christ voluntarily emptied himself of all exaltation to assume the role of a slave, so Christians should choose to give up a self-centered, ambitious, and competitive way of life.

**The Teachings
of
the Epistles**
The Christian's main job, according to the New Testament, is to give witness to the gospel in a pagan world. Jesus calls the Christian the salt of the earth and the light of the world (Matt. 5:13–16). Similarly, in Ephesians Paul instructs Christians to redeem the time, to make the most of each opportunity, bringing God's redemptive process into an evil age (Eph. 5:15–16). Paul also repeats the Old Testament image of God, the worker with his hands: "We are God's workmanship, created in Christ Jesus to do good works, which God prepared in advance for us to do" (Eph. 2:10). The redemptive work of Christ enables believers to give glory to God through their deeds, thereby negating the disastrous effects of the Fall.

The most specific biblical instructions about work in the secular sense refer to individuals and not to society at large. Paul did not wish Christianity to be mistaken for a subversive movement within Roman culture (1 Tim. 6:1), so he was always careful to interpret the import of the gospel for individuals within the hierarchical social order of the time. One of his goals was to instill in believers an understanding of the purpose of work and the attitude Christian slaves *(douloi)* ought to have toward their work and their masters. Paul taught that Christians work because they are to be useful in this world and to share with others. "He who has been stealing must steal no longer, but must work, doing something useful with his own hands, that he may have something to share with those in need" (Eph. 4:28).

In describing the attitude of the worker, Paul always refers to the *doulos-kurios* (slave-master) relationship. Therefore, we have to transfer his teachings from the quite different cultural context of the Roman Empire to our much more complex society. The writings on work, in the context of the various kinds of labor done by slaves, appear in the "Household Tables" of the Epistles: Ephesians 6:5-9; Colossians 3:22-4:1; 1 Timothy 6:1-2; Titus 2:9-10; and in the non-Pauline letter, 1 Peter 2:18-25. These clearly indicate that the worker is to be sincerely obedient to his or her master and is to do everything with excellence to the glory of God. "Slaves, obey your earthly masters in everything; and do it, not only when their eye is on you and to win their favor, but with sincerity of heart and reverence for the Lord. Whatever you do, work at it with all your heart, as working for the Lord, not for men" (Col. 3:22-23). All the Pauline passages repeat these themes, while 1 Peter emphasizes that this revolutionary attitude toward work in an adverse situation is to include the slave's relationship to harsh masters. "If you suffer for doing good and you endure it, this is commendable before God" (1 Peter 2:20). Slaves who endure suffering are following Christ's example.

**Work and
the Roles of Women
in the Bible**   Made in the image of God, men and women are first of all human. The Genesis story of creation underscores the fact that self-worth derives from our reflection of the divine nature, and the New Testament account of redemption shows that self-worth also depends on the unmerited love of God as revealed in Christ. Although our roles in society and our functions as males or females are intertwined with our sense of personhood, they are not to be confused with this essential identity as humans. Men and women are to procreate and work; the marriage relationship most perfectly allows these activities to be carried out, and the physiological differences of men and women indicate that they are complementary to one another. Only as cultures and societies emerged over hundreds and thousands of years did fixed social roles for men and women evolve, and a complex set of factors governs these roles in each society. If we consider how American society has changed with respect to what was expected of our grandmothers and what is expected of women today, we have a slight indication of the differences between our culture

and the first century A.D. or the time of Abraham, thousands of years ago. In reading the Bible, we must be careful not to project our culture and our values on those of another time and place. Nevertheless, we must seek the principles in Scripture which are valid for all times and places.

Although the Bible portrays the evolution of culture from herding and early tilling of the soil to the rise of fortified towns and then cities and empires, the Hebrew tradition maintained patriarchal and hierarchical social structures. The fabric of society was a type of extended family in which the woman functioned as wife in an arranged marriage and as mother of the progeny of her husband. Women often had a powerful, if backstage, voice, and they had many responsibilities. In a nonindustrial age, being in charge of a family meant spinning, dyeing, weaving, grinding corn, baking bread, and the like. At times, it also meant working with one's husband in the fields or in a craft. The Old Testament ideal was the chaste and industrious wife and mother, but the woman of Proverbs engaged in a remarkable range of activities, including selling and buying land, weaving and selling garments, giving to the poor, as well as her usual household tasks (Prov. 31:10–31). Because she was an exemplary figure, she illustrated all the potential of a godly woman in her culture, both in the pragmatic activities of life and in the wisdom of her fear of the Lord. The feelings of incompleteness and the stigma which Sarah and Hannah experienced when they were unable to bear children also indicate the importance Hebrew culture placed on bearing progeny.

Economic values, as well as religious beliefs and cultural mores, affect the role of women in a society. For instance, because of the wealth they brought with them in marriage and their ability to bear children, women were the prized possessions of their husbands in early Hebrew society. In our age, the economic issues are quite different. The traditional household tasks (baking, spinning, weaving) have been taken over by industry, and labor-saving devices have reduced most household work to a minimum. In our society, the "problem" of working women has been, for the most part, a problem of the middle class. We accept the fact that poor wives and mothers must work. We allow unmarried women to work. But we have trouble dealing with the middle or upper-class mother who works outside the home when her children are young or the married woman who works when she does not have to. Some Christians, brought up with a hierarchical view of the family and church, also tend to be uneasy about the ascendancy of women to management or leadership positions, even in a secular work environment.

The Old and New Testaments provide enough exceptions to the portraits of women as wives and mothers to suggest that a woman's work should be related first to who she is as a person before God and then to the norms of society. Deborah the judge and Huldah the prophetess were two of the exceptions in the Old Testament. Two women in the early church, Lydia and Priscilla, illustrate that in the Roman Empire, which embraced an enormous range of cultures, a variety of work was done by women. At Philippi, Lydia was converted to Christianity under the preaching of Paul and Silas, becoming the first European convert. Her name is not Greek, but Lydia was from the Greek town of Thyatira, known for its purple dye. Lydia was a dealer in this dye, and she was apparently successful in her business because her home was large enough that she could open it to Paul and his party as a place to stay, and to the believers at Philippi as a place to gather (Acts 16:13–15, 40).

What we often fail to realize is that the work of the exceptional woman of the past is now much more the work of the average woman of the present because of the changes brought about by education, technology, communication, industry, and government. Today, women cannot be placed in a single category any more than men when it comes to the types of work they do or the roles they play.

Paul's attitude toward Priscilla and her husband Aquila shows that his understanding of the role of women was more flexible than many people think. He and Luke mention them several times (Acts 18:1–3, 18, 24–26; Rom. 16:3–4; 1 Cor. 16:18; 2 Tim. 4:19). Priscilla was, with her husband, a tentmaker and co-worker with Paul. Driven from Rome by Claudius's edict which expelled Jews, they went to Corinth where Paul found them. They accompanied Paul to Ephesus, and Paul claimed that they risked their lives for him. Teachers of doctrine, they explained the way more fully to Apollos. Hospitable, they opened their home so that the church could meet there. Paul always mentions Priscilla and Aquila together, suggesting their true partnership in both sacred and secular work.

Paul is much more progressive in acknowledging the active role women played in the early church and their freedom in Christ than one might expect, given his conservative rabbinic education. The context of Paul's remarks on the role of women in the church and in marriage indicates that he wished to avoid disruptive excesses and strains in the order of the service. Women at that time had little training or experience in public worship, let alone teaching, although they did prophesy (1 Cor. 11:2–16; 14:26–40; 1 Tim. 2:11–15). He did not want the personal lives of men and women to distract from the work of the gospel (1 Cor. 7), and he wished to maintain the sanctity of marriage at a time when the structure of the family was becoming endangered (Eph. 5:21–6:4; Col. 3:18–21). The issues of slavery and submission are linked to marriage and the family in the household tables, and Paul's stance is always the maintenance of the established social structure (Rom. 13:1–7). Yet, the model of the relationship between believers is one of freely chosen submission to each other, following the example of Christ's servanthood. The community of believers is a body where all differences of class, station, gender, and race disappear. Each part of the body is unique in its gifts and is necessary to the well-being of the whole (1 Cor. 12; Eph. 4:1–16).

There is a revolutionary thrust to Paul's approach to the question of authority and hierarchy in the church and family. (He does not deal with women in positions of leadership or authority in secular work.) Women who had been viewed as inferior within the rabbinical tradition are given full equality in Christ (1 Cor. 11:11–12; Gal. 3:28). Yet, Paul does use the rabbinical example of a hierarchical order within creation when he discusses marriage. He does so in the context of a spiritual model for the home. The relationship of the husband and wife is to rest upon a selfless love which mirrors Christ's voluntarily chosen servanthood and love for the church. The mutual submission (expressed as "submission" for the wife and "love" for the husband) is freely chosen, not imposed. The principles set forth by Paul do not dictate a single pattern for every marriage, but allow for a variety of ways, according to personality and circumstance, for the relationship between husband and wife to be worked out.

In the instance in which Paul uses the rabbinical interpretation of the Creation and the Fall as a justification for his opinion, "I do not permit a woman to teach or have authority over a man" (1 Tim. 2:12–14), the context and vocabulary suggest the situation within the early church. Jewish women had been excluded from participating in worship, and Paul is concerned about improper behavior by them and other untrained women who might elbow their way past more experienced men to control the worship experience. Again, it is the abuse of freedom to which he is responding.

The doctrinal passages in the New Testament which deal specifically with women must be read against the patterns set forth by Jesus in the gospels (the subject of a later chapter) and the immediate ecclesiastical and cultural context. The Pauline passages, in particular, justify the work of women and the worth of women in a progressive manner. Few late twentieth-century Christians would condone slavery because Paul and other New Testament writers accept it. Why then should we limit the roles open to women today when the thrust of New Testament teaching is to liberate the individual to do good work?

**The Salt
of
the Earth**   The women to whom we talked expressed a number of different attitudes toward work: work as a "calling," as glorifying God, as an opportunity for excellence, as an adverse circumstance to be accepted with faith. These attitudes are all extensions of the New Testament teaching on work. Another dimension to that teaching, however, is that the working Christian can be an example to society. The values of the Christian will be different from those of the secular world, and

Christian women can bring a unique perspective to their work which can bring healing and wholeness to contemporary society. Joanna is a good example. Divorced and in her thirties, she has one daughter. After a long journey toward emotional and spiritual maturity as part of a charismatic Episcopal parish, Joanna has changed her attitudes toward her work as she has grown as a person. At first, work was therapeutic, a part of learning to cope with reality as a divorced person. "I really believe in the therapy of work. Whatever the situation is, just go to work. I said, 'Bother about what I want to do or what career thing interests me, I've got to face reality. I've got this kid.' So I got a job at one of the hospitals doing clerical work, and it drove me crazy, and the kid was driving me crazy, and sitting at the house and meeting bills and buying a car was all just driving me crazy. I was in a rage most of the time, but I knew that I needed to keep going to church and that God was doing something wonderful in my life. I was scared to death, but I knew it just all had to be. I griped and grumbled, and yet I knew that I needed to do it."

After working a year-and-a-half as a clerk, Joanna was ready to assume more responsibility and looked for another job. "It was the most marvelous thing that had happened to me in a long time. It was an ego booster. I had worked some place for a year-and-a-half! That's almost unheard of in our culture any more, especially in a clerical job." She had several opportunities but decided on a job in a downtown office. At lunchtime she would go to eat in a little sandwich shop. "It was such a nice place. I loved it. Kind of on the fringe of everything. I got acquainted with the owner and his wife. One day they had a help-wanted notice on the bulletin board that said 'manager.' And I said, 'That's my job!' I just knew it. I just knew that was where I was supposed to be working, and so I took the job. It didn't pay well, and it was really hard work, but our family ran a little summer resort, and it just gets in your blood. It reminded me of that situation which I had loved.

"I like my work. But in our culture today everybody is struggling so hard to get to the point where they don't have to ever do any physical work. We're becoming a nation of white-collar workers, so by all rights, if I have my act together, I'm supposed to be wanting some sort of executive position to be accepted in our culture. What I have chosen as my work was totally unacceptable to the kinds of people I want to be accepted by. I had to really work at that. When kids quit, you have to do their work yourself. So there I was. My friends would come in and see me scrubbing tables. And, oh, my pride! It was just awful. They'd kid me about it. That was the worst difficulty I had to get over—choosing something that in our culture is not really acceptable."

Joanna has a real ministry in the way she relates to customers, even if it is only briefly, and her relationships with the customers are the most satisfying aspect of her job. "It's fun just to be there and to serve people and see that they get their little needs met. It's so appreciated because downtown is so plastic. People are just starving for someplace where there is a human being."

Anne provides another example of the special sensitivity Christian women bring to their work. She is about forty and is the mother of four children who are now in college or finishing high school. She married before finishing her own college degree and later returned to get an undergraduate degree and master's degrees in English and library science. Now she has taken a year's leave of absence from her job as a librarian to work on a doctorate. Her aim is a management position within a library.

Anne is particularly concerned about the need for humane and well-read leaders in libraries. "I was doing a paper last year on politics and librarians, and I was struck by how few top administrators that I interviewed had read Aristotle, Plato, Machiavelli, or had any kind of grounding in political theory. And I asked another question about what literature they had read as children. A number of them had read classic literature, but the younger the persons I interviewed, the less they had read. I was horror-struck. I thought, 'What's going to happen to our libraries? There's a real lack of leadership in our libraries.'"

From that experience, Anne developed a sense of mission about going back to school herself. She has noticed, however, that something "dreadful" happens to the dynamic women who move into leadership positions. "What happens, to our dismay, is that most of them, instead of having a more humanizing leadership style than the men they are replacing, become just as bad or worse. I don't know which comes first: they're corrupted by the system, or it's just too much for them." Anne believes women in leadership positions must use their experiences as nurturers in order to humanize the organizational structure in which they find themselves. "I think that nurturing is important. I guess I wish women would realize it. We do the civilizing things in the world, and if women are going to stop doing those, and if men don't think they're important, who is going to do them? . . . The sense of community—the neighbor who is there when someone falls and breaks a hip and who takes the person to the hospital. I think this kind of thing has got to be taken more seriously, and men have to start doing more of it if we're going to survive as a civilization. I really believe that very strongly, and that's where Christian principles come in.

"People say, 'When you become an administrator, Anne, you'll be a terrible one because you're not tough enough.' Well, why do you have to be tough? What's wrong with being nice? I don't think there's such a thing as being too nice. . . . We should celebrate the nurturing instincts, make room for them. They should be viewed as strengths, not weaknesses, and used to humanize the workplace." Anne observed that there is a Christian evangelical movement within the library profession as in other professional fields. "I see this wherever I go now in professional groups, that there are these little pockets where people are concerned about the destructiveness that comes with competing in the corporate or the academic world."

Women are making the exciting discovery that they can provide a missing element in contemporary American society by modeling their own humanity and Christian womanhood in the workplace. Joanna described the nature of this discovery very succinctly: "Our humanity is part of our witness: the things that we struggle through, our long-suffering, and the reality of our struggle. Like every human being, we struggle. . . . We had a marvelous series of teachings at the church about being the salt of the earth, and I believe that's what we're called to be. Salt is a very quiet thing. It's almost a mysterious thing." And society cannot survive without a quiet revolution in values—the very values that Christian women can model as the salt of the earth.

VOCATION

What Is a Vocation? Christians like to use the words "vocation" and "calling" to describe their work, sometimes without understanding the history behind what they are saying.

For believers from many backgrounds—ranging from Catholic to Fundamentalist—a "call" or "calling" is usually equated with an inner compulsion from the Holy Spirit that one is to be ordained or to serve as a missionary. The apostle Paul's missionary work in Europe was initiated after he had a vision of a man from Macedonia begging, "Come over to Macedonia and help us" (Acts 16:6–10). The Macedonian call can still be heard, and many young women and men have judged the degree of their spiritual commitment by their willingness to say "yes" to it.

In the Catholic tradition and liturgical Protestantism, "vocation" was for centuries connected with serving God on the highest plane by entering the priesthood or a religious order where one's single-minded goal would be glorifying and serving God and achieving spiritual maturity.

Today, Christians often speak of their secular jobs and of their work at home as "a calling" in this same religious sense. We also use the word "vocation" in a secular sense to mean one's lifework or profession. All sorts of vocational counseling services are available for planning careers and career changes. In the secular sense vocation appears to be connected with planning and choosing work, whereas a spiritual calling or vocation seems almost beyond personal control because it is the work of the Holy Spirit. Christians sometimes go as far as thinking that planning one's lifework and being called by the Holy Spirit are antithetical to each other.

How did all these confusing uses of the words "vocation" and "calling" come about? First of all, the Latin root of the word "vocation" is *vocatio*, and it literally means a "calling" or "summoning." In Middle English, *vocacioun* meant a call to a religious life. Our modern dictionaries have retained this more narrow meaning, "a predisposition or calling to a certain kind of work, especially a religious career," but the primary definition is the broader, secular meaning: "a regular occupation or profession for which one is especially suited or qualified."

In the New Testament, the word for "calling" is *klesis*, and the church is the *ekklesia*, the "called out ones." Consequently, in one sense, vocation (the equivalent of *klesis*) means basically God's call to follow Christ in repentance and become part of the community of believers. Paul also speaks of the Christian's place in life (married or single, slave or free) as a calling (1 Cor. 7:17). Taken in its radical sense, the call of every Christian is to work first for the kingdom of God; making a living is of secondary importance. Exercising a gift within the New Testament church—serving as an apostle, prophet, evangelist, pastor, teacher, or in some other capacity—consumed more ultimate devotion than secular work (1 Cor. 12:28; Eph. 4:11–13). Yet the writers of the epistles counsel Christians to do their secular work as unto the Lord.

One problem in trying to discover the meaning of vocation for the Christian is that society and the structure of the church have changed dramatically since the time of the New Testament house churches. Today, most Christian lay people would say that the demands of their jobs, homes, and extra-church commitments are so great that they could not in all honesty describe the work of the gospel as their primary vocation, although they would like it to be. Despite the charismatic renewal, the average congregation or parish places little emphasis on the theology of the gifts of believers, a subject to which we'll return. Members are busy, but often with organizational duties that keep the building and the guilds and the committees operating. Organization within the church is not bad in itself, but it often complicates the search for the true meaning of vocation and the discovery of spiritual gifts on the part of individual believers.

History also colors our use of the words "vocation" and "calling." In the Middle Ages, the call to follow God came to be equated with the call to monastic life. (The Middle English word *vocacioun* reflects this.) Whether trying to discover God through contemplation or serving God through work, members of religious orders were viewed as superior to the average Christian. The reasons for the rise of monastic orders are complex, but the orders served an important function in the medieval church. However, in the decline and decay of the late Middle Ages, the excesses within monasticism generated a new view of vocation among the reformers of the sixteenth century. Luther and Calvin changed once and for all the Christian view of vocation.

The Reformers protested against the double standard of monastic life and secular life, wishing to show that the poorest laborer could discover God without withdrawing from ordinary life and that God could be glorified in the commonplace. One's secular work could be one's vocation. Luther and Calvin rejected the dichotomy between the secular and the sacred. In his sermon on 1 Peter 4:8–11, Luther claims that Peter "wants to remind everyone in particular to attend to his occupation or office and, in discharging it, faithfully to do whatever is demanded of him. For, as Scripture teaches in many places, no work is nobler than the obedience in the calling and work God has assigned to each one." (First Peter 4:10 states, "Each one should use whatever gift he has received to serve others, faithfully administering God's grace in its various forms.") In his commentary on 1 Corinthians 10:31, Calvin writes that "Paul teaches that there is no part of life or conduct, however insignificant, which should not be related to the glory of God." (The Scripture reads, "So whether you eat or drink or whatever you do, do it all for the glory of God.")

The Puritans derived their understanding of vocation and of work directly from Luther and Calvin. The misused cliché, "the Puritan work ethic," has come to stand for the set of cultural values which white, northern European immigrants brought to America: one's value in life is defined by one's work; work is one of the highest values in life; and one can get ahead by being industrious and thrifty. This set of values was a secularization of Puritan theology and ethics. (Modern Americans even blame their inability to relax on the Puritans!) The Puritans really believed that all work is holy, that each person has a vocation, that work glorifies God and benefits society, and that diligence must be tempered by moderation. For the Reformers and Puritans, vocation was the particular work, sacred or secular, to which God assigned the individual Christian.

The work ethic, not this integrated view of vocation, still dominates American culture. One woman explained to us how she had absorbed the work ethic in her childhood. "Both my mother and dad are of Finnish descent and are very much into the work ethic that was prominent with immigrants to the U.S. in the 1900s. . . . My father came to this country at ten on a boat with his brother with a tag around his neck saying 'deposit me at this place.' Very sad, very heartrending. I can hardly see pictures of Ellis Island without feeling sad. He really had a very hard life in that he had some misunderstanding with his father at the age of ten and ended up supporting himself . . . so he's very much into the work ethic. He did very well, and he worked very hard, but I never felt, growing up, for instance, that people should take vacations or that people should take time off. . . . It's been very difficult for me to learn that rest and relaxation are part of life."

The work ethic is inextricably connected with the Reformation redefinition of vocation, but the distortion of the work ethic, leading to "workaholism," makes work an end in itself, rather than a means for serving others and glorifying God.

Given the long history of the word "vocation," it is not surprising that it has come to mean so many things. But words are very functional, and the ways we use "vocation" indicate the variety of people's experiences of God's call. We should feel free to affirm that the pattern of every life will be different. For example, Lynn, a civil engineer, told us she did not think of her career as a special calling. "I guess I really believe, wherever you go, there is always a ministry for you, and it's not a matter of being led into a specific position because you're following a ministry. When you're there, you discover your ministry, and discovering that can sometimes take time." Many Christians would agree with Lynn. They feel their daily work has no particular spiritual significance, although they are good at it, but that some other activity constitutes their special ministry or service. Other women would maintain the opposite; their daily work constitutes a clear vocation, and they feel they have been placed in a particular place at an opportune moment. Still others have experienced a call to Christian ministry. Sometimes that call has been dramatic; sometimes it has evolved over a period of years.

This book is not the place to argue at length the case for or against the ordination of women. (We will tell the story of Betty and her gradual sense of calling to the Episcopal priesthood in a later chapter.) We do wish, however, to convey in the stories which follow something of the meaning of the call to Christian ministry for the women who shared their hopes and struggles with us. The "problem" of the spiritual vocation of women is very much related to the readiness of people to accept women in positions of leadership in the church. The issue is both biblical and cultural.

Pastor or Missionary?   The major role-models for our interviewees when they were growing up were their teachers; in the church, their heroines were missionaries, particularly single women who were nurses and teachers in a foreign culture. As young girls most of them never knew or heard of women pastors or preachers. Shirley was an exception. Her real heroine was her great-great-grandmother, a Quaker preacher. "I grew up on a wheat farm in Kansas, and I went to school at a Friends college in Wichita, Kansas. My earliest memories of an aspiration are associated with my great-great-grandmother. I had always heard that she had been a Quaker preacher in the Midwest, and I was in the Quaker church. I never did identify it as an aspiration, but I thought to do something like that would be a really great thing.

"This is very difficult for me to talk about. I have really ambivalent feelings about it. The women whom I knew in our church who were pastors to a certain extent were honored in the same way as the men who were pastors, yet I always felt that my mother had a very low regard for women pastors. Whenever the subject would come up in our church [the reaction was], 'Oh, no, we don't want women pastors.' I always felt that it was a thing to aspire to, and yet it wasn't."

Shirley is now in her early fifties, and she and her husband have recently moved to a restored row house in the inner city of a large urban area. Her three sons are in their twenties. She was not working when she talked with us, but was looking forward to developing a new lifestyle in her predominantly black neighborhood. It has been a long, and sometimes agonizing, road from Kansas to her new environment. The pain has been due in large measure to Shirley's struggle to fulfill her call to Christian ministry and to accept herself.

Although many of the dissenting, evangelical sects of the Pietistic and holiness traditions accorded women the right to preach (the Quakers were among these), over the years the percentage of women pastors has dwindled because of the force of cultural attitudes. ("I would feel funny with a woman pastor.") Middle-class culture often proved stronger than the original prophetic power of revival in which new denominations began and in which women played an important role. Shirley's ambivalent feelings as a young girl about women in the pastorate were directly related to this phenomenon. Her model was a woman preacher of an earlier generation, but the message she received from her own generation was that such an aspiration was unacceptable for a woman. Because society values achievement as a male prerogative, a woman who aspires to achieve is sometimes caught in a deep conflict involving her feminine self-esteem. In the context of the church, aspiring toward a role which has been defined as male, even though one may feel called in that direction, can pose even deeper problems, particularly when the individual woman receives little affirmation. Judith Bardwick has noted that successful scholastic or occupational competition is a general cultural goal which need not threaten a woman's feminine identity *unless* she is punished for striving or punished for succeeding. The lack of any affirmation of a woman's call to a traditionally male field of Christian ministry can constitute just such a punishment. Shirley herself commented, "It seemed to me that I had a very low self-image as a girl, so when I thought about something [like being a pastor], I thought, well, I could never really be what I wanted to be as a girl. Therefore, I never had the courage to attempt that."

Shirley's conflicts as a young girl were also related to her experience as the only girl in a farm family. "My mother always said I was a tomboy. I was very independent. If I had a choice, I would rather go out and milk the cow than cook the supper. I always thought my two brothers had a lot more privileges than I did." Only when the boys were gone did her father ask her to help him extensively on the farm.

Going to seminary did not lead to an affirmation of Shirley's sense of calling. "I went to college, and I always had the feeling that whatever I did it had to be something that was a Christian vocation of some sort, but I didn't really know what it was." She then went to seminary where she was in the first graduating class for the master's in Christian education. "The men there would say, 'Oh, pooh, pooh! You girls are just here to get men,' and 'What's a master's of religion compared to a divinity degree?' " Not all the men responded in that fashion, however. Some were from Wesleyan Methodist backgrounds and had no problem with women being in seminary.

"I always felt that as a woman you had to be at least twice as good as a man before you were ever asked to do anything. Also, I had a problem because I was so timid and afraid. When I did graduate from seminary, I was offered the possibility of taking a church with one of the Friends groups in Indiana, but I turned it down. I just didn't feel that I was ready to handle anything like that. I don't think that my training had in any way prepared me for pastoral work." Shirley decided instead to go to Japan as a missionary. "I felt that was kind of a resolution of the conflict that I felt, feeling that somehow I had a call to some kind of a Christian ministry, but not having enough confidence in myself because I was a woman. I thought that missions was kind of a compromise."

Shirley was in Japan just after World War II; there she met an American serviceman who was to become her husband. After their marriage, Shirley eventually embarked on a new role in the United States as a pastor's wife and as mother of three little boys. "When my children were still in elementary school, I took a job one year on an emergency basis teaching in a parochial school. They needed a teacher, and I thought I'd try it and see. I didn't like it. I was trying to be a mother and teacher at the same time, and that was not within the range of my capabilities. I was exhausted. But I did feel that as a mother and as a woman I did need something to look forward to, thinking 'suppose something happens to my husband' or 'suppose I would have to be doing something, I should get ready.'" Shirley returned to school part-time, intending to get a certificate to teach social studies on the secondary level. (In addition to her graduate degree from seminary, she also has a master's degree in history.) Due to the difficulties her youngest son was having in school, she became interested in learning disabilities and eventually became certified to teach reading on the elementary level.

Shirley taught reading for ten years, retiring when she moved to the inner city. "It was rather fulfilling because I was working with children who were disadvantaged and really appreciated the attention. The most satisfying thing about it was being able to see the progress in children who had great difficulty." Going back to school and establishing an identity for herself proved vital to Shirley as a pastor's wife, a role in which she had never felt entirely at ease. "I had a hard time being a pastor's wife. After having two years of seminary and going into the pastorate with my husband, I found that I was a zero-plus. I had a very difficult time accepting that, and my self-esteem went *way* down." Shirley felt rather shy and didn't enjoy entertaining, but she did teach children in Sunday school. "That was not exactly fulfilling because I enjoyed Greek and would have preferred teaching adults. In most of the churches there wasn't much opportunity to serve." Returning to school and then to work were invigorating experiences. "I'll never forget the first day I walked into a class. We were asked to give our names, and suddenly I realized my name is Shirley. I'm not John's wife; I'm not Kenny's mother; I'm just me. I had never thought about it before."

We asked Shirley why she thought her lack of identity had been a problem for her. "I think that part of the problem in my life is that I've assumed that your identity is what you did, and I never thought that I did anything. I always wanted to crawl in a corner and hide because 'who am I?' I'm not sure that that's true any more. . . . Just the fact that in a group meeting I can speak without my voice going all trembly is a big thing for me. That's something I struggled with for years and years and years. I thought, 'Oh, what an awful affliction to have!' because I always had things that I wanted to say, but I usually couldn't do it. Just being able to say, 'well, I can accept myself the way I am and today as it is,' means I don't have to run after unrealistic goals."

Aside from the love and support of her husband, Shirley has traveled most of her personal road alone. What advice would she give to someone else suffering from low self-esteem? "The main thing you can do for someone like that is to reinforce them as they are and let them know that who they are is quite acceptable. That's something that's hard to learn from anyone else. It's a long road, and you have to take it by yourself."

Spiritual Gifts   Shirley's story is by no means the exception within the church. One wonders how much less painful her life might have been had the church aided her early in identifying and affirming her gifts, directing her in her sense of call, for one of the encouraging signs of renewal within the church in recent years has been in precisely this area: the development of a theology of spiritual gifts.

The New Testament teaching on spiritual gifts has a direct bearing on one's understanding of vocation and need for affirmation. The Day of Pentecost initiated the age of the Holy Spirit, and the early church was marked by the energizing of the Spirit. If the church is a body where every Christian has a significant function and is necessary to the well-being of the whole, it is because the Spirit indwells and blesses each woman and man. Gordon Cosby of the Church of the Saviour (Washington, D.C.) has called the church "a gift-evoking, gift-bearing community." The basis for the gifting process is both vertical and horizontal: believers are to present their bodies as a living sacrifice to God, and they are to realize that they belong not only to God but to the other members of the community (Rom. 12:1–8). The Holy Spirit gives each believer qualities of life and capacity for service. The qualities or fruits of the Spirit—love, joy, peace, patience, kindness, goodness, faithfulness, gentleness, and self-control—become more marked as the Christian matures. The gifts of the Spirit constitute the capacity for service of each person within the body of believers.

The major teaching about spiritual gifts is found in 1 Corinthians 12–14, Ephesians 4:7–16, 1 Peter 4:7–11, and in the passage in Romans cited above. Spiritual gifts are described in various ways. They are called the ministries of prophecy, serving, teaching, encouraging, helping, leading, showing mercy. Sometimes the gifts are equated with more recognizable roles in the early church such as those of apostle, prophet, evangelist, pastor, and teacher. Elsewhere, the gifts are viewed in terms of results—wisdom, knowledge, healing, ecstatic languages, and the like. The variety of the gifts demonstrates that God recognizes the variety of human nature, and every Christian is promised at least one gift to be affirmed, developed, and used (1 Cor. 12:7). And while gifts differ, all are to be used to the common good (Rom. 12:5–6). Christians are called to be faithful in using their gifts (1 Peter 4:10), and this exercise of the gifts within the body is vital in achieving maturity or "the fullness of Christ" which is to be the goal of all believers (Eph. 4:11–13). Undergirding use of all the gifts is the motivation of selfless love (agape, 1 Cor. 13).

Our innate abilities are not necessarily our spiritual gifts.

Often a natural ability is channeled and perfected as a gift within the context of the body of believers, but sometimes Christian ministry entails quite a different set of qualities than those identified as natural abilities. The discovery of one's spiritual gifts constitutes the recognition of spiritual vocation, even for those with full-time secular jobs. Sometimes there may be considerable overlap between one's profession or job and one's call to use one's spiritual gifts; sometimes there may be few obvious points of contact. Generally speaking, though, the nourishment and development of one's gifts within the church spill over into one's secular work.

The teaching that *all* Christians are gifted frees women for service within and without the church. Joel the prophet announced the promise for the Day of the Lord: "I will pour out my Spirit on all people. Your sons and daughters will prophesy, your old men will dream dreams, your young men will see visions. Even on my servants, both men and women, I will pour out my Spirit in those days" (Joel 2:28–29). Peter cites this promise in his sermon at Pentecost (Acts 2:17–21). Later, the daughters of Philip illustrate its fulfillment in the early church, for they are described as having the gift of prophecy (Acts 21:8–9).

Jill, a member of a Catholic religious community, explained the liberating power of the Christian message as one of "empowerment" for women. Working to improve the reading skills of a group of women in prison, Jill sees herself as an enabler in this process of empowerment. Women who are free to use their God-given gifts are first of all freed from being the victims of life. Once they have power over their own lives, they can then proceed to serve others.

**Community
and
the Calling Forth
of Gifts**   The movement of the Spirit within the church is evidenced in the wide range of new and reformed communal groups which emphasize the calling forth of gifts. Many of the traditional distinctions between Catholic and Protestant structures have become blurred as both move in

similar directions. Jill, for instance, is part of a teaching order of nuns in Detroit, but at least 50 percent of the 1100 in the order are in non-teaching positions. Many are engaged in a "ministry of presence" as "leaven" to the secular world. How an individual sister will carry out her call and use her gifts is decided through a process of discernment by both the person herself and the leadership of the order. Jill, who is a convert to Catholicism, described her decision to enter an order as a growing inner compulsion which she could not avoid. "It's nothing I can rationally argue about because as a Christian I could have done a number of things. The pull came most to share my values." Her progressive religious community has given her the support she needs to carry out her work of sharing the message of empowerment with other women.

Jackie, on the other hand, is an elder in the Sojourners community in Washington, D.C. She and her husband share the care of their small son, Peter, and Jackie has begun to attend seminary to better prepare herself in her role of giving pastoral counseling and spiritual direction. As a leader, Jackie sees that gift as emerging from the group. "My basic sense, which has emerged through participating in life in this community, is that leadership—sacramental leadership, pastoral leadership, prophetic leadership, servant leadership—comes out of a group of people who see those leaders emerge from among them and affirm them. . . . I feel like I'm ordained by this group of people to be a leader."

Although most of us may not be called to a more radical form of commitment within a religious community, we can experience the same qualities of the shared life in Christ within individual parishes or congregations which seek to promote and facilitate the use of spiritual gifts. Marjorie Bankson described for us the process by which her gifts were called forth while her husband served two terms of duty in the Vietnam War. "I believe that we each bring our skills and our needs to the body, and in the body they become gifts." Originally a teacher, Marjorie discovered pottery when a friend asked her if she would like to use his potter's wheel in the evening. Since she had no children, Marjorie ended up spending several evenings a week working with clay. "It was really the beginning of my spiritual journey. It was almost like entering a silent chapel when I entered the studio. . . . I really began to value physical activity and to care about a more speculative, intuitive, wondering side of myself."

During her husband's second tour of duty, Marjorie discovered what the real nature of the church as a community of believers could mean. "That was probably my first experience of what it meant to belong to the body of Christ. There was a family in that community, a couple with two children, who invited me to dinner every single Sunday that year. About the third time I said to them, 'You know, I'm not going to invite you back because I don't like to entertain when I'm by myself.' And she said, 'Marge, the deal is finished. You don't owe me a roast beef for a roast beef. You bring me news of the outside world, and I give you dinner. You don't owe me anything.' The other thing was that the husband in that family had taken on a commitment to write to my husband as part of his church tithe." Marjorie brought her need to the church and was affirmed. "That year was the first time I got in touch with the real depth of my loneliness and my need for other people. I think probably that was my major contribution—to simply be a wounded person in that community, willing to stay with that and speak about it. . . . Because of the church body, I had the energy to give outward."

Marjorie began her career as a professional potter by setting herself a time limit and a financial goal; it was both a test of herself and a "fleece" to see if God would affirm her gift as a call. He did, and she now belongs to a professional cooperative. Potting is only part of her call, however. "I really feel called to a teaching ministry, but potting is my groundwork. It is my place of reflection and silence. I know when I don't have a daily time of working with clay and being in my studio, pretty soon I dry up and don't have anything to say. It is important for me to be making functional, graceful, beautiful things that people can really use at a price they can afford, rather than something that is fancy."

Now living in the Washington, D.C., area, Marjorie usually teaches a course at the Church of the Saviour. "I generally offer a course on what my growing edge is. I love it; I love the discipline of preparation. The structure of the church and the emphasis on adult education have been a context in which to continue my own growing as well as giving me a place to offer it." She also leads retreats and conducts workshops, often for the Faith at Work organization. Frequently she combines her gifts of potting and teaching in a single workshop, illustrating spiritual principles by means of the clay she works with. Her call and the use of her gifts are still unfolding. This is an exciting prospect for any woman who sees life and the Christian walk as a continuous process of growth. "I want to be faithful to my call, and I see that call unfolding and changing. I am beginning to write seriously for the first time in my life. I see potentially that I will drop the production of pottery in favor of using clay in ministry full-time. I'm not sure that's the direction I'll go, but I think that's the direction the signs are pointing to right now."

Women in Missions   The history of mission work is dotted with heroines—strong women laboring alone, pioneering, teaching, and training converts in foreign cultures. Until recently, women missionaries have been the only role-models for many girls because this was the only spiritual calling open to women within many segments of the organized church.

Patricia Mortenson has been involved with missions all her life. She was born in China of missionary parents and remembers being airlifted into India during the war with Japan. "I have vivid memories," she told us, "of the sad things brought on by war: people starving and Chinese soldiers walking barefoot in the snow." One of her early role-models was a missionary in India who ran an orphanage. "Many of the girl babies were just thrown on the trash heap, and she went around and collected them, and people brought them to her. She was always a very special person."

Pat became a nursing educator, fulfilling her own childhood ambition and subsequent call to be a missionary. Her early goal of going into missions "needed to be reevaluated. I needed to make sure that it was not just a childhood whim. As I got into nursing, I began to understand some of the medical needs in the world and the importance of teaching in order to multiply your efforts by training others, so I got into nursing education." After receiving a degree in nursing and studying missions on the graduate level, Pat spent two terms of service in Rhodesia. Her work ranged from directing a school of nursing to running a bush clinic. She was active in village evangelism and literacy training and also taught at the Evangelical Bible College. "We always seemed to be operating at an emergency or disaster level because the need was so great and the staff was not sufficient. When I first got into the work I felt that if anybody can't work an eighteen-hour day, they just better not be here. Fortunately, my values have changed somewhat."

After giving so much of herself to the intense life demanded by the needs she felt so keenly, Pat's health deteriorated; she finally had to realize that the door to mission work abroad was being closed for her. "I had lost about fifty pounds, and it finally got through to me that I couldn't keep going like this. I just realized that if the Lord was closing the door to this, then he had something good for me. I couldn't keep looking back. I had two requests of the Lord. I wanted, if possible, to close that chapter completely. I wanted to see people, former students I hadn't seen for a while, and others, and have the sense that I was able to bring things to completion there. That happened. The second request was this: I really didn't see myself going into nursing here in the States, and I did not have a clue as to what else there might be for me, but I prayed that somehow it would be in connection with foreign missions."

God opened a wonderful new ministry for Pat in training missionaries. In 1975, she joined Missionary Internship, a training center for missionaries from many different mission boards. At first she was the missionary-in-residence; now she conducts workshops, counsels, and develops educational materials. Although Pat is a gentle, unassuming person, her vision and intensity have led her to develop a series of workshops for women, "Woman in Mission," which are potentially far-reaching in impact.

In an article on "The Role of Women in Missions," Pat has observed that in the last thirty years there has been a shift in the understanding of the role of women in many missionary organizations, a shift away from the recognition of the individual woman's own gifts and calling. "More often than not the woman is considered to be merely supportive of the man. Many missionary wives and mothers believe their role is totally circumscribed by the home and family. Thus they may never learn the language or enter into relationships with nationals. Single women are often placed in institutions rather than in direct evangelism or teaching ministries. . . . In many sectors of the church today we hear how a woman is to submit and what a woman must not do. But do we balance this with how God affirms woman in all the possibilities and challenges that face her in her life?"

When Pat first proposed her workshop idea, she received a great deal of support from other members of the Internship staff, but elsewhere people "were very fearful of the whole thing and thought we were going to open a Pandora's box. I don't know that I would have had the courage on my own because of this very negative feedback which now seems astounding. A group of furloughed missionary women were going to get together and discuss issues. Now why is that so threatening?" The workshops emphasize that the message of the Bible is for women in all aspects of their personalities and lifestyles; that a healthy self-concept is vital for effective work in missions; that women are accorded spiritual gifts which are to be nurtured, developed, and used on the mission field. They give women practical guidance in finding their gifts and in evaluating their responsibilities and priorities. Issues such as the biblical principles for male-female relationships and cultural conditioning about male-female roles are also discussed.

"Some women have really experienced a freeing, a new sense of personhood. That's been a very exciting thing to see. I think of one very gifted woman who had felt that she had to really take the back seat as far as her husband is concerned since he was the seminary graduate. Therefore, she would get all her spiritual instruction from him. She didn't have anything to add. Then on the field she was easily going ahead of him in language learning, and she thought, 'This shouldn't be. I just better shut my books and stop.' At the workshop she realized, 'I didn't have to do any of that.' It wasn't that she had an insensitive husband. He would have been supportive. It was just this frame of reference that she had which she felt was right and biblical."

Women who do not use their gifts are often bound by frustration, lack of fulfillment, and even guilt. Pat recalled a woman in France "who had basically been doing secretarial and hostessing work." She became involved in home Bible studies "and realized 'This is where my gifts are!' She struggled with this for ten years. She was told, 'You can't do everything you want. This is part of the sacrifice of being a missionary.' She was laboring under the guilt of that, and then she came to realize, 'No, it's the other way around.' After recognizing that her gifts were to be used, not suppressed, she's now involved in a full-time, Bible-teaching, discipling ministry. She's saying, 'It took me ten years. Isn't there something I can do to help so that others don't have to go through the same struggle?' She's done a master's thesis in that area."

Called to Work in the Inner City   As we came to know the women who appear in this book, one of the important lessons we learned is that there is no limit to what God can do as he works through women. He calls us in various, but specific, ways, and he puts the right woman in the right place at the right time. This truth is strikingly illustrated by two women who are engaged in two types of social action.

Doris Dennard moved to Harlem in the mid-1930s when she was six years old. Her father was a dishwasher; her mother worked first as a domestic and then as a beautician. They left Norfolk, Virginia, in the midst of the Depression for a Harlem which was a far different place from what it is today. Doris learned the alphabet out of the Baptist hymnal, and education was an aspiration encouraged by her family. She went to college but married young without completing her degree. At the age of twenty-two she was unexpectedly widowed and left with two small children. It was obvious that she ought to go back to college, so her father commuted from Harlem to Brooklyn to baby-sit for her five evenings a week so that Doris could complete her last year of college by taking classes at night. After holding several jobs in social agencies, Doris completed her graduate work and became a psychiatric social worker.

In the mid-1960s she was working with adolescents in a secular agency and feeling restless. One day she came across a copy of the August, 1966, issue of *The Reader's Digest* and happened to read a little article called "The Bible's Timeless—and Timely—Insights" by Dr. Smiley Blanton, a well-known psychotherapist, who was the director of the American Foundation of Religion and Psychiatry which he and Norman Vincent Peale had founded. Aware of the spiritual vacuum in the lives of many of her clients and their parents, Doris was intrigued by the article in which Blanton maintained that the Bible, if one is wise enough to use it, contains keys to dealing with the problems of the unconscious. Blanton listed a number of his favorite passages which, when memorized and put into practice, give clues for good mental health. Doris was so interested that she wrote Dr. Blanton, asking for information about the Foundation.

"It must have been three or four months later. A Friday afternoon. I was sitting at my desk, minding my own business, behind in dictation as usual, and I got a call from a nice young woman who said, 'I'm Dr. Blanton's secretary, and I'm calling to set up a luncheon appointment for you and Dr. Blanton.' Well, now, wait a minute. I was waiting for literature in the mail. I certainly was not ready for someone saying Dr. Blanton wants to have lunch with me."

Doris went to lunch with Blanton, thought he was a very warm, outgoing person and that they had shared a pleasant luncheon, and that was it. But the next Monday she received a call from the head psychiatrist at the AFRP, who had also been at the lunch; this time Doris was asked to send a résumé. Doris was reluctant, but she finally agreed to do it and to spend an afternoon visiting the Foundation.

"I called my minister and I said, 'Hey, something's happening here, and I don't understand this, and I'm getting kinda suspicious.

I got a feeling I'm being guided somewhere, and I'm not sure I wanta go.' He said, 'Well, you know the Holy Spirit behaves this way.' I said, 'I know, but the Holy Spirit and I are having some conflicts about this!' " Doris visited the AFRP and was offered a position on the staff. "You know, Dr. Blanton very much wants you here," she was told. After making all sorts of excuses, she finally agreed to think over the offer, although it was not attractive to her at all. "Then for some reason I could not sleep. I'm not a person who's given to insomnia, except at times when the Holy Spirit is determined that he's going to get my attention. The insomnia lasted for three days while I was busy saying to myself, 'No, Lord, we're not going to talk about this. I'm not going.'

"The insomnia persisted until I prayed about it. . . . I have never prayed for the power of speaking in tongues. I have never had any particular opinion about it one way or the other, but while I was praying about this conflict, suddenly I began to speak in tongues, and that didn't particularly impress me. But after that I suddenly became aware that a force of some kind was making it impossible for me to move. In my stubbornness I said, 'Of course I can move. This is ridiculous.' I got up, but as I got up, I fell backward. . . . It was not a fall that hurt me, but the room shook. I was aware at that moment that I was being very firmly told to go to the American Foundation of Religion and Psychiatry. So I said, 'Okay, Lord, I'm going under protest, and I will tell you quite frankly that I'm afraid not to go. I know you are omnipotent; I know you are omniscient. I'm going, but I know who's telling me." One of Dr. Smiley Blanton's last acts was to hire Doris, for he died unexpectedly, and she began work on the day of his funeral.

Why had Doris been told so forcibly to go to the AFRP? For several months she was miserably unhappy and saw no reason for the move. Then she heard about a branch of the AFRP which was operating in Harlem. The budget was very low, and there was just one, struggling pastoral counselor. "Nobody knew what they were going to do with it. I was intrigued. After I met Rev. Dennard who was the clinical pastoral counselor, I understood why the Lord insisted I go to the AFRP. He was telling me, 'If you want to build an agency in Harlem, here's how to do it.' I wasn't at AFRP very long, only about six months, before I came full-time to the Harlem Interfaith Counseling Service and found it delightful to be God's fool."

Largely through Doris's vision and that of Rev. Dennard (to whom she is now married), HICS has mushroomed into an agency staffed by about fifty people. Initially, Doris recognized the need for a mental health agency for families "that would take into account the cultural uniqueness and the spiritual belief systems of the people of the community." When she returned to work in Harlem, she "fell in love with the people all over again." Her title is "assistant to the clinical director," but she still carries a caseload of twenty-five while she handles program development and assessment. Her special burden is for black high-school dropouts. In Harlem, 89 percent of black young people never finish high school. One of the programs of HICS is a therapeutic classroom which aids young people in obtaining their high-school equivalency diploma.

"Today a young man came in and brought us his General Equivalency Diploma. He passed. He's nineteen, and we met him three years ago. Three years ago he was chronically truant. He has an alcoholic mother and doesn't know where his father is. One of several children. He has had three years of individual treatment and four hours a day on the third floor in a therapeutic classroom. If he is not in class by ten o'clock on any given day, his therapist knows, and the therapist is going to go find out why. We've been with this kid when his mother left him, with him through every crisis of his life for the last three years. That's why he has a diploma, and he's working in a training program as a printer at this point."

There is a painting of the Last Supper hanging on the wall in Doris's office, and the Christ is black. There is a Bible on top of her bookcase. "When youngsters come from very traumatic and discouraging socio-environmental realities, they need to know that God is their father. And they need to see the love of God in the way that Jesus saw it. I may not always, depending on the frame of reference of the youngster or the adult, use the word 'Jesus,' but I sure use his teachings. It's what he taught more than his name that people need to internalize, and if they can do that, they can grow. Of course, they know what I believe. It's all over this office. Kids are fascinated by that picture. They say, 'Jesus is black?' . . . Each of us is supposed to see him like ourselves. That's what's important."

HICS emphasizes preventive care; its primary concern is to promote health. It maintains dialogue with the Harlem community so that the community decides program priorities. Its services include crisis-intervention, individual and family counseling, parental guidance in the education of children, marital counseling, theme-oriented group therapy sessions, as well as the therapeutic classroom. HICS is developing a multimillion dollar Creative Life Management Center in the heart of Harlem that will attempt to help juveniles restructure their lives spiritually, intellectually, and socially. The new Creative Life Management Complex will symbolize the revitalization of Harlem. One of the groups HICS sponsors is a Saturday Spiritual Workshop for people who can't find what they need in congregational life alone. It consists of prayerful ministry among the participants as they engage in dialogue with one another. Doris calls it "the outpicturing of the living church in action." The same might be said of the ministry of the Harlem Interfaith Counseling Service.

Mildred McWhorter represents a quite different type of social action ministry, but she is a visionary like Doris Dennard. When Mildred was growing up in rural Georgia, she never dreamed she would be the founder and director of two Baptist centers serving about five thousand people in Houston, Texas. "At the age of sixteen as I read my Bible and as I went to Sunday school and church, or any time I read about any type of work helping people, I had a very deep conviction in my mind and heart that this would be a real great way to spend your life. But, somehow, I had never known a person like that. I grew up in rural Georgia; all I knew was what I read. I had never seen a live missionary. In fact, I didn't even know there was such a thing. . . . The most outstanding people I knew, though, were schoolteachers. . . . I just liked those people and kind of modeled after them."

Mildred went to college and majored in home economics. As a teacher, she soon found herself talking to students who stayed late after school to make up work—not about family living, but about

Christ. After three years of teaching, she volunteered one summer to teach Vacation Bible School in south Georgia. "I really wasn't dedicated to the Lord all that much, but I had three months without anything to do, and somebody asked would I help with some Bible schools."

During the missions emphasis in the VBS, the study materials indicated that the teacher should ask the young people to consider what God would have them do with their lives and whether they should be missionaries. "I would do what it said in the book, but it boomeranged. Always I had this conviction, 'What about you? What about you? Why ask these to go when you aren't willing?' At that time I knew nothing about missions in the U.S.A. All I knew about was Nigeria missions or Peru or Chile or somewhere else. I surrendered my life to go into foreign missions.

"While I was in Louisville, Kentucky, in seminary, in social work study, I became acquainted with riverfront missions there on the river in Louisville and dearly loved it. I had a group of thirteen-year-old girls who puffed cigarettes and cursed like ninety and were rough as could be, but it challenged me. . . . From that time, I prayed that if the Lord wanted me to stay in the United States that he'd open the door. He did close the door to foreign missions; I failed the physical. That was a real blow. I was so frustrated for a few months. I went back into teaching and taught two more years, thinking I had gone back and got my master's to do nothing.

"One day, out of the clear blue, a man I had met when I was a summer student worker in Christian social ministries called me. This man had moved from Wichita, Kansas, to Port Arthur, Texas, and he said every time he prayed for a mission worker, he would remember me. But he thought I was already in Peru. He said he prayed for weeks, and every time he prayed he still would remember me. He called my parents and got my phone number. After he contacted me, I flew out to Port Arthur and began work there a few weeks later. You may be delayed, but I feel if God calls you, he will get you where he wants you."

Mildred worked in Port Arthur for five years before she was invited in 1963 by the inner city Baptist churches of Houston to try to establish an outreach for Christ through social action ministries. She emphasized to us that her aim was not to make Baptists, but to serve the community, which is mostly Mexican American, and to declare the Word. "At first I started just visiting to find the needs of the people, but I made a vow to God, too, and I really did feel this very deeply. I said, 'God, if you'll bless my efforts to meet the social needs, I'll always teach your Word. Every time there's any activity, I'll teach your Word. I'll witness for you.' And he's multiplied our efforts a thousand times. We started off with nobody. In fact, I visited for thirty-one days before I got one person in any activity—I mean eight or ten hours a day. Now we have approximately five thousand enrolled in our activities at two locations. . . . God did it. I just happened to be the figure on the scene.

"I have taught the Word. I never have a ball game without Bible study. Never have a literacy class without Bible study. We have planned parenthood, nutrition, cake decorating, beauty classes, but we always have Bible study. . . . I feel like you can put shoes on their feet, clothing on their backs, food in their stomachs, but if you don't win them to Christ, they die and go to hell. I really believe that. I don't try to scare them out of hell; I try to love them into heaven through faith in Christ. I like to call my work 'creative evangelism.'"

Mildred's way of showing love is to make each person feel important. "I get a real thrill and challenge out of seeing people come to realize they are really somebody." When we talked to Mildred, it was late in the evening, and we sat in her office just off the gymnasium at the Center. A teen-age boy was playing basketball, waiting to ride home with Mildred because she was giving him temporary shelter until she could find housing for him. He had walked two miles to her home on a recent evening to get help because his older brother, home from prison, had beaten him. Despite being tired, Mildred showed her remarkable sense of humor and buoyancy. She commented that God had given her a sense of humor to help keep her sane and to aid in witnessing, especially to the older boys. "I feel that if I've been called to any age group it would be teen-agers from thirteen to twenty. These are the ones I'm especially happy to work with."

We asked Mildred what she thought about being a woman in a leadership position. She said she felt "the women's movement is kind of foolish," and then went on to make some astute observations. "I've had a few people, mainly preachers, who couldn't understand God calling a woman as a director of a work in a ghetto. But God knew what he was doing. These people wouldn't kill me when they might have killed a man doing my work. They have respect for their moms. They have respect for Catholic sisters.

"A man who is mature in his thinking, who is stable in his job, sound in his faith, does not resent a woman in a leadership position. I find sometimes I have to be a little more dogmatic than a man might have to be. And I might have to let them know that I know what I'm talking about, and I have to be sure what I'm doing.

"I do not resent being a woman in today's world. It's been very interesting. Very unique to sit in the pastors' conference. They sit up and take note when I talk. A few days ago I spoke in the annual meeting of Southern Baptist churches in Houston, and I flipped out one of my switchblades which I'd taken away from a boy I'd won to Christ. He traded it to me for a Bible. We must have had seven hundred or eight hundred people in the building when I flipped that knife out, and I'm telling you I didn't have to say a word to get their attention!"

Mildred said that no one should consider becoming a missionary anywhere if she felt it would be a burden or thought she would really be giving up something. "God's a God of joy and excitement and dependability. I've never given up anything really. According to people's standards, maybe I have, but God has given me tenfold everything I've ever given away."

**How to
Discover
Abilities and Gifts**   Practically speaking, most of us have not experienced a call to a special ministry in the dramatic way Doris and Mildred did. We may feel we don't have a variety of natural talents, and we may be unsure just what

our spiritual gifts are. The parable of the talents in Matthew 25:14–30 teaches that all are expected to be useful servants of God, whether we have one, five, or ten "talents." There are no excuses for women, just as there are none for men. How, then, do we identify our talents and gifts and put them to use?

The elements of the search are *prayer* ("God, show me my gifts"), *study of Scripture, assessment* ("What gifts appeal to me? What do I enjoy doing? What do I feel I'm good at?), and *action* ("When I do a task or serve in an area on repeated occasions, do I improve and see results?"). A gift discovered will be blessed and used. It will be affirmed by those in the community around us—by friends, family, brothers and sisters in Christ. A gift may also be identified and called forth by members of the community itself. God may lead us into circumstances which permit us to discover and use unexpected gifts. Just as life is a process, unfolding before us, so the use of our gifts will evolve and change; they can be used in unending combinations and in varied situations. We are not limited to one vocation; in fact, many people change vocations several times. God only asks us to have the courage and flexibility to be open to his leading and to take short first steps.

This process of finding our spiritual gifts can overlap the way in which we discover and use our natural skills. Many women do not realize how much they have learned by doing volunteer work, housework, or odd jobs, by listening and interacting with people. They don't realize that they can try out an interest or skill by volunteering in an area before deciding to seek further training or before trying to find a paying job. Our dreams, our feelings, and our bodies give us additional important clues as to whether we are frustrated and ought to be doing something else. As someone we interviewed told us, "Keep track of your feelings. I really think that our bodies give us signals about what the Holy Spirit has in mind for us, and if we pay attention to that, the path will be fairly clear."

A Christian vocational counselor suggested that a vision of the future is also important in determining how to use our abilities and gifts. She pointed out that it is clearly advantageous to acquire some insight into what future hiring trends are likely to be, where the greatest economic growth will probably take place, and what new industries and occupations might be expected to emerge. "If you have a vision of what's out there," she said, "you can act on it and find your place." (The appendix lists several sources of occupational outlook information.)

Jackie Shelton Griffith, another counselor, commented to us that there is no shortcut to discovering the work that is right for the individual. "I'd begin with prayer, because God does know what gifts he's given us and he desires for us to use them. Also, it is always useful to go and talk with four or five people who know you and ask them what they think your gifts, abilities, and weaknesses are. They have to give evidence for everything they say. They're not allowed to just say, 'I think you're wonderful.' No flattery allowed. I've found this process to be so useful. When four or five people begin to say, 'Well, I see this in you,' you also start to say, 'Hmm, maybe I can acknowledge this after all.'" A fulfilling vocation is the consequence of the acceptance of our abilities and gifts.

THE TOUCH OF LIFE

Some women have responsibility thrust on them by the changing circumstances in their lives; others seem to have a clear sense of direction or vocation. Still others are afraid of taking responsibility for their own lives. Why do so many Christian women struggle alone and in silence with their fear and sense of worthlessness?

No discussion of the relevance of belief to the feelings women have about themselves and their work would be complete without treating the centrality of Christ to the lives of Christian women. For the women we interviewed, inner liberation has come through the acceptance of their personal worth which they have found in Christ.

The stories in this chapter provide an overview of the changing roles and lifestyles of contemporary Christian women as they search for authenticity and identity as individuals. Despite differences in background, geography, education, age, and role, these women share distinctive qualities as Christians. Their lives offer hope to other women struggling to assume responsibility and to take the risk of accepting the freedom which Christ offers.

Jeanne   Our interview took place in a small, cluttered office at the rear of a Christian bookstore. The story we heard that fall morning celebrates the life-giving touch of Christ. There were several interruptions and the heating pipes clanked in the background as Jeanne described her reactions to her job as manager of The Way Bookstore. "I've never felt so fulfilled in my life. And I've never felt so equipped to do something in my life as now. All the experience I have has immeasurably prepared me for this ministry, so for this reason it's sort of the apex of my life."

The Way is a Christian bookstore located in an eastern university town. It was founded in 1972 as the project of an ecumenical prayer group. Not long after the opening of the store, Jeanne's husband Ed used money from a legacy to buy the business, and he asked his wife to manage it. She was forty-six when she began this unexpected career.

"I would never have conceived of myself as a manager," Jeanne confessed. Managing a bookstore has provided an outlet for the gifts and emotional qualities of this intense woman in a way that no previous experience in her life has. Before her marriage, Jeanne chose to become a secretary because it seemed practical. "I never liked it much. I hated typing because I made so many mistakes. I really felt like a loser. The endless typing was very nerve-racking. It just didn't suit my personality. My work as a secretary really gave me a bad feeling about myself because it was my vocation and I was bad at it." Marriage and motherhood did not give her complete fulfillment, either. "We had three children, and they kind of overwhelmed me. I never felt really comfortable as I raised them, although I loved children. Rearing my own children was a threatening experience because I never had a strong, consistent personality; I never felt confident that I was doing the right thing."

Not long before The Way was founded, Jeanne came to a turning point in her life—an experience that freed her so she could exercise her "gift of helps," as she called it. In the 1960s she went back to school to get an undergraduate degree at the university. At the same time, her older son kept getting into deeper and deeper trouble. He began to be picked up by the police and was involved in drugs. Jeanne recalls that during this traumatic time, "What was going on inside me and my relations in the church seemed to be two different worlds. People in the church did not have any idea what was going on inside me until it was over. I probably just didn't want to share my anguishes; it was too painful."

Then her mother became very ill with pneumonia. When Jeanne flew to Minnesota to be with her, she couldn't tell her mother that at that very moment her grandson was in jail. Her mother was being fed intravenously and was very, very ill. "I began to minister to her needs and feed her. And she got better and better. I also ministered to the other patients in her room; I massaged them and tried to cheer them. I spent much time at the hospital, and my mother got better and better. Previously they thought she would never come back to the nursing home alive. Until that time I felt I had the touch of death on everything—and this to me was just like the Lord had given me the touch of life." There were remarkable aftermaths to this experience of affirmation. Jeanne's mother lived two more years. Soon her son entered the Teen Challenge rehabilitation program, became a Christian, and completed the program in seven months. At the same time, Jeanne herself recaptured the experience of her own youthful conversion. "This joy, incredible joy, returned and has never left."

The Way is located on the main street of the town, opposite the university campus. It carries a fine stock of books and religious materials for both Protestants and Catholics, providing resources for spiritual growth. Its real ministry, however, is on the emotional level, and Jeanne's sacrificial life of intercessory prayer contributes to this ministry. "The students come from big, square rooms across the street, and they have to give their whole history every time they walk into a store in order to cash a check, and nobody knows who they are from Adam. They come into our store and they get hugged; we know the names of practically everyone who comes in and never ask for their history. All we want is their telephone number when they write a check. They mention several times a week how much they love to come in here. It's the one place they are cared for." Students are not the only persons who find The Way a center of emotional warmth. "There's an elderly widow who comes in. I know she has never recovered from the death of her husband. When she comes in, I always go over and give her a big hug, and I have the feeling I'm the only person who touches her.

She comes in more frequently in the fall and wintertime when it's cold out. She comes in to get warm spiritually and physically."

**Liberation
in Christ**

Jeanne's story is representative, for the meaning of work for the Christian woman is bound up with what it means to be both a Christian and a woman seeking to fully realize her potential. How we respond to life is directly related to whether we see meaning in it. For the Christian, a faith encounter with Jesus gives purpose to life. As a result, in the day-to-day process of living and in the perspective of time, the Christian begins to see her life take on the outlines of a story with a beginning, a middle, and an end. It has turning points and crises; it contains the possibility for creativity and for service, for suffering and for joy. The meaning she sees in life is also related to her understanding and experience of redemption, grace, providence, and the sovereignty of God. The Christian woman may not consciously relate her personal story to theological doctrines, but she certainly affirms them through her lived experience. In our interviews, we discovered that the most ordinary people, when touched by grace, often lead the most extraordinary lives.

If faith in Christ brings meaning to life, it also brings acceptance and the promise of completeness as a person. The pattern of Jesus' life assures the individual woman of his acceptance. In John 4 his encounter with the Samaritan woman illustrates how he broke down barriers to completeness for women. As a rabbi, Jesus would not have been expected to speak to a woman in public; as a Jew, he would not have been expected to have any contact with a Samaritan. Yet he revealed himself to a Samaritan woman as the Christ, the Messiah. He extended acceptance to a person doubly removed from him by the conventions of the Jewish culture of his day. "Whoever drinks the water I give him will never thirst. Indeed, the water I give him will become in him a spring of water welling up to eternal life" (John 4:14). Eternal life welling up *within* the individual insures the possibility of inner-directedness and authenticity to the woman who is a believer. This fullness of life is explained in theological terms by Paul in Galatians 3:26–29. Eternal life and life here-and-now in Christ are available to all in the new covenant. Jews and Gentiles, slaves and free, men and women are now figuratively the offspring of Abraham. "You are all sons of God through faith in Christ Jesus, for all of you who were baptized into Christ have been clothed with Christ. There is neither Jew nor Greek, slave nor free, male nor female, for you are all one in Christ Jesus. If you belong to Christ, then you are Abraham's seed, and heirs according to the promise."

**The Struggle
to   Believing themselves to be accepted, for-
Be Free   given, and free to be themselves has**
proved to be particularly difficult for women, even for Christian women. All of us are governed by the images of what it means to be female and male which we absorb when we are very young. We learn scripts within the family, the church, and society which we act out again and again when we are adults. Often the scripts Christian women repeat subconsciously are at odds with the gospel message of freedom and acceptance. Furthermore, the scripts are often so strong that they become themes in the stories of their lives—themes that hem them in, blocking the path they would like to forge toward personal authenticity. Helen de Rosis has described some of the attitudes and roles of the "traditional woman" that many women unconsciously adopt:

> depends on someone else for her primary sense of security
> tries to please at all times
> tries to avoid all arguments
> needs external approval to maintain a sense of worth
> tries to maintain harmony at all costs
> cannot express anger
> can be extremely skilled and competent, but tends to discredit herself
> experiences guilt quickly and often

is quick to assume blame
is other-centered
expresses opinions apologetically
places her own needs second to those of family and others
is nonassertive in many respects
can meet many of her own needs only covertly and deviously
hesitates to accept leadership roles
works behind the scenes.

Young girls learn that some roles are more "female" than others and that some jobs are more acceptable for women. One of the most common attitudes women unconsciously adopt is that early decisions about their lives are unnecessary and unimportant because they will soon marry, raise children, and care for their husbands. Despite the revolution in the working world, young women still drift into work before marriage, thinking their jobs are only temporary. The work they choose is often governed by the limited number of roles in which they have observed women who have been their models. Subconsciously, a woman often believes she has fewer options than does a man, and these options are almost always in traditional pink-collar jobs. For example, Jeanne became a secretary before her marriage because it seemed a practical course to take, but she hated her work once she started because it did not suit her skills or her personality. For most women, work still means being a homemaker, nurse, elementary schoolteacher, typist, telephone operator, secretary, hairdresser, waitress, nursing aide, seamstress, domestic, or factory worker. These are also the jobs most readily available for a woman who must find work.

There are three basic patterns followed by women after leaving school. The first is to work for a while until they have children, stay at home for a few years, and then return to the labor force on a basis that won't conflict with family responsibilities. Sometimes this return to work is forced by divorce or early widowhood. The second is to work until marriage and then remain homemakers for the rest of their lives; of course, homemaking is a demanding and difficult job even though the homemaker is not counted as being in the paid labor force. The third is to remain continuously and full-time in the labor force until retirement. Both single and married women follow this pattern, which until quite recently has been considered typical of men.

Given the roles and scripts they learn early, women enter life and vocations with certain expectations about themselves and about others. Working women constantly experience conflicts and disappointments as these expectations run up against the reality of the expectations of other people in a world changing so rapidly that the traditional roles of men and women are blurred. Many women are also shaken when they discover that life demands flexibility and responsibility of them or when they learn that they never knew who they really were when they made some early key decisions.

Betty   Jeanne's emotional involvement with her work, her evolving sense of personhood, and her strong feeling that her life has a pattern in which work is central are themes repeated in fascinating ways in other stories we heard. For instance, Betty. Betty is in her early fifties and is married to an attorney; they have four children and three grandchildren. Recently, she was ordained an Episcopal priest, and she now serves on the staff of a suburban parish in a large southwestern city. Her calling is to pastoral counseling.

This well-groomed, gracious person didn't appear to be a pioneer as she sat serenely in her office, dressed in a clerical collar and fashionable skirt. In fact, she said that it felt "scary, frightening" to be a path-breaker. The role and the values with which Betty grew up were really those of a Southern lady. "You went to college. You studied liberal arts; math was not necessary because girls were not good at it. You went to Sweetbriar or Hollins. You didn't go East because those young women were likely to be liberal and hard. . . . I joined a good sorority. I didn't make a debut, but many of my friends did. I married a young man who lived five blocks from where we lived. Next we built a house and had a baby. If you needed money, it was very suitable to teach school, so I did."

Betty's sense of calling evolved as she worked in the church as a lay person and outside the church as a volunteer. Eventually, she began to study theology, but when she looked for a salaried job within the church, she found that "in the Episcopal church you have to be ordained to be employed to do anything except run the Sunday school. Finally I realized I was going to have to be a priest."

Pursuing theological studies was not easy. She took her first course at a Catholic seminary where her teacher was an elderly priest. "The first day I was there, he came in and he said, 'Good morning. Are you a sister?' And I said, 'No, father, I'm a married lady.' He said, 'Which parish are you from?' I said, 'Well, actually, I'm an Episcopalian.' Whereupon he moved all of the young male students over to the far side of the classroom and had me sit on the other side. He taught with his back to me up until just before Easter. Along about Easter, he began to turn slightly because I was the only one paying attention and handing in papers with any degree of regularity. After Easter, he began teaching with his back to the boys. At the end of the term he asked for retirement because he said he had only one student who paid attention that year, and she was a Protestant!"

That first fall Betty was so angry that she drove home gnashing her teeth and clenching the steering wheel. Later, when she had to study away from home and live in a dormitory or an apartment, "it was very lonely. I would be there Sunday night through Friday afternoon, then be with family over the weekend. I would clean house Friday afternoon and cook on Saturday, cook Sunday dinner, and leave. It was at that time that my vocation became very firm. I knew I was going to be a priest, and I knew for sure that I was never going to be without one good close woman friend again in my whole life."

Margaret Asked what advice she would give to a married woman who feels a sense of calling such as her own and wants to pursue a vocation within the church, Betty commented, "You can't do it unless your husband is totally in favor of your doing it—whatever it is." The struggles experienced by many young homemakers and the stresses placed upon marriage by changing roles for women are present in the story of another remarkable woman.

Beneath the surface of Margaret's story we sensed much pain, but pain that has been channeled into positive energy. Margaret is in her early forties and has two children, already in their twenties. She has just begun a new career as an assistant professor of historical theology at a prestigious divinity school.

"My intellectual and theological development began when I was about twenty-two and had a punctured ulcer. I was married to a Presbyterian minister and had two small children, and I was a bored housewife. I think now that my punctured ulcer was caused by trying *not* to use my head. I had the idea that I needed to be primarily a good minister's wife, run the women's association, cook a lot, and things like that—which were all right, but not totally fulfilling. That punctured ulcer, painful as it was and really quite dangerous, was a strong enough incentive to push me to analyze my life. After that I had about seven years of good psychotherapy. Suddenly, instead of being bored, I felt a great deal of energy. That immediately took the form of wanting to read and think a good deal. I did that for a couple of years, and then my children were in school, so I started going back to school on a part-time basis, always beating them home from school. I just got a stronger and stronger feeling that I wanted to understand more about the world than I did. It took me thirteen years, from reentering school on the junior college level, until I completed my doctorate.

"My going to school was not acceptable to my husband, and we were divorced. That was a terribly painful and sad aspect of what was mostly a very joyous feeling that I was getting stronger and healthier and more useful. The change in me had a negative effect on my husband who had, when we married, really expected me to be a good minister's wife. And I honored that as long as I could. That was our initial bargain, and I was really the person who was unable to keep it. I wish there could have been mutual growth that could have encompassed that change, but there wasn't."

For Margaret, the discovery that she had a mind she could use and then the using of her mind were keys to her healing. They were also keys unlocking the door to love. "My own capacity for loving human beings needs to be fed by fruitful work. This has been an important and humbling thing for me to learn. Before, I thought you just grit your teeth and determine to love . . . rather than try to learn how to enjoy and do the kinds of things that nourish you and result in being a loving person." Hers is not a story of self-seeking at the expense of others, but of what happens to an undernourished self when it is cared for. As she herself has learned, "It is important to learn how to love yourself, how to nourish yourself so you have something to give other people rather than trying to squeeze it out of nothing."

Nourishing work brought with it a price, however. Like other women of the 1950s, Margaret grew up with "certain expectations. The most important thing was to be a good wife, and then a good mother, and then a good minister's wife." In the context of her evangelical background and her role as a minister's daughter, she also inherited certain expectations. "There was a strong idea that Christians don't really participate in the larger world. I had no notion of myself as acting within a wide range of possibilities, either as a woman or as a Christian." In explaining her feelings about the changes which have occurred in her life, Margaret sees a basic distinction between guilt and personal pain. "Guilt is something that paralyzes you, but pain can be productive. I think that pain has been useful—the pain of changing my own idea of who I was and what I could do in the world."

Becoming responsible for her life in a new and more complete way led Margaret to the discovery of a pivotal theological principle: "I now see my life as a gift of God, not in the sense of being passive and feeling that things are dropped on me, but as exactly the situation in which I can come to learn what I need to understand next. Each situation in life is exactly the event that will rub me in a way that will polish me up a bit or bring out something that has not been worked on or has been underdeveloped. With this attitude, you approach things in a different way than if you see yourself either as deciding and moving on the external world so as to set yourself up in the ideal situation, or if you see yourself as entirely passive and a helpless victim. Either of those extremes is quite destructive. Receiving from God is high activity, and you have to work with what you get. You have to come to terms with it."

Ellen   Responsible choice does not necessarily mean that one breaks out of traditional roles or patterns of work. Ellen is a homemaker in her mid-thirties who feels her vocation is to be wife and mother. "About 1973, I went through a period when many women around me were going to work. And I wondered, 'Should I go to work? What am I doing here at home? I have a college education. Am I wasting it?' I decided that, no, what I feel called to do is to be a good mother and a good wife. So these conflicts were overcome, and I started to really pray about having joy in doing the everyday things. And the Lord answered my prayer."

Ellen explained how her approach to homemaking is integrated with a total approach to life. "We try to keep a simple lifestyle. I see it as a challenge. To be a good steward it's not necessary for me to use conveniences that might use more electricity or more water." As a result, her housework takes a great deal of time "because I do some of the things in, I guess people would say, an old-fashioned way. I consider myself a conservationist. Therefore, I do not use a dishwasher or an automatic washing machine. The foods that I can or freeze are more wholesome than those I could buy at the store. They don't have the preservatives, and the vegetables are clean when I freeze them, and they're made the way we like them."

Ellen's commitment to a simple lifestyle is a natural consequence of her upbringing in a rural Pennsylvania German environment. Ellen's seventy-eight-year-old mother Amy, widowed for thirteen years, lives alone in a home which was originally built by a civil-war veteran. Until fairly recently, she pumped her water outside. She still carries her own coal in winter, tends her garden, and maintains a busy schedule of church and community activities like helping prepare dinners to benefit the volunteer fire department. Ellen has chosen to follow the model set by her mother. "In the midst of that simple lifestyle, six of us graduated from college, one from trade school, one from nursing school. And another went to nursing school for two-and-a-half years. . . . I felt very close to my mother because she was there when I needed her. I think that has greatly influenced me in wanting to be at home, to be available to my children when they want to talk, when they want to tell me about what happened during the day at school. Even before they went to school I felt it was important for me to have as much time as possible to pass on to them the values that my husband and I have as people and as Christians."

Education had been the way to get ahead in her family, and Ellen herself thought she might want to be a physician or a chemist. She switched to biology in college and worked as a research assistant for two years after her graduation. Gradually she realized that she did not have the ability to go on for a graduate degree which would be necessary for a career in biology; at the same time she began to move toward her feeling that her role as a wife and a mother was a "calling." Only after long struggles did Ellen come to experience real joy in doing housework. When we asked what fruit the Spirit has worked in her life, she said, "Patience."

Kay   While Ellen chooses to stay at home, Kay combines a career with her roles as wife and mother. A newspaper reporter on a large paper in Texas, Kay is twenty-nine and has a small son. "When I was a kid, in the Baptist tradition the big deal was to walk the aisle when you were ten, eleven, or twelve and surrender your life to the Christian ministry. For a girl, that meant being a missionary or a missionary nurse. For a boy, it meant being a pastor or minister of music. I so much wanted to feel the call, but I knew it wasn't to missionary work. Finally, at a very early age, it crystallized in my mind that I wanted to be a journalist. I walked down the aisle and told my pastor that I was called to be a journalist. I remember he kind of skirted the issue when he turned to the congregation to explain why I had come down. I have steadfastly held to that calling to be a newspaper reporter. All of this was to the great consternation of my mother. To this day she thinks I'm going to go back and see the light and become a concert pianist or something like that."

Kay is a small, vivacious person who knows what she wants. Her energy and determination are evident in the way she describes her single-minded commitment to journalism. "I edited the high school annual; then I went to Baylor and majored in journalism. That was the main thrust of my time at college. I was single-mindedly a journalist, and the work that I did on the Baylor paper was probably my best and the most professional I've ever done.

During our interview with Kay, her husband Louis sat with us in the living room of their suburban home and made supportive comments from time to time. Louis is the religion editor of the same newspaper Kay works on, and he and Kay are very much a team. They met while working on the student paper at Baylor. "We both knew we would have to marry someone in that field. We realized that our individual and mutual dedication to journalism was something that would always be there. Louis knew full well before we got married that he was marrying a 'career woman.' We never had to go through any hassles about that."

Then Louis commented, "When we were married, our minister was very much aware that Kay's career was just as important as my career. He worked it into the wedding sermon by saying: 'Your first devotion is to God, your second devotion is to each other, your third devotion is to your family, your children, and your fourth is to your careers.' He made it clear that he was talking about both careers."

After four years covering news in the civil courts and county government, Kay recently took a one-year leave to have her son; then she returned to the paper, but to a new area, writing for the "lifestyle" section. She did a series of articles on adoption, including the current trend among many adopted children of seeking out their biological parents. Since Kay herself was adopted, she and Louis discussed the possibility of finding out the identity of her own biological parents. When they decided to go ahead, they sought the information through an intermediary. After the intermediary learned who Kay's parents were, his first words were, "You won't believe this!" Kay explained, "One of the first things I found out was that I was a fourth-generation journalist! Both great-grandparents were newspaper editors. . . . My feeling was one of relief and 'Well, of course, of course they're all journalists!' It was really a great feeling of validation."

Kay also had an important role-model. Like Ellen's mother who modeled an old-fashioned approach to homemaking and a simple lifestyle, Kay's adoptive mother had a special career which influenced her daughter. "For her time my mother did things that were very unusual. When I was about a year-and-a-half or two years of age, she opened a business in our house. She just cordoned off about half of the house and made it her office. She did public mailing and addressing. In our small town she was the only person doing work of this nature. She had an advantage in that she was there in the house to take care of my needs, but she was doing something none of her friends were doing. She was a role-model for me. Even though she did not work outside of the home, it was very much a part of her life."

Kay was able to manage her career and marriage quite well until the birth of Matthew, when "the real struggles" began. She had arranged in advance with her boss to take leaves of absence from her job for the birth of any children. "I wanted a year at home with the baby." During that year I got involved in seeking out young mothers in similar situations and primarily became involved with friends at church. These women only knew me as homemaker and mother, although I always talked about the fact that at the end of the year I would go back to work. At the end of the year, I did return to work and had absolutely no idea what sort of opposition we would run into.

"In our group of friends, most of the husbands were ac-countants or junior executive types and the women were dropout schoolteachers or people who had absolutely no identity except that of being wives and mothers." Although two-career families are numerous, Kay and Louis found little understanding from those in their middle-class, suburban, Southern Baptist church. When they placed their son in a day-care center, "there were all kinds of rude comments like 'I'd never leave my child in that day-care center.'" One other woman in her group of church friends went back to work solely because of financial need. "That they could accept and that they could support." The problem for Kay's church friends was not that she worked, but that she was a career woman; they thought she should be at home caring for her child on a full-time basis. "This was an extremely traumatic time. Not only were we going through the usual difficulties over leaving our son in day-care and my going back to work and picking up after a year, but I had also been ill with post-partum complications and we were gravely in need of money to pay medical bills. This was a time when we needed our friends. Support—that is what I believe a church should give. We got just the opposite."

Kay explained that even a one-year leave from her job affected her writing skills. "After a year's leave, it was very hard for me. I was terribly rusty. You have to write daily, and you have to keep your mind going daily, and you have to keep up with your skills—talking to people and learning how to find contacts and make contacts. It was extremely difficult to pick that up after a year. If I had put it off for six years until Matthew was in the first grade, it would have been so difficult to return I probably could not have done it."

Louis and Kay have learned to be very assertive in their local church. (They switched their membership to a different Baptist congregation after the lack of affirmation they experienced when Kay went back to work.) "The basic church structure is geared to the husband who works and has a wife at home who has plenty of time to volunteer. Some of the churches we have been members of like for you to be there Sunday morning, Sunday evening, Tuesday night visitation, Wednesday prayer meeting, and on the weekend some kind of fellowship. We have learned to be very assertive and say we will be active in our church, but we're not going to become slaves to it." Because they believe there should be a definite ministry within the church to two-career families, Louis and Kay now teach a Sunday school class. "This class meets at 8:30 on Sunday mornings, so the people who come are those who definitely want to be there. The folks who are there are very good friends of ours and are very supportive. There's acceptance. We call the class 'The Alternatives.'"

Hilda   Hilda is a Mexican American who lives in southern Florida. She works out of her home and laughingly calls herself her "husband's office" because she handles the accounting, tax reports, and financial affairs of their harvesting-contracting and packing business. According to the season, she also handles all of the payroll checks and forms for from 50 to 150 migrant workers. Hilda is in her forties and has five children, including one married daughter. As she described the many changes which have occurred in her life, a glow seemed to come over her face.

Hilda had finished school, including two-and-a-half years of business training, and was working in a bank when her family moved from Mexico to Texas. To learn English, Hilda went to the public school along with the second graders, staying after school to get help with additional vocabulary words from the teacher!

When she married, Hilda took on the lifestyle of the wife of a migrant farm worker. "I don't know how I did it because when I wasn't pregnant I was breastfeeding a child. And then on the road I had to drive. I followed my husband when we were on the road until my oldest was five years old. But my husband was a good husband and a good provider, and I got a lot of help from my parents." When her children were old enough to go to school, Hilda and her husband settled down in southern Florida where there is a great deal of truck farming.

The DeLeons started their business "little by little. We bought one teeny, tiny truck that was about nine years old, and as soon as we had enough money we bought another one a little bit better and so on. Then we met the Lord, and he changed our lives completely. After we became Christians and became aware of our Lord, of the Creator who was over us, everything just flourished."

Hilda has done the business work since 1962; she began when she had three children at home, two of them babies. "I would give them a bath in the morning and would put them down for a nap between ten and twelve. Then I would do my office work and put something in the oven for supper. When the children were sick, it was hard of course." Hilda also took evening classes at a branch college campus in subjects like American history, bookkeeping, and accounting, as well as attending government seminars on handling forms for items such as workmen's compensation.

Valuing education and being sensitive to the problems of migrants, the DeLeons are actively involved in their community toward which they feel a special responsibility. Hilda has participated in parent-teacher groups and is currently involved in a neighborhood committee of six mothers (Mexican, black, and white) who are working for better education for migrants. Her husband is a city commissioner, and they often attend evening political activities together. "If someone represents the people, he or she should be a model." And in their own business they take pains to give personal attention to workers who may be in need.

Looking back, Hilda observed that she used to be an introvert and that God has opened her up and enabled her to relax. "For a long time I wanted to leave everything in the Lord's hands, but I always kept on worrying. Then through the years and through study and prayer, I have come to realize that he will take care of everything if I just give him a chance, just leave everything up to him. I have my work, my family, and my church. I've matured to a point where I've always wanted to be."

What fulfillment does her work bring her? "I think it's the realization that I can do it. One day you just get up and you realize, 'I can do it.' If something happened to my husband, if he wouldn't be able to work, I could carry on through the help of the Lord. I don't have to rely on anybody. I don't have to be dependent. It's confidence. It's a great feeling."

Joan   Thus far, the stories in this chapter have dealt with married women. Joan's personal quest is a dramatic example of the meaning of work for a single woman who has discovered how to integrate all parts of her life. Her story begins in 1969 when Joan was a senior in college; it was a very unhappy time for her. "A part of my unrest was that I was not communicating with my parents. I felt the relationship wasn't real and that they didn't really know me or care about me as a person. To go through the motions seemed somehow artificial, and I just kind of stopped it. I guess I felt the same way about my relationship to God—that I had been going through all the motions of having a deep relationship with him, but that it was not all that it should be. I can remember saying, 'God, all my life I've heard that you really care about me and love me, but I don't feel it. And if I don't feel it, what good is it?' I was no longer willing to accept an intellectual relationship with God. I wanted something more than that. I wanted it to affect my life at the deepest level, and if it didn't, then I wasn't going to play Christian. Looking back, I see that as the beginning of finding a relationship with God that was meaningful and profound."

For four years Joan stopped pretending that her relationship with God was significant. She graduated with a major in psychology and spent a terrible year as a social worker in New Jersey. Then she moved and found a job as a secretary. It was the right job for her then because she could get something concrete accomplished at the office even though she wasn't managing her personal life. "I could go there at eight o'clock in the morning, and as long as I got papers out by the end of the day, my job was fulfilled. It was very satisfying to have a tangible kind of job after trying as a social worker to fill up needs that had taken years to come about and were not going to be met in any short period of time, if ever. My job was the happiest place I could have been at that time."

Outside the office, things weren't going quite so well. She began to see a psychiatrist on a weekly basis and kept going because she felt he was supposed to be able to help her. "I had gotten to the point where I really didn't want to live any more. I didn't see any hope of any changes taking place. I felt powerless to change; I felt powerless to change myself. I think the crux of the whole thing for me was not knowing whether or not God really cared about me, whether he loved me as a person."

As a last resort, Joan decided to go to L'Abri, the community and study center in Switzerland founded by Francis and Edith Schaeffer. One of her friends had gone there, and her life had been turned around. Joan thought that perhaps her life might also be changed. It was, but not in a way she ever could have anticipated. At L'Abri she didn't find love in a particular person, and she did not find the emphasis on study particularly helpful because her problems were more emotional than intellectual. She began to realize that her concept of God's love was that he had to do certain things for her in order for her to be happy. Someone had given her a book, *Your Half of the Apple*, which she had put off reading. One day she picked it up, and the moment of change occurred. She really wanted to believe God loved her. As she read, she said, "God, I'm going to step out on a limb, and I'm going to trust you, and I'm going to believe that all that this is saying is true." There was no profound change at that time, but she really believed it was a moment of trust. "It was like taking a risk with him and really believing that apart from anyone or anything in the whole world, this personal God has the power to fulfill my life. Period."

Now in her early thirties, Joan conveys inner serenity and joy. She exudes a sense of physical well-being, too, for she is now in business for herself as a teacher of creative modern dance. She also has a part-time position as an administrative assistant in a church. An odd combination? Joan would say, "No." She believes that Christians should be involved in the arts, and she is now involved in a new ministry of using dance in the context of the church.

Joan had taken tap and ballet lessons as a child. "I gave up dance consciously when I was in high school. The church that I was involved with really frowned on dancing, drinking, smoking. I really took that to heart because I didn't want to displease God." When she was working as a secretary, one day she saw a sign for a dance class. "It was kind of just a fluke. I saw the sign and got some of the girls from the office and said, 'Hey, let's go.' I knew the first time I whipped across the floor that this was something I really needed to do. This was a part of me. It was a part of me that I really needed. It was a physical outlet, and it was also a creative outlet."

Joan wanted to take more lessons after her first course was finished, so she began to study with a teacher who eventually told Joan that if she would apprentice with her for a year, Joan would have sufficient background to teach on her own. At that point, Joan left for L'Abri and dropped the whole project.

Upon returning to the States, Joan reestablished her relationship with her parents. She also realized that creative dance would allow her to integrate her interests in people and in the arts. (In college she had been an art education major before becoming a psychology major.) Joan discussed with her parents the possibility of an apprenticeship, and they prayed with her about her decision. "My parents prayed with me about whether or not I should go into this apprenticeship, and I'm so glad that God did it that way. That made them a part of my decision. I didn't have my heart set on it; it wasn't like I just had to do it. We prayed that God would clearly answer as to whether or not this was something I should do, and God clearly directed that this really was the way to go. He provided a part-time job, a perfect housing situation, and he made all the conditions right to allow me to be engaged in the apprenticeship." Becoming an apprentice was a risk; there would be no diploma or certificate which would assure her of a job afterward. Joan's teacher, however, encouraged her in time to begin teaching dance classes. Gradually, she developed her own clientele, and the time came for her to leave the studio and launch out on her own.

Joan cannot support herself through the classes she teaches to children and adults, so she works part-time as an administrative assistant at her church. Among her activities at the church there is a creative dance class for women, followed by a Bible study, which she gives on Tuesday mornings. More and more, Joan has begun to share dance in a Christian context, presenting workshops on movement and dance as expressive art forms for local churches and regional Faith at Work conferences. The response has been overwhelming. Her local church has been supportive on a personal level and has never made her feel that she is unchristian in her attempts to integrate dance and worship. On the morning after our Saturday evening talk with Joan, we worshiped at her church. As part of the morning worship service, Joan presented a dance based on God's call to Moses from the burning bush. Tears trickled down our cheeks as we watched, moved by both the dance and the story of her life which we had heard the night before.

Making just enough money to pay her bills, Joan barely "squeaks by." She has the anxieties of any small business owner. Will her classes be comfortably full? Where can she rent adequate studio facilities? How much will her transportation between classes and the church cost? She mops up the floor before her students arrive and carries heavy supplies to and from her car. Joan realizes that her current situation is temporary. "I'm in holding; yet I'm happy."

What are her feelings about marriage at this particular phase of her life? "To find someone who would love God to the degree that I do and would have the same heartfelt commitment and desire to do his work—I guess it would be really special to me to join my life with someone who has those same aspirations. I don't pine for marriage or long for it. I just think about it from time to time and realize that there could be real strength in having two people with that commitment as their goal who would be able to pursue it on the kind of intimate level that marriage would provide. I haven't met anyone who has those same aspirations."

Like other women whose struggles we have recounted in this chapter, Joan has discovered the serenity of inner freedom. Liberation in Christ enables women to express themselves through creative work and service. The creative potential of Christian women is one of the untapped resources of our society.

⑤

CHRISTIAN WOMEN AT WORK CREATIVITY
AND WORK

**The Creative
Potential
of People**   Work, by its very nature, is creative;
taking an infinite number of forms, it is
effort directed toward the production or accomplishment of something. The God who is at work in Genesis is the creator of the
universe. The Old Testament describes men and women at work
using their skills to create handiwork or to make the earth productive. Hebrew tradition is careful to give to God alone the power
of ultimate creation (of making something out of nothing). Yet,
because we are made in God's image, as humans we have an inherent need to express ourselves through creative activity.

Psychologists Abraham Maslow and Carl Rogers have observed that people who realize their full potential are marked by a
creative approach to life and work. They approach even the ordinary events of life with openness, perceptiveness, and lack of fear of
ridicule. They can be spontaneous and don't worry about all the
pressures of society on individuals to conform. In many ways, such
people have retained or recovered the joyous openness with which
the small child approaches life. Because they are free as persons,
they approach whatever they do in a creative and caring manner.

If we think about our own personalities, we find that we are
many-faceted; however, we often have one side that is more fully
developed than any other. Consequently, we live lopsided lives,
crippled in some areas and healthy in others. Our goal in Christ

should be wholeness or the integration of our many selves. John Sanford, a Jungian analyst and Episcopal priest, has described wholeness and health as a journey or process. If we are open to becoming integrated individuals, we can be assured that life will bring us the opportunities we need for the pain and conflict which nourish growth and creativity.

In the Christian life, whenever we ignore the doctrine and presence of the Holy Spirit and shut out the fulfillment which comes from life in the Spirit, we are less than fully creative. The theology of gifts, if put into practice, allows individuals to find their creative center. Thus, a special kind of creativity consists of our God-given potential of personality. Our spiritual gifts are the means whereby we can fully express ourselves and simultaneously serve God.

The Christian's goal is not so much the "self-actualization" or "individuation" of secular psychology, as it is fullness of life in Christ. He promises the development of our creative potential—and much more. In the Gospel of John, Jesus proclaims, "I have come that they may have life, and have it to the full" (10:10); and, "If the Son sets you free, you will be free indeed" (8:36). In Romans 8, Paul describes the resolution of the struggles between opposites—the law and grace, sin and righteousness, death and life. Christians have not received a spirit which makes us slaves to fear, but have instead received the Spirit of adoption, becoming free children of God (8:13–17).

The work which is right for us as persons releases our creative potential and can be an important factor in our journey toward wholeness. Marjorie Bankson, the potter and retreat leader who described in chapter three how she discovered her creative gift of working with clay, believes "everyone is called to be creative and called to be an artist." She doesn't mean that everyone will become a painter or poet, but that all are called to the freedom in their inner being which lies at the root of all creativity. "Someone said once, 'A craftsman needs to know how a thing will turn out; an artist does not.' I think I grew up in a very craftsman-like background where I needed to control how things turned out. (Sometimes that is appropriate. For example, if I have a plumber coming to repair the plumbing, I don't want him to be artistic and wonder how his work is going to turn out.) When we really apprehend what grace is about, we give up control and enter into something—any experience, a relationship, a task—with a kind of freedom and are willing to experience crucifixion because we believe in a resurrection. A mother who tries to control her children is behaving like a craftsman; a mother who can enter life as an adventure with her children is being an artist.

"It isn't the role which is important; it's what you bring into it. When you really, finally, understand grace—that you don't have to earn your salvation, it's been given—then you're ready to enter into anything with a kind of freedom that calls forth whatever creativity is appropriate."

For Marjorie, freedom and wholeness have meant finding a hidden, underdeveloped side of her personality which she had never nourished. She told us that right now her call is both to teach and to create pottery from porcelain, but she started her adult life as a teacher. In her words, she fostered first the "Mary" side of her personality. She needed to discover that she was a "Martha" as well, reconciling and balancing these two selves in her work. Marjorie explained this in terms of her relationship with her mother and her grandmother.

"I spent the World War II years with my Dutch grandmother. My father was drafted at the age of thirty-five; he's a physician. My mother promptly got tuberculosis. I spent those years with my Dutch grandmother who had a fifth-grade education. She was a seamstress. She made ladies' undergarments for big, fat Dutch ladies on her pedal sewing machine. . . . I realize now that my grandmother was my model for what it meant to be a woman. She worked hard with her hands. She grew her own food. She kept three houses—roofed and painted and did all the yard work—and rented out two of them so she had a little cash income. She was a very self-sufficient woman; she really was an energetic, wise manager with a broad range of skills.

"Think about Mary and Martha. My grandmother was a typical Martha with all the good side of Martha. The organizational skills, the practical planning, the self-discipline I have needed to be a potter—almost all come from her—the valuing of my hands. . . . My mother is a Mary. She has always been much more interested in reading than doing. She comes out of an educated, 'Southern belle' background. She really gave me the socialized answers of what it meant to be a wife, and for ten years after I was married, I did her thing. My hair is naturally curly, and I straightened my hair and wore it on top of my head and wore nice clothes and taught school. And that was my mother's role.

"I realize that as I began to pot I picked up the strengths of my grandmother again and really have gotten much more in touch with my ethnic background. My grandmother was a Dutch immigrant, and my grandfather, too. I really feel like I have claimed a wholeness that I was divorced from during the years that I was being my mother's daughter. I am an eldest child, and so I internalized my parents' values, and I've really had quite a struggle to let go of that and to allow the Spirit to transform—I don't mean get rid of—to fill it out, to flesh it out, give it some color."

**Imagination
and the**   Dorothy Lomenick and her husband own
Creative Impulse   and operate a private school in Miami
Beach, Florida. Dorothy has designed a curriculum for children from preschool through the third grade in which emphasis is given to the arts in order to develop the imagination and self-expression of each child. Dorothy herself is blessed with an outgoing personality, plenty of energy, and a creative impulse. She has been a music educator on and off for twenty-five years and has always been involved in musical performances, shows, and drama. "Creativity," she told us, "is a true asset from God. What an exalting thing for a human being to be born with a gift of creativity. When you want to put something together, it's just there. I can't explain how it is. You can go into the art closet and see an old piece of junk, and you can't understand why the teachers can't take that and create something fantastic because in two seconds you put it to-

gether in your mind. It's the same with putting together a show." The imagination, that mysterious faculty, allows us to create and give shape to beauty, to think original ideas, to capture feelings and sense impressions and recreate them in concrete symbols, to experiment and dare to do new things with color, sounds, materials, and forms. The capacity to create is present in all of us; but a few people, as Dorothy observed, are granted a larger and more intense imaginative capacity. They are our writers, musicians, and painters, and they are compelled to create by an inner need or drive. Since children exhibit more active imaginations than adults, it is apparent that the socializing process we go through as we grow up does much to curb, if not kill, the imagination.

Studies of unusually creative adults have shown that they are more flexible in their thinking, have a greater ability to concentrate and work long hours, are bolder, freer, more spontaneous, and more experimental than other people. They resist the stereotypes and socializing conformity of much of society and, therefore, retain something of the child about them.

Although it is sometimes maintained that women direct their creative urge into childbearing, something that men can't do biologically, there is no evidence for this. We found an equal number of unusually creative women with and without children. If women have not achieved greatness in the creative arts to the extent that men have, it is because they have been more heavily pressured to conform and to take fewer risks in life than men.

Dorothy described what the arts mean to young children as a means of imaginative self-expression. "Music for preschool children is just a vital part of their growing experience. I don't think I have a child who doesn't love it. I start them when they're only two years old. . . . I work with them in drama. Playacting is a big part of my school. We have a whole playacting room. Since that is my field—drama and music—I have accumulated fantastic costumes over the years, and you can go into my playacting room and just create anything you want to. Nothing brings a child out of himself like putting on a hat. . . . We have three performances a year, using every age. I try to do them in a very professional way, try to teach the children what a real performance is."

Children whose gifts are recognized and fostered grow up to use them. Take Dorothy, for instance. "I learned music when I was just a little girl. I lived on a farm and walked to school—about a mile every day—so I sang all the way to school. Oh, I just sang to the heavens. The neighbors laugh about it to this day. They could hear my little voice as I walked to school. I think that walk to school caused the peace that I have. I remember the beauty of walking in the country, crossing the ditches, climbing over the fences to my little school. My first grade teacher took an interest in me. . . . Miss Pearl spent time with me at the piano when I was six years old. I learned to play by ear. My mother tells the story that I was just driving her crazy, and she said, 'Dorothy, take your foot off the pedal!' I said, 'Well, Miss Pearl said she keeps her foot on the brake all the time.' She wasn't very good, as I learned later on, but she was good enough to show the love and interest in me to get me really going."

Not all creative persons, however, discover their gift as children. Frequently homemakers become artisans as a result of doing crafts in their homes, but it is a long road from so-called "cottage industry" to professional work in the arts. Working informally, without much pressure at home, provides great creative fulfillment for many women who weave, sketch, do ceramics, sew, and the like. Often they place pieces on consignment in shops or participate in fairs or shows. These crafts have been a natural route for many homemakers who have moved into new careers as professional artists. If a woman is truly gifted, she will feel an inner compulsion to create and will be frustrated until she finds a way to create or perform on a regular basis. The decision to then become a professional brings with it a commitment to discipline, technical excellence, and business acumen.

Barbara Heyl is a partner with her husband Daniel in a wood-design and antique restoration business. She describes herself as a folk decorator, and she finishes all the original furniture which her husband makes. Barbara is an expert in early Pennsylvania decorative art, and she is entirely self-taught. "I was always interested in crafts and working with my hands. About twenty years ago, the only place we could find was a big, old farmhouse. We had no furniture, and we started buying what would be classed today as antiques and started fixing them up. Just from working with old pieces we learned a lot about design. Everything we've done has been learned by doing as well as by going to museums. . . . I was a housewife, and Daniel was with the fish commission when we really started making things." After years of working part-time at their crafts, five years ago they went into business full-time. It is still a struggle for them financially because of their high overhead and the high caliber of their work which weeds out many customers who cannot afford to pay for quality.

How did Barbara discover her creative ability and special interest in early folk art? "This is ridiculous, but in college I was in science. I never took an art course, and I could just kick myself. I never even took an art history course, and I would love to know more about history. I didn't want to teach. I didn't know what I wanted! I must not have thought. I think that those of us who grew up in the forties and fifties weren't that much concerned with our futures. When a girl got married, that was pretty much it." When Barbara and Daniel began to restore antiques, and then to make reproductions, she became interested in folk painting and decorating. "I think the first thing I ever did was a dower chest. It just went from there. I love the folk art." Barbara feels that God gave her and her husband complementary talents and the inner urge to create. "We both think that creativity is a God-given gift, and he says, 'Whatever you do, do it heartily unto me.' I think we both enjoy doing our best in something that we're qualified or equipped to do. I don't have any idea what I'd do if I didn't do this."

Barbara has acquired her expertise through years of study and technical experimentation. She has a library of reference books and an extensive collection of early folk designs. She has copied important designs which exist only in single examples on privately owned pieces of furniture. Barbara explained to us the extensive historical knowledge and the careful restoration process required when an old dower chest, for example, reveals only a few traces of its original painted design. "Basically, you have to have a feel for the design itself and to understand what those early Germans and English did. My main interest is in the Pennsylvania dower chest which was painted, oh, most of them were painted between 1770 and 1810. It's a primitive sort of painting. You have to have a little understanding of those people at that time. They had a feel for this art form. Their sense of balance and design was just fantastic. They were really orderly. Every space is filled perfectly. . . . If you want to restore an entire chest, you have to almost become that particular artist.

"Even from the beginning it was very exciting to me to get a chest that had everything taken off of it. You can see just a little bit of the original design. It's detective work. And then to bring it back to life and to see the finished product! . . . I think perpetuating the original craft is important in this day and age. There's too much hideousness today, and that could go for all forms of art. I like the purity and the simplicity of the early art. There's just a grace and beauty I think this age could use."

Creating Beauty Versus Serving Society   As a Christian artist, Barbara is in a somewhat enviable position because she and her husband create furniture and restore antiques which are both beautiful and useful. Barbara also sees a direct correlation between the purity and cleanness of the designs with which she works and the need of our society to rediscover handwork and the beauty of simplicity. Many Christians, however, work in art forms and styles which do not seem obviously "useful." They are sometimes misunderstood by the church at large. Although Christianity for centuries integrated beauty and art into worship (one need think only of the great medieval cathedrals or of the symbolism of the Catholic mass), much of the Protestant tradition has neglected the arts. Post-Reformation Christians have frequently maintained that we are called to serve God and the world directly. The artist does not fit too well into such a definition of vocation where service is given a very narrow meaning. Yet, many Christian sects and denominations have always placed a high value on handcrafted work done with skill and care. Frequently, artists are the daughters and sons of people skilled in the crafts.

Where, then, does the creative artist fit within the body of believers? Is her call as valid as that of the person called to serve in the inner city? Is the Christian artist bound to create only art which overtly teaches or gives witness to the gospel message? The Bible gives due place to beauty in our world. Beauty is essential to our survival as humans, for the world which God created was intended to be good. Psalm 8, which we cited in chapter two, suggests that God's handiwork reflects his glory and majesty. In the making of the Old Testament tabernacle, great care was taken that it would be beautiful and symbolic in every detail. The artisans who worked on the tabernacle are described as skilled, their ability God-given. Moses says of Bezalel, one of the designers, that the Lord "has filled him with the Spirit of God, with skill, ability and knowledge in all kinds of crafts—to make artistic designs for work in gold, silver and bronze, to cut and set stones, to work in wood and to engage in all kinds of artistic craftsmanship." Bezalel and his fellow-artisan Oholiab taught others. They were filled by the Lord "with skill to do all kinds of work as craftsmen, designers, embroiderers in blue, purple and scarlet yarn and fine linen, and weavers—all of them master craftsmen and designers. So Bezalel, Oholiab and every skilled person to whom the Lord has given skill and ability to know how to carry out all the work of constructing the sanctuary are to do the work just as the Lord has commanded" (Exod. 35:30-33, 35-36:1).

Jesus himself embodies the power of true creativity. In the Gospel of John, he is called the Word, the *Logos*, through which all things were made (John 1:1-4). This passage recalls the opening of Genesis in which the Spirit of God moves over the waters and creation occurs when God speaks. Christian philosophers have seen the human creative process in which we speak or create imaginative symbols as a mirror of this initial creative activity. The Incarnation also teaches something about the nature of symbols in art. When God revealed himself in human form, the spiritual was inextricably present in the concrete. Such is the mystery at the center of art.

Paul describes the Incarnation in a well-known passage in Colossians 1:15-20. Here Jesus is portrayed as the image of God and the agent of creation:

> He is the image of the invisible God, the firstborn over all crea-
> tion. For by him all things were created: things in heaven and on
> earth, visible and invisible, whether thrones or powers or rulers or
> authorities; all things were created by him and for him. He is before
> all things, and in him all things hold together. And he is the head of
> the body, the church; he is the beginning and the firstborn from
> among the dead, so that in everything he might have the supremacy.
> For God was pleased to have all his fullness dwell in him, and
> through him to reconcile to himself all things, whether things on
> earth or things in heaven, by making peace through his blood, shed
> on the cross.

Christ offers the supreme example of wholeness and creative potential. He embodies the creative imagination, for he is the creative
power of God. Paradoxically, by taking on human form he is the
firstborn *(prōtotokos)* of creation, the image *(eikōn)* of God.

The word *eikōn* has aesthetic overtones; it is the root of our
word "icon." The Greek word means "likeness or image," but it
can also mean "form, appearance, or statue." An icon is an image
or symbol, while iconography is the study of symbols. Thus, Jesus,
God incarnate, teaches us the true nature of symbols, the basic
fabric of art. When we try to take the life out of a symbol, to
abstract the truth from a work of art, it is destroyed. No true artist
sets out to teach a truth or convey a lesson; rather through her art
she expresses an inner vision which is larger and more complex,
more mysterious and elusive, than a simple statement of moral or
theological truth.

The biblical justification of beauty, artisanship, and creative
activity makes the struggles of Christian artists all the more poignant. Although the climate for the arts in Christian circles is changing today, for years creative artists have met with indifference and
misunderstanding within the church. This situation has merely
added to their financial worries, for most artists cannot earn a
living from their art alone. Furthermore, the artist struggles continuously to establish her identity in a secular world where values
are often different and recognition is hard to come by. When the
church could have fostered and supported creative artists, all too
often it remained silent.

Erma Martin Yost is a Mennonite artist who lives with her

husband, a photographer, in an old brownstone in Jersey City, New Jersey, across from Manhattan. Erma is primarily a painter, but she also works in ceramics. The Yosts support themselves by teaching part-time so they can carry out their creative work. Erma admitted that it would be very difficult for her to be a painter were she single, for she would have to work full-time and would have much less emotional support.

Erma grew up in Goshen, Indiana, in a strongly Mennonite environment with a tradition of Christian social service. In that sense, the tradition did not affirm an artistic calling, although Mennonites did value working with one's hands. "Doing things with your hands was one thing that was rewarded in my family. My father was a carpenter, and he had quite a reputation for being the best carpenter, the most meticulous one, in the area. My mother was quite a quilt-maker." Erma started painting very young, and her solitary childhood fostered her innate gifts. "I was the last child. . . . We were a rural family and had no neighbors. I had no one to play with, so I entertained myself. . . . The way I entertained myself was drawing and painting. My mother always kept me supplied with a little pan of watercolor paints. They were like nineteen cents thirty years ago, and as soon as one would be used up, she would get another one. We had this bushelbasket of old ends of wallpaper in the attic, and I would unroll them from one end of the upstairs hallway to the other and paint from one end to the other. Also, my sisters were hiding *Seventeen* magazine in the attic, which as Mennonite girls they weren't supposed to have, and I would copy the Breck girl on the back.

"We lived near Goshen College, and from the fourth grade on, I went to every lecture-music series at Goshen College. I think it's very unusual that my family went because my parents are uneducated. My mother has a fourth-grade education, and my father an eighth-grade. But my sister who was nearest me in age wanted to do it very much, and I wanted to do it. . . . I can remember the first orchestra concert. There was that special connection there, even though nothing related specifically to the visual arts. The evening with Marian Anderson, you know, there was that connection there. I knew that this was something very special and very different that

I just related to. Some of those concerts just stand out so clearly, but I was not musically inclined."

Erma's intense response to aesthetic experience ("that special connection") was just another reinforcement of a growing sense that art was "what I wanted to do and kind of what I should do." She also learned the invaluable lesson that art is born of inner pain and self-reliance. "As a child I experienced very severe epilepsy, and I really internalized so much pain with that. I need painting as a way to express myself. That whole thing I think almost gave me a sense of direction because I had to depend on myself more or less. . . . I've always had a very strong sense of who I am and the direction I want to go. I think it's what some people would call the Lord's leading. It wasn't a voice from the sky, but it felt very right."

Once she got to high school, Erma insisted on taking art instead of some of the required subjects in the pre-college course. Her art teacher encouraged her. It was very difficult, however, to make the decision to major in art in college. "While it was okay to see this kid do cute things, it was a different thing when I wanted to decide to major in art. My family wasn't really all that discouraging, but I really didn't ask their advice. But people that I did ask were very discouraging. It was not 'a service.' I think, too, it was partly that they didn't know any advice to give me, and one of the easiest things to do was to discourage me."

Erma has forged ahead with her painting because of a basic inner strength. She is, however, gifted with an eye for the special atmosphere of the natural world. Her paintings express this natural atmosphere, most recently as she has experienced it in the Southwest. (She and her husband have spent extended periods of time in Arizona.) "I'm always very intrigued with atmosphere—atmospheric things that go on. I grew up in the tornado belt. I saw a twister take up a row of houses. I saw up into the eye of a twister once, which was really incredible. I was standing under it as it formed. Then it closed in and turned on its side and just took a row of houses right across the street. So I've always been aware of atmospheric things and forms in nature, changes in nature, and if my work is about anything, it's just the mystery of all that. My work does not show any of the abuses that man does to the landscape. You don't see 'golden arches' in my landscapes or telephone poles.''

Good art has spiritual qualities to it because the creative process itself is a kind of inner journey, but no true artist, Christian or non-Christian, sets out to convey a message or an exact picture which she has clearly in mind. "I think the creative process itself is kind of a spiritual experience. I don't start out with a sketch and say this is what I'm going to do. I find my way as I go. I have notions of what I want to paint when I begin, but then I let the painting suggest itself to me. It's a process of finding one's way. For me it is sort of a spiritual journey. . . . What I paint is very, very significant to me, and that's about as far as I can take it. There's no hidden message. I think all art that is great art has spiritual elements to it; all good art does, regardless of whether the artist is Christian or not. I think my work has spiritual elements to it, but I don't set out to have some specific message."

Struggles of the Christian Artist
We've been using the term "artist" in a broad sense to include any professional whose primary work is in the imaginative arts, whether painting, composing, writing, designing, crafting, or performing. (Although performing, which is a special kind of interpretation, may not require the same primary act of the imagination as composing or writing, it still requires intuition and creativity, coupled with technical achievement.) The struggles of the Christian artist are both like and unlike those of other working women. We've just looked at the issue of whether art must be "useful." The answer is that good art does not exist, first and foremost, to be useful. If art does exist for this purpose, it ceases to be good art and risks becoming trite. There are, however, many other practical problems which face the Christian artist; many of them relate to the question of what it means to be a "professional."

Having a gift does not make a person an artist; that gift must be trained and developed over a period of years. A professional earns her way because she is qualified by temperament, talent, and training and because she takes her work seriously. She does not dabble in art but works seriously on a regular basis. A tremendous sacrifice of time and energy is required because a writer, sculptor, or painter must have blocks of uninterrupted time on a regular basis and must enjoy the solitude of the creative process. The life of the artist is particularly difficult for a woman with small children who wishes to continue her creative work.

Luci Shaw   Luci Shaw, a widely published poet, says her "bread-and-butter" work is the editing she does for Harold Shaw Publishers, a firm which she and her husband felt led to start twelve years ago (poetry has never paid well!). Luci has five children; four were born during the first six years of her marriage, and during those years she did almost no writing. "When I was first married, I was a very uncertain person. I don't think I was really ready for motherhood, and we had four children in six years. I was fairly insecure about this whole business of raising children. There was a lot of trial and error, which was hard on the kids. I felt frustrated in many ways because I knew I had gifts that were not being developed, and yet I also had this sense that, 'Well, this is only temporary, this exhausting business, this twenty-four-hour day. And though it's an emotional drain, it is also a great satisfaction.' Having children has the promise of both tremendous satisfaction and awful hurt." Then, very significantly, Luci went on to say that "home life, with its ordinary and extraordinary stresses and crises, is a matrix out of which real writing and real growth can come."

As her children grew, she began to do editorial work at home for a publisher. Then when the family publishing firm was begun, she took on the full editorial load at home until fairly recently. Luci's love of words and her editorial skills complement her husband's managerial expertise. Luci feels a multiple call to writing poetry (she has published four volumes), editing, and being a wife and mother (one child is still at home). Thus, her problem is one of priorities, for she also travels frequently to lead workshops, read poetry, and lecture on creativity. She admits that she is fortunate to be a poet. "I think poetry is one of the few arts which is possible in the context in which I live. If I were a novelist, I would have to relinquish the everyday work of an editor, disciplining my time in a very different way. Because each poem is a unit on its own, it's independent of my other work. I can do a poem and finish it and put it away and not have to keep that particular train of thought alive as I would if I were writing a series of newspaper articles or a novel. Poetry is really tailor-made for my particular situation.

"My own creative writing rises out of the cracks between everything else, and that's an unpredictable factor because I never know when I'm going to get a seed idea which will need to be developed. What I generally do is write down the ideas immediately and file them away. When I do have some leisure time, I use it to develop these seed poems. Sometimes the ideas for several poems will come at once and not be developed until later, perhaps six or seven in a burst of creativity when the juices are really flowing."

Luci is a professional, not because she has written individual poems which are published, but because, as she expresses it, she is "involved in the building of a body of work that is representative of me, my ideas chronologically as time passes, different perspectives that I see, and, I hope, growth. A great many people call themselves poets and think that it's just a matter of writing some good poems. To me it's much more than that to be a poet. It's a whole direction of life—my vocation."

Poetry demands a particular technical command, not just a feeling for words. In a sense, the poet's mind is always at work, storing up mental images in her memory, seeing correspondences between things, looking for the miracle which transforms the mundane into the symbolic. "Poetry is different from autobiography in its concentration. It's like an essence; it's like perfume as compared to cologne. It's a much more crystallized, closely focused work of art."

Although Luci explained that her biggest conflict arises from determining her priorities among writing, editing, and serving her family, she conveyed an inner glow as she sat at her desk, a manuscript in front of her. "God may call us to several different things and expect us to use gifts in a diversity of areas at once. I just have to ask the Lord every day to bring into my life the opportunities and responsibilities that he wants me to fulfill on that particular day." A clue to her joy is that none of these callings is a heavy burden. "I love doing all these things—writing, and cooking, and gardening. I love my home. I love parenting. And I love to edit. It's not a struggle. It's something that comes naturally." She finds editing marvelously creative. "Most of our authors are people whom we know personally. They're friends, and we try to put their ideas into books that they will be proud of and happy with, and also to promote them, not just as a business venture, but as a ministry and as a token of real friendship and confidence."

The issue of professionalism raises another question for the Christian artist. No creator or performer works in a vacuum. Readers, viewers, and listeners are important. Although a creative person is energized by a God-given impulse, some ego-drive is always present in the need for recognition and the striving for excellence. There is a precarious balance between the human need to be affirmed and heard—to feel that the sacrifice of creation has been worthwhile—and the self-centered need to be recognized because of what one has created.

Jeannette Clift George   The actress Jeannette Clift George had a professional career in off-Broadway, summer stock, and repertory theater before she founded the After Dinner Players, a Christian repertory company in Houston. The aim of the company is to present original plays which draw on Christian material in order to show the relevance of biblical truth for today. In this instance, drama is conceived as both an art form and a statement of witness. Jeannette serves as playwright and director, and she spoke with us while the rehearsal of a play was in process. As we talked at the ADP theater, Jeannette spoke frankly of the problems of ego-drive and professional discipline as they relate to Christians in the theater.

"Only now is the company at the level of professionalism that was my way of life when I started it. That was very difficult. The first time somebody didn't come to a rehearsal for a casual reason, I couldn't deal with it. Rehearsals in the commercial theater were missed, of course, but never for a casual reason.

"There is a kind of ego-driven commitment in theater that many of us in Christian theater do not have, and until we find the spiritual counterpart for that, we're going to offer that which is less than excellent. I feel the spiritual counterpart to that is real and will goad us to excellence. Christian theater is a marvelous opportunity for witness within the fellowship of craftsmanship. It is a marvelous statement to the marketplace because the marketplace responds to theater, and we have not had any statement there unto Christ. . . . Christians have not had equal representation in theater, but I don't think we've deserved it because our craftsmanship has been so below par that we couldn't earn our right."

We found that Christian artists who have received recognition in Christian circles have to struggle with the demands made on their time to speak, lecture, teach, or give workshops. Many women feel they have ministries in these areas, but they must accept only a percentage of the invitations they receive in order to continue their primary creative vocation. Some have the added struggle of dealing with a certain celebrity status within the church. After Jeannette played the role of Corrie Ten Boom in the film *The Hiding Place*, she became a "Christian personality."

"It hit me like a wet halo in my face. It was a shock. It still shocks me. I tried to deal with that in my book *Some Run With Feet of Clay* because it was a real blow to find myself suddenly a Christian personality. I'd been a believer for many years, and I was finding my way as a believer in the world in which God had placed me. After the film, I was doing some things I had done before, like speaking, and suddenly, for the first time, I was swamped by an autograph group. I'd done autographs after a play and particularly in summer stock where you'd have your little fan club, but I had never known people to come up for an autograph with whom I had not shared any time. It was bewildering. I did not find it an immediately pleasing thing.

"I also resented, not so much the invasion of my privacy as the inflexibility of that invasion. People would ask me questions in public that I would never ask anyone unless I had already paved the way for such a question in a personal relationship. And then finding that I was asked to give Corrie's opinions! There was a great deal of resentment, feeling that I suddenly was not only a Christian personality but was somebody else's person."

On the other hand, recognition by one's peers, especially in the secular world, can be hard to come by. Publicity and timing are important in getting one's work recognized. How far should the Christian go in taking the initiative in order to make her work known? Barbara Heyl, the restorer of Pennsylvania folk art, commented, "The more publicity you get, the better it is for you— newspaper articles and things like that. Any artist would like to have shows. You do want recognition from your peers and people who collect, but it isn't *essential*. We're not pushers. An artist can push into shows all over the country and make showpieces. We haven't done that." Depending on the medium, a cooperative gallery or venture is a frequent outlet used by artists. Erma Martin Yost has found support in the co-op gallery of thirty artists to which she belongs. "There is a group that just sort of gravitated toward each other, and about a year later we found that we're all Midwesterners. I think it has to do with our priorities. Many of them come from Protestant backgrounds. While they're not practicing an institutionalized type of religion, their values, their upbringing, you know, just make them different. They have not been born and raised in New York."

Luci and Harold Shaw provide a publishing outlet for Christian poets by including poetry among the titles which their relatively small firm brings out, but Luci spoke of the difficulty good Christian poets have in trying to place their work in excellent secular journals. "What I try to do is to make the orthodox exciting and new and not stale. I used to write poetry about the way things should be between God and man, and now I try to write more honestly about the way things are. If there are problems, I try and express that and not always give this idealized relational picture." Such poetry does not find ready reception in secular journals. "Secular poetry journals are open to every human experience, no matter how perverse, except genuine Christian belief. That seems to be too simplistic, and it's a taboo subject. It's frustrating to be a serious poet and have that aspect of one's life negated."

Madeleine L'Engle   Madeleine L'Engle, best known as the winner of the Newbery Medal for *A Wrinkle in Time*, has recounted the story of her struggle to publish in her autobiographical book, *A Circle of Quiet*. During her thirties, when she and her husband and their three children lived in rural New England, she met rejection after rejection for *Meet the Austins*, *A Wrinkle in Time*, and other novels. On her fortieth birthday, yet another rejection slip arrived in the mail. That was enough. She decided to renounce writing, covered her typewriter, and walked around the room sobbing. Suddenly she stopped short because she realized that her subconscious mind had already started to plot out another novel—on failure! It was a moment of decision. She recognized her undeniable inner impulse to write, uncovered her typewriter, and vowed to continue even if she never found a publisher.

Now in her sixties, Madeleine L'Engle writes at her desk in the library of the Cathedral of St. John the Divine in New York City. We had an appointment to talk with her on a beautiful Friday morning in late October. On the preceding Sunday, an article about her had appeared in the book review section of *The New York Times*. The writer had noted that Miss L'Engle was about to set something of a record, for during the next twelve months eleven of her books were appearing; two were new books, and the others were reprints or new paperback releases. When we asked her about her recent recognition, she replied that it was "particularly gratifying because of the long years of failure. Several of the books being reprinted are books I found it almost impossible to get published. "When we were living in the country those nine years, I had no support group whatsoever. Not many people read books, and certainly nobody wrote books. Why do you write books if they're not being sold? I mean I sold practically nothing. That was my decade of rejection slips, and I was desperate—I really was. The only support group I had, by the way, was my high school Sunday school class. I had more nourishment from those kids than from anybody else because they were asking all of the cosmic questions."

Looking back, she acknowledges gratefully the support of her publisher, Robert Giroux, who accepted *A Wrinkle in Time* and has subsequently encouraged her to write exactly what she wanted. She can see that some of her books were ahead of their time and that delayed publication has borne out her inner conviction that she should write. "I realize that, for instance, if *A Wrinkle in Time* had been published when I first sent it out instead of over two years later and after all of those thirty-odd rejection slips, it might just have fallen into a dark pit of oblivion. It was published at what was for it exactly the right moment. I'm not sure why, but I have some ideas why the reading public is ready for multi-leveled books. I think it's because the world is in a chaotic mess, and we need something to affirm reason. This need is general, whether the human being is Christian or not. We need affirmation of meaning."

Madeleine L'Engle writes first for herself and then for others. "I don't think that a book which is exclusive serves any purpose. If I wrote only for Christians and only Christians read me, how would I be spreading the gospel? I like my books to be read just by a general audience, and they are indeed. No particular age level. . . . I deplore this tendency to label. We want to put people into pigeonholes, and I don't like pigeonholes. That's why I don't like being called a Christian writer. I don't like being called a children's writer. I don't want to be labeled. I'm worried that when I'm called a Christian writer, it's going to deter non-Christians from reading me. What I want to do is share."

While we chatted, the family's friendly Irish setter appeared from time to time in the cathedral library, wanting to be petted, and the phone rang twice—one a call from someone arranging a conference where Miss L'Engle would speak and another from a friend in need. In speaking of her schedule of lecturing, writing, and being a wife, mother, and grandmother, she emphasized three themes. First, she makes time for people. "Sometimes it gets pretty frantic. I try to balance it out, but I think people are terribly important, and if I reject people, then what am I going to be able to say in my writing?" Second, she makes time for writing. "I write every day. It's like playing the piano. I think it was Rubenstein who said, 'If I don't practice for one day, I know it. If I don't practice for two days, my family knows it. And if I don't practice for three days, my public knows it.' Last summer at a writers' conference, one of the writers said, 'If I leave my work for one day, it leaves me for three.'

"You do not write when inspiration comes because, by and large, inspiration does not come before you write; it comes while you're writing, during the work. It's exactly like prayer. You don't start out praying well. You just do all those dutiful prayers—the words—and then maybe something else happens and you stop words and listen. But you have to start off with the finger exercises."

Finally, Madeleine L'Engle keeps learning anew the lesson Jesus taught—that unless we are as little children, we will not enter the kingdom of heaven—a truth she sees as essential to creativity. "I mean he kept on saying unless you *are* as little children, you will never enter the kingdom of heaven. It's an ability to be open." Citing the mystic Thomas Traherne, she said that we have to keep learning anew the joys of all the five senses and unlearning the devices of the world. "This unlearning has been the largest part of my growing up, and it's a constant process."

What are her goals? "The continued grace and bliss of work and love. When a young poet complained to the French novelist Colette about not being happy, she replied, 'Who asked you to be happy? Work!'"

FACING CHANGE

**Work
and
the Life-Cycle**
One of the most popular books of the late 1970s was Gail Sheehy's *Passages*, a study of the predictable crises which adults face between the ages of eighteen and fifty. Drawing on the work of psychologists such as Erik Erikson and Daniel Levinson, Sheehy illustrated their theories of adult development and change by means of interviews. One of the reasons for the popularity of *Passages* was that most adults had never realized that the patterns of transition and change are as pronounced for them as for children and adolescents. Aside from realizing that there is a "mid-life crisis," adults had never really dealt with the stages of their own inner growth. Given the rapid pace of modern life, the breakdown of family life, the dangers of modern armaments, and the increase in inner anxiety which has accompanied these changes, readers turned to *Passages* for clues as to how to cope with both the internal and external changes of their lives.

In various papers, Erikson had explained that the human personality unfolds through phases of psychosocial crises in childhood and continues to develop as the individual progresses through the life-cycle. He identified eight stages within this cycle: infancy, early childhood, play age, school age, adolescence, young adulthood, adulthood, and mature age. In the three stages during which adults work, the basic needs and concerns of the individual shift. Young adults struggle to establish intimacy as opposed to isolation; mature adults face the conflict of generativity, or producing offspring, versus absorption in the self; older individuals wish to establish the integrity of their lives rather than give way to despair.

Sheehy took the concept of the life-cycle and popularized it. The "trying twenties" is the decade in which we try to shape the dream which will structure our lives, to find a lifework, and to seek intimacy in marriage. The early thirties are marked by putting down and extending our roots; commitments are deepened or altered. The "deadline decade" between the ages of thirty-five and forty-five is characterized by a crisis in which we search for authenticity and question previously held goals. We either renew or change our life dream or resign ourselves to failed dreams. During the mid-life crisis we become sensitive to the onslaught of time, to the limitations imposed on us by the experiences of life, to the need to integrate our lives and do meaningful work. Finally, when we have weathered the "dreadful decade," we enter the fifties able to accept and approve of ourselves at last.

Most of the transitions of adulthood are gradual; they are not dramatic crises. Life is, after all, a continuum; it is not usually a series of peaks of ecstasy interrupted by crashing periods of despair. Change is the means by which personal growth can occur, and there is an impetus toward such growth in every healthy personality. Consequently, the "passages" of the life-cycle are generated from *within* the individual. External circumstances interact with these changing inner needs, sometimes creating "marker" events which we remember as particularly meaningful. At such juncture-points in our lives we are usually faced with significant choices.

The general pattern of the life-cycle applies to both men and women, but the rhythms of the male and female cycles differs. The differences are related to the physiology and social roles of the sexes. Sheehy has categorized the paths which women typically choose to follow. These life patterns, established in the twenties, also affect the transitions of the later years. The *care-givers* marry young and envisage their lifework as centered in the home. *Either-or women* feel compelled to choose between work and marriage. Those who marry postpone their career until later; others put off marriage or childbearing or both in order to get established in a career. *Integrators* try to combine marriage, motherhood, and work during their twenties. The *never-married* are women who will remain single, often playing nurturing roles in helping professions such as nursing or unconsciously serving as "office wife" to a male boss. Finally, *transients* are women who never settle down in their twenties, but wander from job to job, emotional attachment to emotional attachment, place to place. Of course, Sheehy's categories are merely suggestive of life patterns; they are not definitive. In real life, people cannot be pigeonholed so neatly.

Change and growth are so basic to adult experience that no woman can automatically view herself as "locked into" a single role or career for her entire life. The courage to change is both active and passive; it is the courage to face and accept changes within ourselves and others and the courage to take risks to change the direction of our lives and work.

**Identity, Work,
and
God's Plan
for Our Lives**   Erik Erikson has indicated that in the healthy personality a sense of inner identity begins to emerge as the individual leaves adolescence and enters adulthood. "Identity" connotes several things: a conscious sense of being a unique individual, a feeling of continuity of the self and a striving to maintain this continuity, an integrated "I," and a feeling of belonging or solidarity. During the transitions of adulthood, that "I" is still in the process of becoming integrated or complete, and at times we may feel that our sense of identity has become confused or lost as we try to discover new sides of our personality or launch out in new directions.

Christians struggle, just like non-Christians, to find their authentic "I." In chapter four we saw that women in particular have had to learn the lesson of acceptance by Christ and responsibility for self, both keys to a healthy concept of the self. Identity is so intertwined with the life-cycle and the choices we make in our twenties that our job can be an important and valuable way by which we establish our identity and self-esteem.

An additional factor in the attitude of Christian women toward their identity and their work is their understanding of the sovereignty of God. One of the most quoted clichés in Christian circles today is "God has a plan for your life." The New Testament unmistakably indicates that there is a divine purpose for each life, a purpose related both to redemption and to spiritual vocation. Jesus speaks of the fulfillment of the divine purpose as the central factor of his life. "My food . . . is to do the will of him who sent me and to finish his work" (John 4:34). Paul comments, "It is God who works in you to will and act according to his good purpose" (Phil. 2:13), implying that the Holy Spirit is constantly empowering us to be obedient to the will of God. And in the well-known passage on predestination in Ephesians 1:3–14, Paul develops a theology of the sovereignty of God by which God wills or chooses that we should be redeemed and adopted as children in the divine family.

Nowhere does biblical teaching indicate that the purpose or will of God is a blueprint to which no alterations or additions can be made. In reality, God's will unfolds for us just as our personality or identity unfolds in time. Being open to change and finding the courage to change, while being conscious of remaining in God's will, are signs of spiritual, as well as psychological, maturity. Paul Tournier has described the essence of life as movement. Grace is not extended to us in a rigid, fixed way; it is granted within the natural dynamic of the life process. God's purpose and his grace may lead us to dramatic moments of choice, but the stuff of life is made up of imperceptible, gradual change leading us to those choices.

One lively woman in her forties summarized this openness to change. "One thing I really believe is that life is full of so many different stages that you're not locking yourself in if you do one thing fully and wholly. There's still time to do more. I see this with my own children; they're afraid that if they decide to go to law school, they're going to have to be lawyers for the rest of their lives. And they aren't. Look at my life. I've been an actress, teacher, mother, Bonwit Teller merchandiser, sales clerk in a shoe store. Those things aren't really related. And those were all very full lives for a moment. I don't think you have to be so scared. The commitment to the present isn't going to preclude something else happening that you can't even plan on. So go ahead and make the commitment fully with as much enthusiasm as possible, 'cause you can't program your life anyway."

The Twenties   Marisa was engaged and looking forward
                       to her marriage when she talked with us.
Although her concerns are representative of many women in their twenties, she is refreshingly flexible about her future roles and future work. She teaches government and history in a Catholic high school in a working-class area near Boston. Her fiancé is a journalist and a nurse. Marisa views her identity as quite distinct from her work. "I have never been a very career-oriented person. My teaching is an outgrowth of my Christian commitment and my sense of needing a ministry which uses my gifts. I never felt that my career was something that was walled off and that had to go on no matter what. I could stop teaching high-school students. I could have children. I could have a part-time, or maybe even a volunteer job where I teach something to someone, and that would be fine with me. I don't need to be professional or even to be paid to feel that I have a career.

"I have a friend who is definitely career-oriented. For her to be 'out of the market,' and out of the struggle of being on top and being known professionally, would be death. Her identity is very tied up with that; mine is not." Marisa continued by explaining that her future husband, although committed to being an artist, was not career-oriented either. "He has a strong sense that family comes first. I can see Michael and me sharing a lot of home responsibilities. I think he will be with the kids as much as I will be with the kids. He feels that the man should be doing that. He doesn't have this rigidity about roles."

We found that the relative importance of work to the self-esteem and identity of individual women varied tremendously according to background, personality, and where they were in the life-cycle. For example, Marisa was about to enter a stage where her primary role would be within the home. Although she expected to work outside the home in the future, having a career was relatively unimportant to her. Barbara, on the other hand, faced a struggle over the issues of career and marriage. She is in her twenties, married, and has two sons, aged five and four. She never envisaged herself as staying home with small children, even on a temporary basis. "I never liked to baby-sit. I never liked to cook. I had never been shopping until I got married. It took me about two hours to do our first week's shopping. I just didn't have the interest. . . . I was really frightened about having no identity, and I saw being a mother as having no identity. The reason that we decided to have children was that two couples we knew who had children remained very active in a lot of things and really enjoyed their children and had their children be a part of things."

Barbara and her husband moved to Washington, D.C., and became part of the Sojourners community. She now serves as director of the day-care center sponsored by Sojourners. "We had a lot of struggles after we came here. Both of us are easily employed, and a good many of the people who live here are not easily employed. They have social science degrees but no particular skills. When we first came here, my husband had to get a full-time job and be a wage-earner, and that left me, of course, at home. That was really hard, especially when the children were younger. At one point I got so frustrated and said I couldn't stand it any more and wanted to get a job. He offered to stay home with the kids while I got a job. That was toward the end of our first year here. When it came right down to it, I decided that I really didn't want to do that because summer was coming, and there was a lot I could do with the kids as they were getting older. I had also become very involved in the daily life of the community and was doing a lot of administrative work. It wasn't that I was bored. I just felt a loss of identity."

Barbara confessed that her struggles about her loss of identity were really struggles "with the way I'd been raised—that your value is in what you do." Living in a Christian community has provided a context in which it has been possible for Barbara, who had training in retailing and accounting, to change her attitudes toward both herself and her work. The needs and priorities of the group are foremost, and Barbara can now say, "My particular vocation changes from time to time according to the needs of the community. Most people, especially middle and upper-class people, are controlled by vocation. We are coming to discover that the primary thing we are called to be doing is to live with other people in fellowship. The primary calling is to the church, and the calling of vocation is secondary."

Since the accepted social pattern has been for women to marry in their late teens or early twenties, those who remain single face a number of transitions which set them apart from the "norms" of society. Beth is twenty-two, a graduate student in mathematics, and a teaching assistant. She is from a rural coal-mining area of Pennsylvania where few women go to college and almost everyone stays in "the valley," marries, and raises a family. "The small town that I come from is such that very few of the women have had college education, and the ones that have are mostly teachers in the high school. A lot of my friends got married right after high school and stayed right in my hometown. Most of the people who have gone away from there have come back and are teaching high school or performing some other traditional role. Very few women have gone on to graduate school, and many of the other women in the town don't understand why I'm going on and why I'm interested in pursuing my education."

We had heard that "senior panic" was often a problem among women students at Christian colleges because pressure to marry is great, from both families and peers. Beth had attended a Christian college, so we asked her whether women felt panic when they had to make serious decisions about their lives during that final year of college. "I felt an inferiority because I wasn't ready to marry. There's a lot of pressure to get engaged during the senior year, especially during the second semester when people are deciding what their futures hold. There's a tendency to hold on to something familiar because so much is changing. The security of being at college is changing. No longer will you be a student. You're going to have the responsibility of being on your own and earning your money and everything. A lot of girls kind of panic over the question, 'How am I going to handle being on my own?' " As Beth indicated, "senior panic" has several dimensions; it does not relate only to finding a husband. Today's college women are hearing the message that they need to have careers. But many have not learned to be decisive, to assume responsibility, or to take risks and initiative.

What about Beth's friends who married right after graduation? Many of them were trained in business and education. "I felt that a lot of them gave up the goals that they had had before they got married. Wherever their husbands found jobs, that's where they went. There was really only one exception to that. Most of the girls really didn't even interview or try to find jobs because their location depended on their husbands. Most of them are working as secretaries or sales clerks. Although they appear to be happy, I feel a lot of them could be doing more with their potential than they are."

Beth concluded that her personal attitude had helped her deal with the transition periods at the end of high school and college. "It was hard in a way because I had to deal with a lot of people who were going through wedding plans. All three of the girls I lived with were engaged. My attitude just had to be, 'I'm not there, so where am I to go?' It helps to have the faith that God's plan for my life is such that when I'm ready to marry, someone else will be ready, too."

At her age, Beth's attitude toward marriage seems entirely feasible. As single women reach the age of twenty-nine and beyond, the desire and need to marry often become much stronger. How do women handle their attitudes toward work and singleness as they get older? Laurie is a vivacious, intelligent woman of twenty-nine who is deeply committed to her work as a nurse. She is a clinical specialist, teacher, and administrator at a four-hundred bed hospital in a large city. Laurie recounted several instances when she had been given a significant spiritual ministry to patients, but as important as her work is to her, she does not exclude the possibility of marriage. Being single is a "waxing and waning struggle," she said. "Someday I would love to be married."

Laurie noted realistically the difficulties which Christian women have in meeting eligible men within the context of the church, and the lack of understanding of the single and divorced among many married Christians. She told us how, when she described her work to a staff member of a Christian organization, he responded, "'Yeah, Laurie's just a career woman.' I really resented that. I said to him, 'I'm not a "career woman." Yes, I love my job, but someday I would like to marry and combine the two.' I do not—comfortably—see myself being single for the rest of my life.

"This morning, having breakfast, I said, 'Lord, I have a struggle thinking about having breakfast alone for the next forty years. I really do.' I feel like the Lord is calling me to continue to pray when it wells up, then to set it aside. It's at his feet. I thought this morning about all the blessings he's given to me, and I just set it aside and was on my way."

The theme of the problems of the so-called career woman within the church came up again during our conversation. Laurie explained that she had been told that she often threatened single Christian men. "I had a man take me aside and say, 'Laurie, I find what you say at dinner so fascinating. You have such interesting points to make, but I'm just going to tell you something. Try to sit back and not say too much because you're threatening these single guys.' I was so angry! . . . Part of the enjoyment of a friendship I have with a man right now is that he does not find me threatening at all. We talk about the Strategic Arms Limitation Treaty and Russia, and it's great."

Laurie mentioned that a particular Christian leader and teacher has counterbalanced her negative experiences by his realistic but positive advice. "He told me, 'Laurie, you will have a tough time marrying, and it may be a long time before you ever marry because you will need a man who is not afraid of your brain, and there are not too many men around like that.' He has meant so much to me because he's allowed and encouraged me to be who I am, and his solution is that what the Christian community needs is more 'red-blooded men who become Christians in their late twenties and early thirties.' All I know is that the men who become Christians a little later in life tend to be a little more gutsy and a little less afraid."

Where does she find her emotional support? "Dear friends—

dear, solid, mature friends in my age group. Women friends who work and struggle with the same things and who are 'with it' women. I don't have the sense that they are losing the battles. . . . I live with a cat, a dear little cat . . . and I love living alone. As much as I enjoy company, I need to go home and unwind and just have it be my little place and serve my little entertaining dinners and do my reading or whatever I need to do. I need that."

Support doesn't come from the singles group at her church. "I've become the administrative leader of the group, and I'm the only one who gets the speakers for the group every Thursday night. I've been ready to chuck that group and have been very frustrated with it. It's an extremely emotionally needy group, very somber. . . . But I'm going to stick it out. I was nominated to be a deacon. I would have loved to have accepted that nomination, but I knew that my job was with the singles group."

**Thirty-Five
and
Beyond**
Gail Sheehy calls age thirty-five the "crossroads" for women, the age when all sorts of unexpected questions force themselves into our consciousness. It is the age when most women send their last child off to school. It is the time when single women take urgent steps to try to marry or else become reconciled to singleness. The end of the childbearing years begins to loom ahead. Women return to work; career women change their careers; wives run away; marriages begin to dissolve. Although men go through a mid-life crisis in their forties, and women may go through a transition connected with menopause in the late forties, thirty-five seems to be the age when women must begin to think of themselves in new terms. In our interviews, we noticed that this shift in consciousness occurred anywhere between thirty-five and fifty. Sheehy adds that women who have gone through this post-thirty-five transition period are the possessors of significant levels of energy. Once childbearing is behind, women seem able to focus themselves and their energy in a

more single-minded way than they did when they were younger. The transition at thirty-five also occurs because women frequently marry before their identities are firm; they have to sort out who they are in their middle years rather than in their early twenties. Think back to Beth's comments that many of her friends were not using their potential, although they seemed happy to have married when they were twenty-one or two. One woman, divorced herself, felt keenly that working for a few years before marriage could help avoid the identity problems women face later. "I think many people spend the first five years after college either reacting against their upbringing or fulfilling their upbringing, neither of which is who they are. It's very dangerous to get married when you're still in the action-reaction stage. That's where a really committed career can be helpful because you can find out who you are. Then if and when you get married, you will have something to give, something definite, something tangible, instead of looking for that identity in somebody else, expecting somebody else to give it to you."

Margaret was in her late forties when she went through a startling transition. Happily married, the mother of two daughters, and a trained musician, she had for years been totally immersed in the life of the church. The wife of a clergyman, she had her own ministry of music within the Christian community. Then she realized she had lived such a sheltered existence that she had never tested herself—she really wasn't sure what she could handle on her own. One detail of her experience was unique; she and her husband had moved four years earlier from another country to a large American city.

"My only experience in America had been in an area of about six blocks that were closely related to the church and the Christian community we were a part of. I had not related in any kind of way personally to anybody outside that circle, and I wanted to meet people and be exposed to the general run of life that's in a city. Coming to America was a tremendous culture shock. I was trying to handle my homesickness, and I thought this might be a way I could put down some roots. What I found was that going out to work in the city was a tremendous challenge to me, to my faith. It's very easy to relate to a group of Christians, you know.

"The thing that I basically wanted was to find out who I was and to be honest. What can I cope with? What can I face?" Margaret decided to find a job downtown, and after visiting employment agencies and then answering an ad in the newspaper, she located a position in the box office of a symphony orchestra. She has since changed jobs and now manages the box office for an opera company. "I turned fifty years old just a little after this, and I began to see that the last twenty years had gone really quickly. My children had grown up during that period of time. I thought, 'Well, there's another twenty years left, and if they go as quickly as the last twenty, there are a few more things I want to experience.

"I've come to the place where I feel I can give an honest answer if anybody asks about God. Before there was a certain amount of role-playing. When we come before the Lord at the end, we'll be alone. We'll stand before him and give an account. I said to the Lord, 'Okay. If that's the way it is, then you are available to me all the time as an individual. Otherwise, the game's not fair because I'm going to be in situations where I'm not surrounded by a group of people supporting me, saying "Yea! Come on! You can do it!"''"

Margaret needed that personal reliance on God because striking out on her own in an alien world was scary. Driving downtown and even walking down the street were anxiety-producing. "I literally, for the first time in my life, had to make myself take one step at a time to go down the street without being intimidated by people. I was afraid of the whole downtown scene, and I could see that I was and wanted to face it. I was terrified of banking and still 'have a thing' about walking into a restaurant by myself. I pretty much avoid going out to lunch if I have to go alone. Now traffic is no problem; I thoroughly enjoy it. I can look with love at the next driver who wants to push me out of the lane. It took me two years to enjoy it, but I really am thankful that I did it because I can feel in myself a strength I never had before, strength there by the grace of God."

Related to the issue of integrating the self and establishing one's identity is the need for affirmation and self-esteem. As children begin to go to school and then leave home, women find less and less affirmation through direct nurturing. They also have more time on their hands. Many women still prefer to serve and find fulfillment through volunteering rather than working for pay, although the pool of volunteers has diminished dramatically as more and more middle-class women return to work. Roberta has three teen-age children and feels a heavy responsibility toward them because her husband's work keeps him away from home a great deal. Although the interests of her children are her top priority, she admitted that affirmation within the home can be a problem.

"There isn't a lot of affirmation in washing and ironing and doing the drudgery. There isn't a great deal of affirmation from the family because you're pretty much taken for granted. I can't fault that because that was exactly the way I was as a kid. I decided to do some things that give me more affirmation, both outside as well as within my home. I get a lot of satisfaction out of creating things. If I'm baking bread or if I'm making jam or framing pictures or doing things like that, I feel very gratified."

At one point, Roberta did consider going back to work, but she decided that the small amount of money she could make was not worth the energy she would have to expend. Instead, she does volunteer work. "I feel that I want to serve in ways that I can't be paid for. I'm doing some volunteer work in a nursery school with kids from disadvantaged homes, and I find that very helpful. I couldn't do that if I were working. I've started to tutor students from other countries. I've found that very gratifying. Having taught languages, I always felt I wanted to teach language again. I've really been enjoying teaching someone else my language and helping them."

Fulfilling
Postponed Dreams
For some women, the desire to do something more with their life once their last child has started off to school is accompanied by a great struggle as to what that "something" ought to be. We've already seen some of

the steps people can take to determine their gifts and begin to use them. Our unmonitored fantasies and dreams constitute a clue about work that we often overlook. *If nothing were stopping you, what would you like to be doing?* Women can and do take steps to fulfill such dreams.

Pat Gundry always wanted to write. She says now that she is not sure whether to describe herself as a "housewife who writes or a writer who housewives." Pat had no formal training as a writer, and until her last child started off to school she was a full-time housewife. Once, when her children were small, she had signed up for a correspondence course, but she couldn't follow through with her plans because of her duties at home. She read, painted, gardened, and played the guitar as her children grew older. Writing, however, "eats at you. It tickles you until you finally give in to the urge."

One day at the public library Pat found a book on determining goals and achieving them by concentrating on a single one. Her goal was to write. She bought an old typewriter with a bent key (which she straightened) and set up a little office in her basement. On the morning that her last child set off for his first full day at school, she began to write every day. She read books from the public library on writing, and she "practiced." In the five years since she has been working as a free-lance writer, Pat has completed, and published, three books.

A great user of the resources of the public library, Pat recommended that other women, puzzled as to what they might do with their lives, should read books on determining goals. In the course of the conversation, she made several useful suggestions for women who want to make changes:

1) "Don't look for pie in the sky by and by. Live your life now, *today.*"

2) "Examine your latent abilities which are there waiting to be used."

3) "Be courageous enough to get help." Find out what training you need and get it.

4) "Remember, you don't have to leave home to find worthwhile work."

5) "Read things on assertiveness. Women always think they're less than they are."

Meg provides another example of a woman who is fulfilling postponed dreams. After graduating from Vassar where she received training in music, she married and stayed at home to care for her young children. When she began to work, she again deferred using her musical training and found a job as a secretary and as a medical reference librarian. Her piano stood untouched. Then, at the age of thirty-four, with two children and a new baby, she began to realize that the reason her duties as a housewife had not been fulfilling for so many years was that she had not been in contact with herself.

"Something within me wanted to get out." This awakening to her self "coincided with a spiritual reawakening." She began to practice the piano, then the organ; organ lessons followed. Within six months she was offered a job as an assistant church organist; this soon became a full-time position. Now in her late thirties, Meg is the organist and choir director in an Episcopal parish with a vigorous music program. "I came to believe it was a 'calling' to a very specialized ministry because one's talents have a purpose. Without that kind of conviction I probably would not have pursued an endeavor which cost me and my family so much in effort and time and conflict."

The conflicts have centered around the issue of time because Meg works during the periods other people have free; her family had to make some adjustments and sacrifices because of this schedule. The constant struggle to choose among priorities and to deal with her responsibilities to church and family is a working out of the redemptive process for Meg personally. She looks to Jesus' responses to the demands on his time as her model. A specific instance of redemption at work within her family occurred recently. One of Meg's daughters had previously sung in her mother's junior choir and, apparently feeling resentful, hadn't thought her mother was a good director or that the choir was very good. Recently, after an outstanding choir performance, the daughter, now sixteen, came and asked her mother, "Can I join your choir?"

Like Pat, Meg underscored that no matter how much a woman

may lack in confidence or how much she may worry about conflicts, she must take courage and act when she is in a period of transition in her life. "One cannot spend too much time evaluating. Plunge in."

Returning to School   Emily Greenspan recently wrote an arti-
and to Work   cle for the *New York Times Magazine* entitled "Work Begins at 35." Her research among women in general
emphasized that those who return to work after being out of the job
market have low expectations and are riddled by anxiety as they
enter a climate of competition. The same reactions occur when
women go back to school for training in a new field. Being a Christian in no way eliminated the anxiety of the women to whom we
talked, although their faith did give them a coping mechanism.

A nurse in her forties who returned to hospital work after an
absence of many years confided, "I was so nervous. I didn't sleep
for a week. . . . And it was hard to get back, but once I had been in
it a couple of weeks, I wondered why I was so nervous. The only
thing that gives you confidence is doing it, and it doesn't come
overnight, either. I'm just starting to feel comfortable there, and it's
been about six months."

A woman with prior business experience went back to school
to obtain her license in real estate. "I was very much up on the
business world before, and then all those years elapsed. I used to
tell my husband, 'I really don't feel like I want to go back to
school.' It's terrible. You feel reluctant, and I think—I'm sure—
it's because you don't have confidence. You aren't sure how you
will fit in. But I've found real estate to be a great career, and it's a
good career for women who do have some age on them."

Sometimes the Christian woman's stress is increased by her
ethical and moral values. Margaret told us of a position which she
obtained through an employment agency and then quickly turned
down. "I'd heard all these wild stories about American businesses;

I had one experience in particular where an employment agency set up an interview for me. I actually went and interviewed and got the job. Then the man at the employment agency called me and asked me to come in and see him. He said, 'I don't think you realize the reputation of this company. I've felt guilty about sending you there.' Then I said, 'What are you talking about?' He said, 'Everybody who works there needs to be available for cocktail hours and weekend visits and this kind of stuff.' I began to realize what he was saying, and I thought truly his warning was the Lord protecting me."

Greenspan has given a succinct summary of the difficulties facing women who return to work.

> Take economic necessity; add the difficulty in making these perceptive transformations [in thinking of oneself in a totally new way]; fold in rusty or outmoded job skills, little or no job experience and lack of contacts with today's job market; garnish with employers who are unwilling to credit previous work experience or volunteer activities as evidence of future potential; simmer with age and sex discrimination, and you have a recipe for today's re-entering homemaker. And she is often willing to settle for low-skilled, low-paying, traditionally female jobs that afford minimal opportunity for advancement and maximal stress.

Greenspan does not comment on the added stress which a recent divorce or the death of a husband can bring the individual. Under the pressures of time and finances in a crisis situation, a woman may have few options available to her other than traditional low-paying jobs.

Pamilla, for example, returned to work to help finance the college education of her only son who was in his senior year of high school. Just two days after she started her job, her husband was stricken with a heart attack which proved fatal. Within six months, after prayer and a sense of God's direction, she sold her home in order to relocate in the town where her son was to attend college. She "had a general plan" which she thought any woman in her position ought to have, but she also had a limited set of options because of the circumstances in which she found herself. Pamilla bought a home with a rental unit in it so that she could have a source of income to help carry the mortgage payments. Then she found a job as a secretary.

Blessed with excellent training and excellent work experience before her marriage, she began her new position as a head secretary with two persons responsible to her. But she has been unable to move to a higher-paying job within her organization and has reconciled herself to staying in her job until she retires. Because she returned to work at the age of fifty-six, circumstances lead her to think that her age has worked against her. When she retires in two years, she hopes to make an interesting career shift by joining the staff of Campus Crusade for Christ; in preparation for this, she has been taking training courses offered in her area by Crusade staff members.

Striking Out
in   For women already committed to a
New Directions   career, the years after thirty-five are often marked by a shift of direction, an enlargement of vision, or a dramatic job change. Women returning to work, on the other hand, bring a variety of life experiences and a richness and maturity of outlook which give them an advantage in the workplace; often they turn into the visionaries of the organization which they join. Older women can strike out in new directions once they have a surer sense of self; they have discovered that one set of challenges, met and mastered, gives the skill and the confidence to meet a new set of risks. Mature women also discover new aspects of generativity; childbearing may now be out of the question, so they need to perpetuate themselves through their work.

Rev. Nellie Yarborough, the single black pastor of a Pentecostal congregation, recounted one of the most striking stories of career diversification that we heard. Nellie grew up in North Carolina, and after graduating from high school joined a traveling evangelistic group led by Bishop Brumfield Johnson. She traveled around the country helping to found and build churches, eventually studied at a Bible college, preached, and aided in the administrative work of the church. "The bishop always felt that women had a definite part in the ministry, and he encouraged me as much as possible." Since 1962 she has been a pastor, and in her late forties she returned to school to obtain a master's degree in religion.

Nellie also received a second master's degree, this one in administration and management. She has embarked on a second career as president of the Lincoln Industrial Supply Company, located just outside Boston. Nellie says that it is terribly important to "be in touch with yourself, your own feelings and really know what you want. What you want is just as important as what anybody else wants. That's a good feeling. And feel that what you're doing is right." Nellie's new business venture ties in with her personal vision to serve the black community where she lives and to enlarge the ministries of her church.

She did her master's thesis on black-owned businesses and then did some research which showed that there was no black-owned industrial supply business in New England. She had always loved business, and God made it possible for her to take over an establishment and to begin under federal sponsorship. She has also benefited from seminars run by the Small Business Administration.

The problem for most people in starting a business, Nellie says, lies in not knowing the right people in the right places and in not counting the cost. "Decide that you're going to spend a lot of time in the embryo stages of the business. You're going to have to relinquish some time you might have for yourself. You have to almost forget about a social life and do your socializing on the telephone." There are trade-offs you have to make. "It takes approximately four to five years to get a business on its feet. I came with the attitude that I would not take salary for sixteen months to two years so that I can build up the cash flow. I've been working here every week [in addition to pastoring], and I have not taken a cent out. This is what I mean by trade-offs. But if you really like what you're doing, it's easy."

Nellie's first goal is to expand the business so that it can take in roughly fifteen employees from the neighborhood who could eventually buy stock and become owners. A second goal relates to the use of the income. "If the business takes off as I believe it will, I'm looking forward to opening up a Christian home for senior citizens. I want a beautiful home where they can have fellowship." Then she'll remain as senior pastor of her church and serve the residents of the home. Nellie believes in working with God to bring dreams to fruition.

Emotional Support   No woman can make the kind of transitions we have described without the support of people to whom she feels close emotionally. Social scientists speak of "support systems" as enduring "attachments among individuals or between individuals and groups that serve to improve adaptive competence in dealing with short-term crises and life transitions as well as long-term challenges, stresses, and privations." In other words, support groups help us cope and adapt to change. They give us emotional control over the situations we face. They provide honest feedback which reinforces our sense of self-worth. Supportive friends can provide a reality check whereby we can test our appraisals of a situation and our reactions to it. Such groups can offer us guidance about ways to deal with conflicting forces in our lives.

A stable, integrated family is the basic unit of support for any person. When the family is broken or a person is on her own, she must seek other types of relationships. Even loving, caring families cannot be the only emotional support of those women who are blessed with them. Too often women who learned as they grew up that they should act to please men in general and their husband in particular have forgotten the strength which is to be found in healthy, mature friendships with other women. Betty, whose story we told in chapter four, learned this lesson when she experienced the loneliness of studying for the Episcopal priesthood and determined that she would never again be without a close woman friend with whom she could share her concerns.

Christian communities provide the support of an extended

family for many women, as do small sharing groups within the more traditional church structure. The advantage of such groups is that they permit enriching friendships with both men and women. Many working women are experimenting with participation in an "intentional family." In such an arrangement, a small group of people make a commitment to live near each other and to function as a family. A single social worker described for us her intentional family of five persons. "Even though we live in separate households, we feel like we have a special bond of intimacy and a goal to work together as a family. We originally came together because it seemed silly to have three washing machines between us and not to take some of the economic burden off each other."

The most vibrant, radiant Christians we met were those who have learned to carve out time for meditation in order to know themselves and to hear God's voice in their lives. They also maintain the disciplines of reading the Scripture and of prayer. Such Christians have learned the value of praying on a regular basis for specific, deep needs and concerns with a close friend or small group of friends. The most poignant moments in our interviews often arose when women confessed that they had few close friends or worked such long hours that they preferred just to be alone in their rare moments of free time. When we asked one busy executive if she had any emotional support outside of her family, she looked startled and then thoughtfully answered, "No. That's not a good situation, is it?"

Women told us marvelous stories of the strength of Christian marriage when, during times of change, husband, wife, and children agree on a course of action. Husbands and children have frequently seen more in wives and mothers than the women have seen in themselves. But many men do not have egos strong enough to handle a wife with a career; they may even have difficulty encouraging their wife to find ways of expressing herself within the home. A scientist, who is also the wife of a pastor, told us, "A man has to be secure in himself and also be sensitive enough to recognize the woman's needs and be willing to let her do her own thing and not try to fit her into a mold—for instance, as a pastor's wife. I've been very fortunate that way."

A nurse gave us a charming account of a summer she spent studying at the University of Rochester in order to become a nurse practitioner. It became a family project. "We moved there, part and parcel, with the whole family. We rented an apartment, and Dick [her husband] became official *Hausfrau*—domestic engineer, I guess, is what he prefers to be called. He was great about it. He was able to make arrangements for the girls to take gymnastic lessons, took them swimming, to the library twice a week, made a point of studying the culture of the American Indians in the vicinity, did the laundry. The kids did a lot of things; he had them organized. . . . I worked very hard. I think I was the only person there who had their family with them, but I was really serious about studying because I thought that was the only way I could achieve my goal. It was very hard. The girls missed the dog. I desperately missed our back porch. But I felt very much that it would increase my skills and make me a better teacher, and it did."

Walking Through the Doors of Opportunity   Life brings us change, but God gives us opportunities. Women who accept risk, we found, usually see the risk as an open door through which God is asking them to walk. When God wills something else, he closes doors. Lois embodies this philosophy of life. She began her married life as a partner with her husband in farming, and she worked with him as they struggled to make a go of it. Now in her fifties, she has become active in politics on the state level because she feels that Christians have no right to complain that "politics is dirty" when they shirk their political responsibilities. When Lois talked with us, she was serving as the area representative for a United States congressman. "I feel that when the time is ripe, things will open up, and you'll know it. I guess that's how I live my life. Everybody laughs at how I flit from one thing to another, doing different things. But I really believe that if you live your life guided by God, you don't know what you'll be doing from one time to the next. He just opens up avenues.

"Ten years ago, if anybody had said, 'You'll be working for a congressman,' I'd have said, 'You're out of your mind.' But I just feel that God thought this job was where he could use me. Every day I can feel him working through me, using me. Maybe something will come up, and he'll have something else for me. He will open the way and say, 'Hey, this isn't for you any more. You're needed somewhere else.' That's the way I've lived my life. My husband has always said farming is a gamble anyhow, and you've just got to turn it over to the Lord and let him direct it. Both of us basically have lived our lives that way."

COPING

The Three-Ring Circus With Side Shows   A constant complaint of working women, no matter what their lifestyle, is that their lives are too full and there isn't enough time in the day. "Time seems to be our biggest enemy nowadays. It's almost frightening. We seem to be running from one end of our life to the other." The most striking image of this frantic pace was painted for us by a woman of fifty, thinking back to the time when she was teaching part-time, studying for a master's degree, looking after her husband and two young children, and participating in assorted activities. "Those were difficult years because the kids were little and we had to arrange for baby-sitters. And what if the children were sick? I had all kinds of guilt feelings. I felt like my life was a three-ring circus with side shows. I was teaching six hours; I was taking six hours of courses each semester; I was running the house and family. Those were the three rings. Then the side shows were the Sunday school class, the Campfire Girls, and missionary activities."

Time also becomes a precious commodity to the person whose job consumes more than eight hours of the day. An executive, who is single, told us, "The loss of my own time—time—is the thing that's constantly on my mind because I have so little that's my own to dispose of. I've learned to value it and use it well, I think. Before I was an administrator, I thought I was a busy person, worked hard and all of that, but I realize there was a lot of downtime, a lot of time just devoted to living and being that I no longer have. I've

153

learned to have the sense of a vacation in one day. You can take a mini-vacation by going to New York for the day on the train. Now, on my business trips I try to build in getting rested up when I'm away from home by sleeping more. And I try to do one fun thing in any city I go to."

Other women don't have the luxury of any time to themselves, primarily because their salaries don't permit them to take mini-vacations or to hire baby-sitters. Take, for example, the single parent who works as a secretary and gets her two young children off to school every morning. "In the morning, I have a small time of prayer, and then I'm on deck. I'm up. I'm making the kids' breakfast. I'm making sure that whatever money or notes they need to go to school is in their knapsacks. I check the weather to see how to dress them for the day, make sure there are enough snacks to go to the sitter. Time is a pressure."

When she was first divorced and her children were even younger, things were still tougher. Her son was constantly ill. "That first year, I think I spent every vacation day I earned home with him while he was sick. I didn't have any time for me—just to get away and read. When they're small, you have to do so much for them. . . . It's so much easier now. They have assumed a great deal of the small responsibilities for themselves. They can put on their own boots and snowsuits. That's a big deal—when you have to get yourself dressed and go out and clean off the car and warm it up and not have to get *three* people dressed and go out and warm up the car. I feel like telling all single mothers, 'If you can make it until they're six, you're going to do all right.'"

The price that a woman pays when the circus gets out of hand is physical illness or exhaustion and a feeling that nothing is getting done properly. An athletic director at a Christian college whose income is needed by her family felt very pressured when she talked to us. Her job includes coaching and traveling with her team; she also has two daughters at home. "I've had many periods over a year's time when I've seen the kids for an hour a day, if at all. It's just not good. I'd like to think they come first, although in actuality I sometimes question that. Timewise there is no way I can do it. If I don't put the time in, the athletic job is just not going to get done.

In many respects, a woman who was single in my position could do a far better job because she wouldn't have these other commitments. I guess I'm getting a little tired of trying to be super woman. I'm holding down two full-time jobs."

The deepest fear of working mothers is that their children will suffer from neglect. Sometimes the children give overt signs that they want attention. Anne, the librarian mentioned in chapter two, described what happened when she was studying and working full-time. "When I started working, there was one summer that was pretty dreadful. I was getting my library degree and working. I left the house at seven, had classes till noon, and I'd go to work until seven. I was gone from seven to seven. I had a marvelous high school girl whose family lived right across the street to baby-sit. Well, the summer was all right, but when the fall came, the children started running away. I realized something had to give. I realized I couldn't work full-time as long as the children were little."

Sometimes husbands rebel, too. Luretha, a medical technician, found that the combination of her job and her commitments to her church groups was harming her relationship with her husband. "Monday night it was missions meeting. Tuesday night we had Bible study. Wednesday it was missions. Thursday it was choir rehearsal. And that left only lonely Friday. I began to pray, 'Lord, put it in divine order.' Now, I divine order every day." Luretha cut down on her church activities and made a concerted effort to spend more time alone with her husband.

Managing Time and Making Trade-Offs   Luretha's prayer, "Lord, show me your order for today," is an excellent starting point for the daily choices we must make as to where our time and energy are going to go. There are also some steps we can take to put our lives in order so that we don't have to reach a crisis, as Anne did when her children ran away, before we revise the priorities in our life.

Some people find that a two-step inventory is an easy way to begin to manage time wisely. Begin by listing the people and activities which are important to you (family, friends, work, hobbies, service to others, prayer), and then numbering them according to the relative importance you would like them to have in your life. The "crunch" comes when you determine how you actually spend your time.

Next, keep track of how you spend your time during a typical week. Use half-hour units and be specific as to your activities. Then compare the inventory of your actual expenditure of time with your list of priorities. If there is a discrepancy between the two lists, set some reasonable goals for reallocating your time, budgeting it the way you would budget money. Most people find that old habits of misusing time die hard, so don't be discouraged if change comes slowly. Begin by making small changes. Build flexibility into your schedule and allow units of free time in which you never schedule anything. Lists can be useful as long as they don't constitute a list of "shoulds" which cause you to feel compulsive about your time.

When they begin to set priorities and manage time, many women face a special battle which stems from their strong sense of nurturing. Women want to be needed and to care for people. The more we do and the more people we help, the more others may come to depend on us. It is hard to acknowledge that we are not indispensable. Ruth, who was exhausted because of over-committing herself, faced this issue. She was a wife and mother and held two demanding nursing jobs. "I like to feel useful. I guess a lot of us find it very easy to get into situations where people are dependent on us. But I do not see the object of nursing as dependence. I see it very much as helping the other grow and encouraging people in self-care.

"I like to be needed, and I think most of us do. I had to go through a process when I actually said to myself, 'What if I got hit by a car or run over by a truck?' Everyone would say, 'Isn't that a shame. What ever will we do?' Then everyone would just go on as they should. What would be better? To be able to carry on or to collapse out of helplessness?" Ruth discovered that she was dispensable and that others would be better off if they were able to stand on their own two feet without depending on her. Furthermore, she realized that her energy had limits. "I am over forty, and I had to look at how much energy I have, and I didn't have enough to keep it up." She chose to give up one job and to continue teaching nursing because she could bring about change more effectively through educating other nurses.

If women are to work full-time, they must make trade-offs—give up some things. With few exceptions, both single and married women said that family and friends remain their first priority. First, most women trade off their ideal of a well-kept, clean house in return for working and maintaining the important emotional relationships in their life. Shortcuts for managing the house and preparing meals can be found. Husbands, children, or apartment-mates share chores. The second trade-off is giving up much of the leisure time necessary to do things one enjoys doing for oneself. The third trade-off is limiting the amount of time one spends with family and friends. "Quality time" was the cliché constantly used to describe the units of time people try to give to others.

"I'm a terrific list-maker," Ruth, the nursing educator, confided, "but if I walk into the kitchen and see that a counter is dirty, instead of saying, 'Oh, dear, I need to do that, I'll grab a cloth and clean it. I can't do that with everything because I just don't have the time, but with the more obvious things, I do the job when it needs to be done.

"The other thing is, you put your pride behind you and say, 'Is it more important that I have my drawers all organized or is it more important that I have time to spend with my children? Is it more important to get the laundry done or the basement cleaned?' Obviously, you do the laundry. I try not to let it be that the wheel that gets the grease is the noisiest, but sometimes that's true.

"I have learned that I can't make a roast beef dinner with exotic fixings on a regular basis. I have learned that I have to feel free to say, 'This is a Burger Chef night.' That also comes from the support of my husband; he's willing to eat Burger Chef food on those nights. On another night we'll have a real nice dinner because there's time.

"I like to sew, but I can't do that any more. I have to buy clothes or hope the girls will learn to sew. I had an extra day at Thanksgiving that I hadn't counted on before company arrived, and I made new curtains for upstairs. So, when I have the time, I use it. And I think that's another aspect that's different when you're not working—you know, you just kind of let things go then.

"I think the one area I'm sorry I don't have more time for is the things that I just enjoy doing. I think perhaps the only one that gets short shrift is myself. I don't have time for fun things for me, but hopefully there will be time for those things along the way."

•Anne, the librarian, explained that she had become much more relaxed about her home. "I think I did more than I needed to. I was very organized. I would get up early, and I would make casseroles for five days. I didn't have to, really. Now I hardly do anything around the house. Warren [her husband] does all the shopping. The kids do all the cooking. We all do the cleaning. My standards have slipped. Things are more relaxed.

"When I was getting my second master's—my master's in English—and I was working full-time, I came home one day and I was just exhausted. I put my head down and cried and said, 'I can't do it all. I can't work, go to school, and run the house.' So I got all the kids a big laundry basket. They do all their laundry. I made a list of all the chores that had to be done, and we divided it up." Her children were eight, nine-and-a-half, ten, and eleven-and-a-half. Now they are teen-agers and college age. "The kids are very supportive. The kids always step in. If I have a talk I want to give, and I need to go over it, they will very often listen. They're really unusually generous and kind about that sort of thing.

"I always allow for personal things to intervene. Like last year my mother got sick, and that was a large emotional, physical drain. I've accepted these family interruptions. I used to fight them and think, 'Oh, I can't get on with my professional life because my family is getting in the way. Now I realize that's silly, and my projects can wait. The people are more important."

The Flexible   These methods of coping by organizing
Workweek   and making trade-offs are representative,
for the most part, of the way middle-class, married women deal
with the pressures on their time. Even though husbands and children often cooperate in the chores at home, the burden of adjustment is placed on the woman who holds the equivalent of two
full-time jobs—homemaker and employee outside the home.

There are other women for whom the pressures of time and
energy are even greater. For example, a single professional who
commutes to and from New York City each day told us, "If I work
a ten-hour day, I can't do anything at night. I don't have much of a
social life that doesn't have something to do with my work, primarily because it takes too much energy to go out of the house. It's
much easier to stay home."

Many women who are in low-skilled jobs are so exhausted by
their work that they cannot expend their peak energy with their
children or the activities of their family. A teacher commented on
the problems of working mothers who are in physically demanding
jobs. "The kind of work they do is not rewarding. They work in
factories or they work cleaning houses because they have to and
they don't have any skills. When they come home, they are
exhausted, and they're not very fulfilled. . . . The time they have for
their kids is time when they're worn out, so working is a negative
thing, an unfortunate thing. If they didn't have to work, they
wouldn't. When middle-class women work, they're generally doing
it because they love it. When they come home, they're excited
because they've spent time doing what they want to do. They don't
resent their children. They're not worn out, so work can be a positive thing. I don't think you can compare the two groups."

Part-time work, while permitting an additional source of income for the family and more free time for a wife and mother, is not
really an answer to the pressures felt by working women. Part-time
workers are normally paid on a lower scale than full-time employees, and they receive few, if any, fringe benefits. Often a part-
time job pays so poorly that it is not worth taking. Furthermore,
part-time workers are not taken seriously by many firms, and they
suffer from a pervasive attitude that they are somehow inferior to

full-timers. A woman reported the deep anger she felt when a colleague, who worked full-time, wanted to discuss a department problem with her and said, "I can tell you; you're a nobody," referring to her part-time, unofficial status.

Some fundamental changes in the working habits and schedules of Americans seem to be in order. The concepts of a flexible workweek with "flex-time" and of part-time jobs at pro-rated full-time pay are slowly gaining ground in some areas of the country. The current industrial workday is structured around the premise that the worker is male and that his wife is at home looking after the children. The eight-to-five schedule mitigates against shared parenting and shared housework because both parents usually work at the same time. The long hours demanded of professionals, managers, and executives mean that both men and women are better off single—or married and childless—if they feel called to responsible positions.

Rosemary Ruether has asserted that "we need to change a pattern of complementary and mutually exclusive roles of work and home to one of shared work for both men and women on both sides of the home—work split." The answer to many of the problems we have outlined may be the flexible workweek in which the number of hours would range from twenty-five to forty, the number of days would vary, and the workday itself would be flexible. Single wage-earners could choose a longer workday and workweek, whereas couples could jointly work fifty to sixty hours (twenty-five to thirty hours apiece). Hopefully, the concept of the underpaid part-time job would begin to disappear. Ruether comments, "With a three- or four-day flexible workweek there is much more possibility of mutually shared housework and child-raising. Each person could be home one or two days while the other is working. Each would feel less pressed to find time for civic activity, self-cultivation, relation to children, etc. The pattern of over-worked husbands and under-stimulated wives could be changed in a real and systematic way to one of mutually shared work and home lives."

The state of California has taken the lead in experimenting with flex-time. In 1976, using federal money, the state funded a center in Palo Alto called "New Ways to Work." The aim of the center is to develop shared jobs in which two individuals are employed in a position usually held on a full-time basis by one person. Los Angeles and San Francisco have begun to offer flexible schedules to municipal workers. Most employees work eighty hours spread over nine days, with an extra day off on the tenth; a few people work four ten-hour days each week. In Los Angeles, all municipal employees can begin the day anytime between 6:30 and 8:30 A.M.; San Francisco permits its workers to put in eight hours between 6 A.M. and 6 P.M.

These are just first steps toward the types of basic changes our society ought to be making. In our interviews we met a few individuals and couples, mainly in Christian communities, who have adopted a flexible work schedule or a fifty-to-sixty hour shared workweek.

Laura played with her infant son Andrew as she talked to us in her bedroom-office. She edits a small church-sponsored magazine which relates Christianity to contemporary social issues, and she is able to run the operation out of her apartment. Her husband Norm is a clergyman but does not have his own parish. They are both committed to working limited hours and to sharing child-care. "I've set real clear boundaries for years now around what I do. I work thirty hours a week in my job. I found that that's the best way to insure that I have time to do the other things that I want to do. We work six days a week and hold Sunday as the Sabbath and really keep it. That is just such a humanizing, wonderful way to live. That day is different. That's for us and adventures and church and sleeping. The other six days our time is completely full. . . . I'm either working or taking care of Andrew. We also try to take one evening or one unit of time each week to be together."

Laura and Norm are committed to life in the city; their neighborhood is black, Hispanic, and white. The parish church where they worship is located in their immediate neighborhood so they feel their lives are coherent and integrated. "It has to do with the satisfaction of having a whole life—living in one place, working in one place, worshiping in one place, and being committed." The city needs professionals who care about it, and the urban setting provides a practical advantage for Laura and Norm, for it permits them to move from one job to another, setting up a flexible work-week. "The city is the one place where we can live and have serial professional involvements."

Guild

Working women frequently experience gnawing guilt, especially if they work because they want to, not because they have to. Guilt is intensified if a person has not really thought through why she is working or if there is a conflict with her spouse or family about her job. Guilt is frequently the result of a set of "shoulds" which we internalize as we grow up: "shoulds" which come to us from our upbringing, from societal pressure, from our belief-system. If we carry around the "baggage" of too many shoulds, we waste a lot of psychic and emotional energy trying to live up to unrealistic ideals which have little to do with God's expectations. Some psychologists maintain that a system of shoulds can tyrannize the individual, locking her into a rigid life system which makes adaptation to the changing circumstances of life almost impossible. Sometimes compulsive shoulds are a sign that we don't really accept ourselves and that we subconsciously think neither God nor our family accepts us, either.

Molly, a homemaker in Maryland, told us, "Society says you've got to be the perfect mother, the perfect housekeeper, the perfect lover, the perfect career woman. Whether you're a home-maker or a career woman, if you try to raise a family, you can't do everything. You've got to decide what is important to you." When we think about our feelings, we often discover that we are experiencing false guilt which is based on a set of priorities made up of inherited "shoulds."

Working mothers seem to feel guiltiest about themselves and their children. One woman blurted out to us, "I tend to feel guilty when I'm doing something I enjoy. Isn't that awful?" Another admitted, "It's been very difficult for me to learn that rest and relaxation are part of life." Although Scripture sets forth the principle that rest from work is good and necessary, many women feel that mothers should never relax or have time to themselves. There is a subtle form of "workaholism" related to the "super-mom" mentality in middle-class American society. In this ideal of motherhood, the super-mom is at the beck and call of the entire family and always puts others first, even if she also works outside the home.

In reality, however, we are nourished by free time—by play which has no useful end, by leisure to rest and think, by time spent with husband or closest friends. Leisure can result in wisdom and creativity because it renews the inner and outer person. In Ecclesiasticus 38:24–39 (Apoc.) there is a passage which is often quoted because of its wonderful description of working with one's hands, plowing, smithing, and potting. Yet, the theme of the entire passage is really that work, while benefiting society, does not lead to the wisdom which is the foundation of culture. Speaking of artisans, the writer says:

> All these put their trust in their hands,
>   and each is skilled at his own craft.
> A town could not be built without them,
>   there would be no settling, no traveling.
> But they are not required at the council,
>   they do not hold high rank in the assembly.
> They do not sit on the judicial bench,
>   and have no grasp of the law.
> They are not remarkable for culture or sound judgement,
>   and are not found among the inventors of maxims.
> But they give solidity to the created world,
>   while their prayer is concerned with what pertains
>   to their trade (38:31–34 JB).

Molly expressed the importance of leisure in practical terms for the mother of young children. "I would encourage her to take some time for herself when her children are small and not put it off thinking things are going to get better in a few years. Make the most of the time you've got. If you can't afford a baby-sitter, there are all kinds of possibilities like cooperative play schools. Community Bible studies have baby-sitters with programs for children. I used to bowl once a week, and they had baby-sitters at the alley. Having some time for yourself enables you to give more to the kids when you are with them."

Some people thrive on challenge, stress, and activity; others have a much lower tolerance for pressure. We need to be able to recognize when the love of challenge and activity is becoming compulsive. A recent study of workaholics indicates that they fear failure, boredom, and laziness and are often acting out, as adults, an unconscious need for parental approval. These people feel guilty if they say no to a request, even an unreasonable one. Sometimes Christians follow the model of parents who pushed the Protestant work ethic too far. Others are motivated by the need to be in control of everything in their lives; constant activity gives the illusion of such control. Workaholics try to maintain the myth that they are indispensable. They are often consumed by details and cannot delegate responsibility.

Florence Seaman suggests that there are four steps to take in dealing with guilt feelings related to our work. First, we can reassess our values to determine if we are motivated by subconscious shoulds which are not really appropriate to our lives as responsible adults. (This does not imply the rejection of the basic tenets of our Christian faith.) Second, we can restructure values to suit our own personality and responsibilities. Third, once we assume responsibility for our own actions and values, we can pay attention to feelings of genuine guilt. They are a sign that something is amiss in our lives and should be changed. In a Christian context, change may include confession and repentance. And four, we can talk about guilt feelings with supportive friends or family members.

Guilt
About   Many mothers worry when they must
Children   leave young children in child-care centers
or with baby-sitters. They are guilt-stricken if their children are sick and they must go off to work. They worry about their children

becoming "latchkey kids" who return to an empty house, get into trouble, and have emotional difficulties. If a mother must work for economic reasons, her feelings may not be quite so severe, but whether she has a choice about working or not, she must be relatively satisfied with the quality of child-care she has been able to find. Many working mothers have to deal with employers who are unsympathetic toward sick children. A mother who returned to work after her divorce said to us, "I didn't want to establish the reputation for being somebody who always stayed home because her kids were sick."

Often Christian friends, family members, and authority figures send mothers on unnecessary guilt trips. For example, an article on the frustrations of working mothers, written by a leading Christian family psychologist, suggests that many mothers have begun to work because they have bought secular propaganda which says that a woman is not fulfilled unless she has a career. According to this article, working mothers have also capitulated to the myth that state-sponsored child-care centers can substitute for the traditional family. The writer argues that mothers of small children who have enough energy to carry out two full-time jobs are rare and that divorces result from just such over-commitment by both wives and husbands. Near the end of the article, the writer suggests briefly that husbands should show their appreciation of the decision of their wives to stay at home and should pitch in and help with the housework. In short, he says, there is a single model for raising a Christian family. In reality, each family is unique and must adopt its own satisfactory pattern which maintains the integrity of the marriage and the loving atmosphere necessary for the sound development of the children.

Several mothers told us that one result of their working was that their children became more self-reliant and independent. In their view, this was good because they had a tendency to overprotect their youngsters. "I tend to do too much for my kids, and my working has forced them to be more self-reliant. They're more independent and more thoughtful about how to help. My working has forced their father to be with the children more, and they've developed a wonderful relationship which was really non-existent before I went to work." While many complaints are raised against mothers who work, we often forget fathers who have not fulfilled their parental responsibilities. One young woman complained forcefully about this issue. "My big gripe is not working mothers, but working fathers. The absent parent is usually the father. Nobody thinks it's a big deal that the men aren't around. From what I've seen of teen-age boys, the fact that their fathers are absent . . . affects them much more than the fact that their mothers work.

"I was a governess in a household where the father was a banker. He was traveling constantly and came home very late and hardly saw the kids. Nobody thinks that's terrible. After all, he's earning money for them. If his wife had gone out and gotten a job, people would think that was awful. But I know from working with the little boy that he needed his father around a lot more." An unexpected side effect of the return of women to work may be the righting of this kind of imbalance in the home.

Real guilt, then, arises when parents fail to make the adjustments toward their children required by the demands of their home as well as their office. These adjustments include a choice of child-care based on a careful investigation of all the possibilities, shared parenting by both spouses or the provision of adequate male role-models when a single mother has custody of the children. Parents should spend units of time with each child in which their full attention is directed toward the child. Mothers can always be available, even if it is by telephone, and can make children feel needed by showing dependence on their ability to act responsibly. If children are too young to come home from school and remain unsupervised, a way must be found to insure that an adult is responsible for them. Neighbors can be located who will be available if a child should become ill while at school.

A single parent called having a sick child "the pits." "It puts together several stresses," she explained. "You've got to pay for medicine and a doctor and, if you're lucky enough to find one, a sitter who will stay all day. Then you stay up all night with this child and work all the next day. It's very hard when they're sick. You can't roll over and hit your husband during the night and say, 'You get up with him this time.' There's nobody there."

A former elementary schoolteacher with two sons felt that mothers of young children should be at home. "I suppose my feeling stems from being a teacher and having to call home when a child was sick and finding that the mother was not there. Sometimes a child would spend the day in the nurse's office because there was no one at home. There are so many times when children need to know that their parents are home. I feel very strongly about being home when the boys walk in the door. If they don't see me right there at the door, they'll holler, 'Mom.' There's just such a short period of time when they are young, and I want to be here."

On the other hand, an executive with two children of junior high and early high school age explained how she dealt with her children's needs somewhat differently. "I'm available by phone at any time of the day. They know they can reach me. They know where I am. In turn, I must know where they are. They have responsibilities. When I'm going to be late, dinner is ready when I get home. They both know how to cook. They both know how to do the washing and ironing. They do things. They're required to. There's no question of 'will you' or 'you should have.' And it's always been that way. We haven't had too many problems with the children, but it's because we run a tight ship."

Studies by social scientists are still incomplete as to the long-term effects of working mothers on children. By the mid-1970s, however, researchers had reached several general conclusions.

1) Daughters of working mothers compare positively with daughters of non-working mothers, especially in independence and achievement. Working mothers model female competence for their daughters. The effect of maternal employment on sons is much less clear.

2) The mother's feelings about working are important. If she experiences guilt and emotional stress, these feelings may interfere with her mothering. Internal conflicts about inadequate child-care and large families cause stress, particularly among lower-class women.

3) Working mothers tend to develop the independence of their children by giving them more responsibility than do non-working

mothers. They compensate for their employment by planning specific times and activities for their children.

4) Children of lower-class working mothers are more likely to be delinquent, probably because the mothers cannot afford adequate supervision of their children. Maternal employment and delinquency may be related in the middle class, but the causal connection has not been documented. Again, much depends on the quality of the supervision given children.

5) School-age children are not deprived of maternal affection when their mother works. Data on the effects of maternal employment on the infant and pre-school child are not yet available. It is not known whether employment interferes with the function of the mother as the stable adult figure in a child's early years. Again, much depends on the quality of the care a child receives while the mother is absent.

In the United States, there is no centrally organized child-care system. (In some countries, day-care centers are located in neighborhoods or at factories.) Finding the right care for one's children requires a great deal of energy and, frequently, money. In 1970, it was estimated that as many as 60 to 75 percent of the children of working mothers were cared for through an informal arrangement with a baby-sitter; 20 to 25 percent were at day-care centers, and 3 percent were unsupervised. One analyst has categorized child-care services as "custodial" (minimal supervision and physical safety), "developmental" (opportunities for learning and well-rounded growth), and "comprehensive" (including even medical care).

Many people are fortunate enough to find a reliable grandmother who shares their own standards of child-care. Sometimes neighbors can organize cooperatives, and individual churches have done much to fill the day-care gap. But the quality and availability of child-care varies dramatically from city to city and region to region.

It is important that parents realize they are consumers when they look for care for their children. Louis and Kay, the journalists described in chapter four, never intended to put their young son Matthew in a commercial day-care center. "Day-care centers are kind of like nursing homes—most of the people who criticize them have never been in one," Kay told us. "We were caught up in all that. Five months before I went back to work we started advertising for a baby-sitter. I called up practically every church in town because my mother's motto was, 'If you want a good baby-sitter, call the church.' We searched very, very hard for an individual to come to our home and care for him there. Of the people who called and applied, two ladies had lost custody of their own children, and they wanted to sit with mine!

"There are two commercial day-care centers in the area. I spent a great deal of time in both of them and chose one which turned out to be satisfactory. It probably would not have been satisfactory had we not played the consumer bit. I went with my copy of the state rules and regulations for day-care centers in my pocket, and I checked everything. Of course, they knew I worked for the newspaper, so we got good care for Matthew. But we played the consumer bit to the hilt.

"So much of what you feel when you go back to work is in direct proportion to the quality of care that your child is getting."

Working It Out
As We have seen that there are various ways
Husband and Wife in which Christian couples handle their lifestyle when both spouses work outside the home. These lifestyles range from a more traditional model in which the wife essentially performs two full-time jobs to partnerships in which the husband and wife work together in their business and share the chores at home to job-sharing where both spouses work half-time and share parenting. Despite agreement between spouses that a wife should work or follow a career, it takes a man of unusual ego to accept the fact that his wife has outstanding career potential. In most cases, the career of the wife is secondary to that of the husband. Frequently, wives with professional training follow the moves demanded by their husband's career and pick up whatever job they can find when the family moves to a new location. An executive

who is also an engineer and a scientist told us that her husband was one of only two or three men she had met during her life who accepted her interests in traditionally male disciplines and adjusted his career to her own strong career drive. She called him "a rare beast indeed!" Another woman who began her career in her forties in a field related to her husband's work and then began to outstrip him in some ways confessed that professional jealousy had been a problem between them. "I think the problem has resolved itself. He had to be assured that his role was not diminished because mine was increased."

Recent secular literature on working couples indicates that conflicts about family and career will be severest at mid-career and that couples are likely to sacrifice their families for their work when they first start out and are trying to get established. In fact, such couples are better off professionally if they have no children. If both partners rank their career first, conflict will be inevitable, whereas if one gives more attention to the family (usually the wife), potential conflict is reduced. Working in related or similar fields can make communication easier, but there can be rivalry, and in some cases, the home becomes an extension of the office. Rivalry and conflict can be particularly intense if the woman earns more than the man. Generally if partners are at different stages of their careers, they tend to be more supportive and less competitive. Finally, job-flexibility, mutual support, and good communication between spouses increase the chances that a two-career couple can succeed at work and at home.

Very few of the Christian women we interviewed showed this kind of thoroughgoing commitment to a two-career marriage where work was an all-consuming activity. Most couples maintained a commitment to a number of people, activities, and service involvements. We were told that family came first and that couples worked hard at giving good care to their children. They admitted that spending time together could be a problem when work loads were heavy or family commitments were great. "Providing quality time for each other is always the thing that goes on the back burner. That's something we have to work on." A marriage counselor told us, "You have to take time to communicate, and that seems to be the big problem. You make time for the things you want to do, so something's got to give if you want time for something else. What I've heard a lot of people saying is that they're aware they haven't made time for each other because they're so busy running here and there and doing things with the children or doing housework or whatever."

Anxiety and Stress

Anxiety can be a normal experience; when we face an important change in our lives, we are bound to experience fear and a general sense of being troubled. We saw in the last chapter that emotional support can be a significant factor in helping us deal with the stress of new jobs and life transitions. Anxiety is also a part of day-to-day living in a world full of stressful situations. In addition, anxiety can originate from internal causes—from a poor self-image and the ensuing lack of self-confidence and indecision, from our perfectionistic expectations of ourselves, and from our desire to be in control of every situation we encounter.

Helen de Rosis has defined anxiety as "a feeling of dread, a nameless fear" that gives a troubled, uncomfortable feeling and is accompanied by an array of physical symptoms. It signals unresolved emotional conflict and frequently is accompanied by tremendous energy. If we feel anxious about meeting a challenge in a work-related situation, a mild form of anxiety can help us do a better job if we channel that anxiety outward in a positive way. On the other hand, prolonged stress and internal conflict can be destructive, focusing nervous tension within our bodies. Christian women often internalize anger because they have been taught that it is not an appropriate emotion; that anger then becomes a part of an anxiety syndrome in which the individual does not recognize that she is angry, describing herself instead as "nervous." The degree to which we can handle work-related stress, whether at home or in outside employment, is determined by how secure and ordered the rest of our lives may be and by how much we feel loved. Readily available stress-scales indicate how quickly stressful events can add up in our lives: a divorce or death of a spouse, a move, or a new job constitute typical disruptions which result in great anxiety. Prolonged stress and ensuing anxiety manifest themselves through a number of common symptoms:

—changes in vital physical functions: sleep patterns, appetite, bowel and urinary activity
—minor physical complaints with no apparent cause: dizziness, faintness, heart palpitations, nausea, skin problems
—fatigue, loss of interest in life, lack of purpose
—irritability, mood swings
—poor concentration, poor memory, troubling daydreams
—lack of decisiveness, poor judgment
—frequent comments by family and friends that you seem "pressured"

If these symptoms are unheeded, the results can be alarming. One woman whose husband was insecure and could not accept her need for new outlets once her children were grown permitted her to work only during hours when he was away from home (and his working hours were frequently irregular). This conflict over work was related to other unresolved issues in their marriage. Over the years, the wife began to show an increasing number of physical symptoms of her internal conflicts: stomach and bowel spasms, heart palpitations, an excessive desire to sleep, and others. Medication and psychological therapy reduced but did not eliminate the problems because the unresolved conflicts remained.

Most working women experience moderate anxiety from time to time, particularly when they do something for the first time on a new job. Patricia is twenty-eight and is an attorney for a prestigious law firm. She has been practicing law for three years and is one of five women among the thirty-seven attorneys in her firm. Her specialty is litigation, and she argues cases in court. "I like to be in a situation where you can achieve justice," she told us. Patricia is bright and competent and has won an impressive number of cases in her short career. "I get the most satisfaction when I win and when I've done a good job. I have only lost one trial, and we're appealing that one." Patricia is married to another attorney, and although both she and her husband are busy, time is not a real problem—pressure is. "I can get very uptight at work and drained. If my husband is, too, we can argue on the way home. We're both at our low points and tired from what we've just done. But by the time I get home, I really do forget about work. My husband helps with the pressure. He'll say, 'Let's pray and ask the Lord to take care of it.'" To handle the pressure of an upcoming trial, Patricia makes sure she is ready for all eventualities. "I'm an over-preparer. I bring in more cases than another person does and am organized. I tend to feel 'I must be able to do a good job; look at all the preparation I've done.'" Nevertheless, "Before I have a trial I feel sick to my stomach with worry. I'm praying, praying all the time, 'Please, Lord, let me do a good job; let me think clearly.'" But afterwards the anxiety is forgotten, and Patricia admitted that her ego-involvement usually comes to the fore. "I'm just so proud of my-self!" she laughed, recognizing her own inconsistency.

Pressure can also be significant for a woman in a traditionally male job or a woman from a sheltered background who suddenly enters the secular work world. One positive way of dealing with such situations is to accept them as challenges, rather than viewing them as threats. Joan was twenty-four and admittedly naïve when she became her husband's business partner, selling parts for heavy construction equipment. She couldn't find a job in which she could use her undergraduate degree in sociology, so she trusted her husband's judgment and helped him start the business. "I have seen God bless that act of trust. I have become a much more confident person by having to learn how to work in a man's world. Construction is a redneck, hard-core field. When I answer the telephone and the caller says, 'Can I speak to someone who knows about bulldozer parts?' and I say, 'Yes, can I help you?' there's a silence for a while. I really took that as a challenge. I got spunky and learned the business the best I could. The next thing I knew, men would come out to the shop just to see this girl who sold bulldozer parts!

"Imagining the person that I might have been had I not come into the business, I think I would be one of those who go sweetly and passively through life. Now I'm a bit more aggressive, much more confident. . . . I enjoy being accepted by the men, but if they don't want to talk to me, I have learned to accept that, too.

"While the business has enabled my husband and me to work in partnership, it has also added pressure to our marriage which we have learned to cope with in different ways. When we worked out of our apartment, I had so much to learn that we really would work from sunup until sometimes eleven or twelve o'clock at night with Bill teaching me. Finally we realized that we had to close the office door at five o'clock.

"The business has brought us into a lot of worldly circumstances and has made us deal with people who have mistresses, people whose business dealings are different from ours. I'm thankful for that because at one point I found myself associating so exclusively with Christians that I couldn't deal with the outside world."

Joan and Patricia both indicated that they found ways of handling anxiety and stress as a result of emotional support, prayer, preparation, and an important decision—to turn off work-related problems at the end of the workday. Many women told us that they had become much more relaxed as they had learned the lesson of complete trust in the providence of God. Others have learned to reduce tension by consciously relaxing themselves on cue. A common-sense way to keep the body in balance is through a well-regulated diet and regular physical exercise. When the source of anxiety is hard to pinpoint or an individual is unable to put emotional distance between herself and her job, she can take concrete steps to handle anxiety which are similar to the inventory we described earlier for managing time. De Rosis suggests using a loose-leaf notebook to keep track of troubling issues. She suggests writing down in a step-by-step manner the ways in which one stressful issue is causing suffering in our lives, how we have tried to deal with it and why this way of coping has failed, our willingness to reduce our suffering, the alternative actions available to us for dealing with the issue, and our choice of action. Once we act, we should write down how this action has worked or failed and what new action we plan to take. This procedure can be repeated as we deal with new stressful situations because it facilitates coping with one issue at a time in a constructive manner.

Handling Conflict   Work-related conflict can also induce anxiety, particularly when we feel powerless and dependent for economic survival upon the person with whom we have a troubled relationship. Many women have been socialized to act out the theme of powerlessness in their lives and have never learned how to confront others by stating honestly how they feel. Nita, a nurse who returned to regular hospital work after a long hiatus, described to us the difficulties she had with her supervisor on her new job. In the orthopedic section to which she had been assigned, she found "such a hostile climate I couldn't believe it. There was a real hatred among the nurses, the aides, and especially the charge nurse on P.M., and I couldn't understand it. I found myself crying to the Lord. I hated work. I was so nervous I could hardly work." Finally, Nita reported the situation to the hospital administration, "not to tattle, but just to say, 'hey, this is the way I feel.'

"The only reason I did talk to the administration was because one night, when the charge nurse had been at her worst with me in front of everybody, I was demoralized and felt horrible. One aide ran after me and said, 'Nita, hang in there. That's the way she is with new people.' And I thought, 'Aha, it isn't just me,' and that's what gave me the courage to talk to somebody about it."

After administrators talked to Nita's supervisor, however, the problem became worse. "She ignored me totally. If I asked a question, she wouldn't answer. She turned the aides against me, too. A lot of it was because I was insecure, and she could tell it and she exploited that." Nita did not transfer to another department because she felt she would be running away from her problem, and the hospital supervisors were not eager for such a move. She stayed in her ward and continued to pray. Eventually, and in an unexpected way, the head of another department arranged Nita's transfer. The climate there was totally different. "Everybody is so supportive and loving, and we work together. It's just fantastic—a day and night difference. It's only been for a couple of weeks, and I'm elated. It's so important to like your job."

Nita was not totally successful in her attempt to handle this conflict, but she concluded that "the whole thing was a growing experience." Her initial response was nervous anxiety, then prayer, followed by a form of assertive action. She felt unable to confront her supervisor directly, but she did find a way of stating how she felt to someone in authority who would listen. That reduced her anxiety even though the stressful situation did not disappear. Eventually, the transfer marked the end of the episode—and the anxiety.

Handling conflict through loving confrontation and assertive behavior is a skill to be learned. Many people equate assertiveness with aggressiveness and the demand for one's "rights." A more accurate description of assertiveness is the ability to choose a behavior or a response consistent with one's value system and feelings. Such action is honest, direct, self-enhancing, and expressive. It reveals respect for the other person, but it also shows respect for ourselves. Confronting another person is a tricky business because we have to learn to express our feelings without putting blame on the other individual. If we ignore our feelings and avoid dealing with them, we can become aggressive or resentful or we can adopt defensive patterns which avoid reality. Furthermore, if we don't act assertively, we allow circumstances to continue which are harmful to others, as well as to ourselves.

The biblical basis for assertive behavior lies in such passages as Luke 10:27 where Jesus commands: love your neighbor as yourself, and Ephesians 4:15 where Paul urges mature believers to speak the truth in love. A sense of self-worth is reinforced by patterns of assertive behavior. A fifty-year-old executive with striking self-confidence told us her strength "comes from my sense of who I am which is rooted in my relationship to God—that I'm accepted by God, that I'm valued. That's the basis, but I've always had that;

I've been a believer since I was five. My sense of self-assurance is a developing thing, and part of it comes with age."

Sense of self is conveyed by body language—eye contact, posture, gestures, facial expression, tone and volume of voice—as well as by the content and timing of what we say. As with the management of time, the handling of guilt, and the reduction of tension and anxiety, assertive behavior patterns and communication skills can be learned. In this case, however, one cannot work alone with a journal or notebook; it is beneficial to belong to a group where role-playing is possible and where feedback is given.

Laurie, the single clinical specialist we described in chapter six, took a course in assertiveness. "It was a six-week course in the evenings, which I think is the best way to do it, as opposed to a one-day seminar. It gave me the opportunity to come back with, 'Well, this week I had trouble with this. What do you people think about it?' We shared a lot and supported each other. My personality is such that I appear aggressive, but I'm really not. Over the years I've had to learn, and still am, about confronting people. I had no problem saying, 'Hi, how are you?' and being really outgoing and friendly but when it came to saying, 'I didn't like what you just did,' or 'It hurt me when you did that,' I did not have an easy time. That's why I took the course, and it has helped.

"I got called into my boss's office on Monday and got reamed up and down and left and right about a Bible study I have been leading. My boss said to me, 'I want you to answer one question. Have you been having a Bible study in your office from 4:00 to 5:00 on Monday afternoons?' And I said, 'Yes.' She said, 'That is totally inappropriate, and I will not allow you to do that any more. I'm very upset with you.'" Laurie explained that she finished her duties at 3:30, that no one was participating in the Bible study during a scheduled period of work, and that no one was proselytizing in the hospital. Her explanation did not resolve the conflict. "I got up and said, 'If that's what you want' and walked back to my office—and cried and cried and cried. I said, 'Oh, Lord, what do you want me to do about this?'"

Laurie realized that she had put her supervisor in an awkward position and that the supervisor had probably been reprimanded by the director of nursing. "I realized that I had been a coward last April when we started this study. I knew then I probably should tell her, but I did not want to because I thought she would say 'no.' So I rationalized and thought, 'It's over and above work time, and it's none of her business. It's in my office, and we're not hurting anybody.' But I knew. I knew all along that sooner or later it would be found out and I would really be in big trouble. I thought about it and concluded, 'Laurie, it's not fair. You put her in a really bad situation, and you must go and apologize.'"

The supervisor could be stern, and the last thing Laurie wanted to do was reopen the conflict, but she knew what God was calling her to do. She left a note on her supervisor's desk, asking her to page her when she had time. "She paged me, and I went down to her office. Once I get started, I'm extremely direct. I said, 'I called this meeting because I want to apologize to you. I am sorry you had to be surprised with something that I should have come to you about directly, rather than your having to hear it from someone else.' She just nodded her head, and there was a firm line about her mouth. I said, 'I will not do this again. I'm sorry.' She said, 'Well, as far as I'm concerned, if you want to meet, you may meet in the chapel, but you have to go through the proper channels.' Then things were fine. Our work relationship was back to where it had been, and I was pleased. But three years ago I would not have been able to do that."

Laurie's experience is a story of growth toward the ability to cope and confront. It is a story which can be repeated in the life of any woman troubled by pressure, conflict, and anxiety. Changing the way we handle such problems requires only the will to change, honesty in facing the situation, a step-by-step program for learning new behavior patterns—and grace.

WORKING WITHIN ORGANIZATIONS

People and Structures

Many people go through life with the unfulfilled dream of quitting their job and becoming their own boss, but modern work is organized in such a way that few of us can really be our own boss. Part of the movement away from the cities in the 1970s was this desire to escape bureaucratic anonymity and the rat race of work, as well as the blight of the city. Rural life became much more attractive to people fed up with urban problems. Farmers would be the first to put an end to any romantic or nostalgic dreams, for successful farming requires business acumen, a knowledge of governmental regulations, and hard work. Yet, there has always been something appealing to Americans about the relative self-sufficiency and independence of farm life.

Martha, a partner with her husband in a dairy farm and bottling business, told us, "It's nice to be at home and still be part of the business and farming, but not have to go out to the barn. I've been able to raise my family right here beside me. For years they were right by me in a playpen by the bottle-filler, and I was doing what I like at the same time."

Farm life has some real advantages. "More togetherness, I guess. Kids have something to do. Our kids never had to wonder what they could do next. We love to go hiking in the afternoon—Sunday afternoon, mainly. At the dinner table somebody says, 'Let's take a walk.' So we do. We have a creek out back, and it's fun to go along it. And we go sled riding and have wiener roasts and hayrides."

The realities of work and family life are much different for most of us. Our jobs are within organizations—factories, corporations, large bureaucracies, or relatively small offices, shops, and businesses. Few of us are without a boss. No matter what the size of the organization in which we work, it is structured in some way. Jobs have titles; official relationships exist between people according to their responsibilities. Usually, informal relationships and groupings are as important, if not more important, than any organizational chart.

In her book, *Men and Women of the Corporation,* Rosabeth Moss Kanter reaches five basic conclusions about the effect of organizational structures on working women and men:

First, work is not just the relationship between a person and a productive activity. The setting affects the work experience of each individual. "Jobs and the relations of people to them cannot be understood without reference to the organized systems in which the contemporary division of labor operates. Understanding organizations and how they function is the key to discovering the ways in which people manage their work experiences."

Second, people adapt to the structure of their organizations; that is, they make strategic decisions in order to survive in their job and maintain their personal sense of worth.

Third, the social structure of the working place limits choices, but most workers have a degree of freedom within the constraints placed on them by organizations.

Fourth, the tasks workers are assigned affect their behavior and interpersonal relationships.

Fifth, competence is important, but it is not easily measured; in fact, the issue of a worker's competence may be obscured by other factors such as sex and social background.

When women enter the work force, they must learn adaptive skills in order to survive, let alone succeed, within organizations. Researchers have found, however, that most women are unaware of the adaptive strategies required by organizational behavior. Furthermore, women have special problems in knowing how to choose responses because the power structure of most organizations is male. Within this structure the patterns of communication, the unwritten codes of conduct, and the prevailing values are also male. In their interviews for their book, *The Managerial Woman*, Margaret Hennig and Anne Jardim were struck by the lack of perception among many women in corporations and businesses. They just did not see the organizational environment in which they worked in the same way that men did. In interactions, they were often unaware of the significance of events which men immediately perceived as important career steppingstones.

A question facing the working woman, no matter what her job, is whether she must adapt totally to the values of the secular power structure in which she finds herself. Can she maintain her individual integrity? Can she bring something new and fresh to organizational life? Can she even change the prevailing values of her organization? The last is a troublesome question because most women feel that any challenge to those in authority might endanger their jobs.

Rosalie is one of the women quoted in the introduction of this book. Her field is interior design, and she works on the managerial level. She is very aware of the questions of perceptiveness, flexibility, and power—both from her training in management and her personal experience. She told us that potential managers should have a good education and get an apprenticeship with a reputable company so that they understand the intricacies of organizational life and the rapid changes in a particular field. "Stay in tune with everything that's going on. Things change rapidly. . . . In this day and age, a field can change or disappear quickly, so it's good to be involved in a couple of things."

**Power
and
Success**

Rosalie learned about power the hard way. "I got fired for doing a good job—which is enough to destroy a person. But it didn't. It just taught me an awful lot." Rosalie was working for a firm where she boosted sales tremendously. In fact, she boosted sales too much. "Everything was rolling along nicely, and I was just starting to make some money. Then I was making more than the sales manager because of the commissions that were coming to me, so they set me up with a tape recorder on the phone." Since she was honest, nothing damaging was gained by bugging the phone. Someone then tampered with an incoming shipment of merchandise which Rosalie had sent for repairs and "reworks," removing all the tags. The "mess" was blamed on Rosalie, and she was fired. "People knew why I was fired—because I was doing too good a job." The shipper realized the situation and closed its account with the firm, but Rosalie did not get her job back.

The unjust firing was difficult for other reasons. "I was pregnant at the time, although I didn't know it and I lost the baby. It was a rough time. I was bitter for a little while. I just couldn't believe something like that could happen. But so many people called me and stood by me that it wasn't as bad as it could have been. One of the accounts that I worked with called and offered me a job." Rosalie's husband Ray was also offered a position, and they moved to an entirely different geographic area. Unfortunately, their troubles mounted. The new firm went bankrupt unexpectedly, and they found themselves without jobs and in debt. Ever resourceful and hard-working, they started their own business. Both worked extraordinary hours until the new firm was stable, and then Rosalie left to take her present managerial position. The unfair use of power by her male boss whom she threatened by her success started the string of disasters which eventually turned out for the good, according to Rosalie. The price she paid, however, was tremendous.

Most women may find themselves in pink-collar jobs, rather than in sales or management, but all are affected by the authority and power of superiors, especially in hierarchical organizations. Power can be expressed in a patriarchal or patrimonial way toward women in the lower ranks, especially in the secretarial pools. Rosabeth Kanter observes that secretaries are often asked to act in total loyalty to their bosses, as in a fiefdom. They are status symbols of their bosses. Michael Korda gives an example of the worst sort of executive privilege in his book, *Male Chauvinism! How It Works*. He quotes a man as saying, " 'I haven't time to mess with details. I need a girl who looks after things for me, a nice, uptight, compulsive, organized girl who needs the money, so she'll work, with no back-talk, because she can't afford to get fired.' "

These two examples of the use of power are really abuses of power, dependent upon the relationship between the strong (those who have authority by virtue of their position in the organization and in society) and the weak (those who are economically dependent upon the strong for survival). Personal power, however, is not based on domination through this type of strength.

All of us have this power—the potential and strength of our personality. This personal power is quite distinct from our status in society or at work. It is a sense of personal worth. In theological terms, personal power is the result of the actualization of the redemptive process and the empowerment by the Holy Spirit. This inner freedom gives us an inner power which counterbalances the external pressures exerted by the realities and injustices of the secular world. Personal power is also expressed in assertive behavior. We are free to enjoy being ourselves and to express ourselves.

A lack of a sense of self-worth translates into a sense of powerlessness which is often communicated to others; we sometimes invite the kind of exploitative treatment we receive. In the preceding chapter, Nita realized in retrospect that her lack of personal power invited domination. Her insecure boss reacted to the very quality she could not tolerate in herself. Nellie Yarborough's advice to women who want to strike out on their own and see their dreams fulfilled also applies to women who may feel powerless in their jobs. "Feel that what you want is just as important as what anybody else wants."

There is still another kind of power. Kanter calls it "the ability to get things done, to mobilize resources, to get and use whatever it is that a person needs for the goals he or she is attempting to meet." This kind of effectiveness leads, usually, to promotions within large organizations and to an ever-widening sphere of influence. Managers who are respected by their superiors and are "visible" within the organization will be given increased responsibilities. Christians often feel uneasy about seeking positions where they can marshall resources to achieve goals. Some of this reluctance may be due to the fact that Christ sided with the power-less. Nevertheless, using power to effect change can be a calling that is as valid as the voluntary renunciation of power which Jesus modeled.

Society has had such a confused understanding of the nature of power and responsibility that many people in leadership positions personalize the notion of power. They think that they themselves own power when the potential to effect change and the foundation of their authority really derive from their job title. In addition, the value system of secular society equates success with power, author-ity, and visibility. If they are honest, Christians in positions of prestige and responsibility admit that theirs is a dangerous route. Although they may not be called to renounce success, they must continuously resist the pressure of the world to remake them in its own mold. One person who had worked in both secular and Chris-tian organizations told us, "I do not believe in success. Power is in the title of the job. Of course, I have the responsibility to use my intelligence, but success in and of itself is the most dangerous thing in the world."

Competition   Little boys are brought up to value competition and success. Although they participate in sports and learn that playing as a member of a team is important, they also realize they are expected to win and to succeed as individuals. Part of the male American dream is to achieve recognition and success in one's work. Research into corpo-rate and organizational life indicates that men learn very early to approach their work in a much different way than do women. For example, Jean Piaget studied how boys and girls regard the rules of games and concluded that, faced with an argument about the rules, girls prefer to terminate the games and do something else. Boys, on the other hand, keep going; they try to resolve the conflict by using the rules. Corroborative studies indicate that in a game situation girls want to preserve relationships while boys want to keep the rules. In the adult world, women and men approach competitive situations in a similar way. According to Georgia Sassen, men size up such situations in an individualistic way, but women approach competitive life quite differently. "Their structure of knowing is more oriented toward preserving and fostering relationships than toward winning."

To rephrase this theory in terms of issues we have already encountered, the nurturing side of women is enhanced by the socialization process, but societal pressure downplays female competitiveness. Women aren't supposed to appear superior to men because that might endanger their prospects of marriage. Hennig and Jardim cite a study of twenty-five women enrolled in the graduate program in business administration at the Harvard Business School in 1963-4. Twenty out of the twenty-five were the eldest in their families, and five had the same experiences as a first-born child. All were close to their fathers and had been involved in a wide range of traditionally masculine activities with their fathers. All were given freedom and family support to pursue their interests, whether or not they were in traditionally masculine areas. These women developed an early preference for the company of men rather than women. These twenty-five women were exceptions and were embarked on a competitive career because they were exceptions; most of their socialization experiences were those an eldest son would have received.

Kathryn, a "faculty-wife" and part-time instructor at the same college as her husband, admitted to us that she had played the role of the dumb blond as a teen-ager and college student. In the Dutch community in which she grew up, intellectual achievement by women was not valued. "In that ethnic group, in the Christian high school where I went, women were not supposed to be intelligent. I can remember coming home in tears over an all-A report card because so-and-so had found out and blurted it out. I can remember one boy in a government class pulling my hair when I got an A on a test and saying, 'You just make me sick.'"

On the other hand, Betsy Ancker-Johnson, an engineer and physicist and the first woman named as a vice-president of the

General Motors Corporation, told us that she grew up in a family where there were no sex roles. Her two brothers were her models, and she was always interested in sports and mechanical things. She described herself as having a strong, competitive drive. At the same time, as a Christian she sees Christ as "the ultimate success," so that any competitive success she might achieve has to be subordinated to the biblical principle that "we are to seek Christ's kingdom first."

Matina Horner, now president of Radcliffe College, made a well-known study in the 1960s of the attitude of women toward success, concluding that most women experience intense anxiety at the notion of achieving success themselves. Much female behavior, she added, is oriented toward avoiding success because society equates success with its expectations of men, not women. Kathryn, the college instructor whom we just quoted, found herself on the horns of a dilemma as she grew up. Her environment gave her the message that women should not seek intellectual achievement, so she played the role of the dumb blond. She avoided success, not by getting Cs, but by trying to hide her As. Her family, however, gave her another message. As the elder of two daughters in a family where there was no son, she received the encouragement of her father who had achieved distinction in the legal profession. "There was an intense conflict between the males in school saying 'you're not supposed to succeed' and my father saying, 'absolutely, you're to succeed.'"

Horner's conclusions have been criticized from a methodological perspective, but they signaled a breakthrough in the study of women. When people began to realize that women had internal conflicts about success, they first thought women should be assisted so they could function competitively and be successful on male terms. Now social scientists aren't so sure. Georgia Sassen suggests that women don't feel anxiety about success; it is the competitive aspect of success that upsets them. Women, with their sensitivity to relationships, have trouble when they enter the corporate world where the managerial ethic downplays relationships. They are much more inclined than are men to refuse a promotion in order to keep close personal relationships.

Since men, too, have a nurturing side which they have too frequently denied, and since the corporate world of competition exacts a toll on them and their families, people are now saying that we need to change our definition of success and the structure of complex organizations. As Anne, the librarian who hopes to enter management, asked, "Why can't someone be nice and also be an administrator?" Why can't someone care and still succeed? Georgia Sassen claims that there is a new agenda for helping women who work in complex organizations. It is no longer appropriate to try to rout out "success anxiety" and replace it with the ability to play by the masculine rules of the game. Women need to focus on affirming the values and world view they bring to the competitive environment of the workplace and "to start reconstructing institutions according to what women know." This means a struggle lies ahead. Changing structures is a long-term goal requiring the cooperation of men and women. It means rejecting the environment which produced the adage, "nice guys finish last." And before women can think of changing organizational structures, they must first get their foot in the door of the organization and learn how it operates.

Leadership   According to Hennig and Jardim, most women describe themselves as hesitant, indecisive, confused about their goals in life, waiting to be chosen or discovered by a man. They don't like to take risks, and they become anxious in situations where there are many unknown factors. How in the world do women become leaders, then? These qualities are the very opposite of those of a leader—someone who takes responsibility, sets goals, takes risks, and makes decisions. Therefore, women who are leaders either have had exceptional experiences growing up or have recognized their potential and have learned how to lead. Researchers have found that women who enjoy leading do not think of themselves as female and different; they see themselves first as persons. Their mind-set, as well as their abilities, qualifies them for leadership. They are oriented toward competence and the achievement of tasks. "You have to have organization, a sense of how to get things done, how to organize a meeting, how to plan for something."

Not only have these women learned to exercise their personal power, but they have also been able to achieve emotional distance in situations which require clear judgment. They are not unemotional, but they have learned to know themselves and to handle their feelings. Ruth, the educational administrator whom we quoted in the introduction, talked to us of her struggles for both emotional distance and empathy. "You have to be pretty strong physically, and I suppose psychologically or emotionally, so that not everything gets to you—and yet the things that should touch you do. It's hard to remain sensitive to the issues that are really important to people when, in the course of all you have to deal with, their personal concerns seem really trivial. I had to learn how to deal with people, how to put myself in their shoes."

Being competent does not mean that Christian women who lead don't care about people. They can fire someone and show personal concern at the same time. Rosalie discussed how difficult it is to fire an employee. "It can change a person's life so drastically. If they're not ready for it emotionally, it can hurt and cripple them terribly. I have fired people, but it's after talking with them and explaining to them exactly why they're being fired. Sometimes a firing really pushes you ahead; it can be a steppingstone."

Having leadership qualities is of no benefit to a woman if she can't penetrate the upper echelons of the organizational structure in which she works. Betsy Ancker-Johnson noted that there are a few women who occupy number one or two positions in industry and government. Below them is a gap—several ranks of managers where there are few women. This is because the women in the top-level jobs are tokens—the exceptions who have been named because they are competent and will be visible. Women who are management trainees are at the lower levels of organizations, and it will be a few years before they work their way up through the ranks. Ruth admitted that she became an administrator because she was at the right place at the right time. She was "lucky."

The male organizational world is characterized by an informal set of relationships—networks—in which essential communication takes place outside regular office channels. Potential leaders learn what is expected of them, what is going on behind the scenes, and who their potential sponsors are via this network. The network is most evident in places like the golf course or the bar. In current jargon, a "sponsor" or "mentor" is an older colleague who takes an interest in a younger colleague, recognizes his potential, initiates him to the "ins and outs" of the organization, and brings him to the attention of the hierarchy. Ruth commented that it is very difficult for a woman to penetrate the upper ranks of an organization; competence is not enough to bring promotion. "Women are more likely either to have to have good sponsors or to promote themselves or to have some other people promoting them if they're going to get a chance."

Christian women can rely on God-given opportunities for entry into positions of leadership, but practically speaking, they also need political know-how. "Anybody who is going to be in administration needs to recognize the political nature of it." It is not unchristian to be realistic—to know who has the authority within an organization, to count one's resources and one's backers in trying to achieve a goal, to bring one's achievements and qualifications to the attention of one's superiors. Christians are called to do excellent work, but they, like anyone else, must achieve visibility; and they must find sponsors if they are to become leaders. Betsy Ancker-Johnson entered management when she felt restless in her position as a prominent research scientist within industry. She asked to change the direction of her career after an analysis by the personnel department of the corporation in which she worked.

Political savvy often comes through bitter experience. One young woman, Nan, was a leading candidate to become the director of a special program in her organization. When the vacancy in the directorship occurred, many of her colleagues told her, "Well, I suppose they'll name you to the job now." Nan left on a scheduled trip for three weeks. She returned to discover that another person had been given the promotion. Her rival, another capable young woman, was named for two reasons: she seized the opportunity when Nan was away and made her interest in the position clear; and her case was also argued by her sponsor, an older man with long managerial experience. Nan had no sponsor. She learned from her experience, however. "I waited patiently for two or three more years, fulfilling all the 'correct' steps in the career-ladder of my institution. I obtained a wide range of experience, a certain amount of visibility, and a reputation for competence. The head of my department then gave me the opportunity I needed." Nan found her own sponsor—again, a male, because there were no women in the middle management ranks where she worked. Her sponsor began to train her to become a department head herself.

Because women are still the exception rather than the rule when they hold positions of leadership, they do their jobs in the limelight; they "stick out." On the other hand, men who lead are under enormous pressure to conform—not to stick out. Kanter makes these observations about the male managers whom she studied in a corporation. "Managers at Indsco had to look the part. They were not exactly cut out of the same mold like paper dolls, but the similarities in appearance were striking." As men move up the managerial ladder, their job responsibilities are less and less structured. There is a great need for mutual trust and solidarity among leaders in the few top positions of an organization. Out of necessity, there is a very small social network at the top, but it is just as conformist as the larger network at the lower ranks of management.

Does the woman who finds herself in the limelight adopt the mores of the male leaders in her organization? Some women do. They choose to act like their male colleagues, thereby achieving invisibility. They prove themselves, often by beating the men at their own game. These women are able to penetrate the prevailing network and to obtain the information they need in order not to be isolated on the job. Other women soon realize that they are tokens. Named to their positions primarily because they are female, they are expected to represent women as a class. They are symbols. Frequently, however, their achievement or their competence on the job is not recognized. They can, however, be powerful role-models for other women, encouraging them to be free to be themselves. A few women, once they have "arrived," choose to become "queen bees." They enjoy the status of being the only woman at the top and do nothing to encourage other women in their careers or provide more opportunities for them.

Women who maintain their individuality as they lead are incredibly strong, busy, and fulfilled. They have suffered all the pressures of being a member of a minority group plus the loneliness inherent in a position of responsibility. In a moment of candor, one woman executive told us how, early in her career, a fellow staff member told her, "You must lead a pretty lonely life." She didn't deny it. As much as the struggling young homemaker with small children, the single working parent, or the two-career couple, women leaders need support. They usually find few persons within their local congregation or parish with whom they can share their concerns, and they are often cut off from other Christian women with more traditional lifestyles and interests. Only in large urban churches have we observed any attempt to meet the needs of professional women, and relatively little has been done to bridge the communication gap between "traditional" and "nontraditional" women within the body of believers.

In style and personality, women leaders are as different from each other as men are, but the stereotypes about women bosses, which are based on societal prejudices, still are very prevalent. People think that women managers are jealous, emotional, petty, perfectionistic, faultfinding, and oriented toward detail. Kanter has astutely observed that these are not female qualities; they are qualities which result from an inner sense of being powerless; they are defense mechanisms. Women who are truly free to be themselves and to feel comfortable in leadership positions are free to allow others more freedom. They do not exhibit the stereotypic qualities of the woman boss. Rather, they are able to think about long-term goals and to develop a personal, creative style of leadership.

Personal styles of leadership differ, but two qualities characterize Christian approaches to responsibility: openness and servanthood. Leading is a matter of drawing out the best in people and matching their gifts with the proper responsibilities. It requires not only the ability to marshall resources to achieve goals but also the capacity to develop trust. The goals of an organization can never be just those of the leader; they must be shared by a much larger group of people. "I get much more pleasure thinking that I have convinced somebody by the strength of my ideas," one woman told us, "than by implying 'you will do this because obviously I have the power to make you do it or to keep you from doing something else.' I try to encourage people to do things. To involve them. To move them. To get them out of ruts, if necessary. I want to lead them, rather than insisting on my own way."

The leader who sees herself as a servant avoids the trap of personalizing the power, prestige, and salary which secular responsibility brings with it. Jesus is the model of the leader with personal power and authority who is, at the same time, servant of all. He was no doormat, but he chose to channel his authority so as to empower others. "They came to Capernaum. When he was in the house, he asked them, 'What were you arguing about on the road?' But they kept quiet because on the way they had argued about who was the greatest. Sitting down, Jesus called the Twelve and said, 'If anyone wants to be first, he must be the very last, and the servant of all'" (Mark 9:33–35). It is in the acting out of servanthood that women leaders can make great use of their sensitivity to personal relationships as they act as facilitators and enablers. They may achieve concrete objectives in terms of the goals of their organizations, but ultimately, they touch lives. "The satisfactions in administrative work are seeing that you're able to help others do good things. The rewards are basically secondhand. You see others doing more than they could do if you weren't there to help them or encourage them or facilitate it or put people together."

**Working Together
as
Men and Women**   In 1978, only 6.1 percent of all working women were in managerial and administrative jobs. Five percent of the people earning more than $10,000 a year as managers, officials, or proprietors were women. Only about 2.5 percent of all those making salaries above $25,000 were women.

There is no way of avoiding the issue of male-female relationships in the workplace. Male power and authority and male attitudes toward women are significant issues in the lives of most working women because of the heavy distribution of women in non-salaried, low-skilled jobs. But the issues of sexism and sexuality are not limited to the secular place of work. The division of labor by sex prevails in Christian organizations, too. A survey of twenty-five Christian organizations in 1974 indicated the following distribution:

	Male	*Female*
Board of Directors	92.2%	7.8%
Managers	83.5	16.5
Supervisors	81.2	18.8
Clerical Workers	21.9	78.1

The sample in this survey was too small for us to draw any real conclusions. The percentage of women in the supervisor or manager rank may actually be a little higher than in the secular world, but the general distribution remains parallel. Men occupy most of the prestigious positions of leadership.

Because of our early socialization, women may defer, apologize, and yield to men both in social situations and on the job. On the other hand, ingrained attitudes in men can make the workplace difficult because they hold the positions of authority. "Chauvinism" may be expressed overtly in a hostile or sexual way, but it is always based on the issue of power. If a woman feels powerless, she will have trouble confronting situations in which she feels she is being exploited. Stereotypic attitudes and behavior patterns are also embedded in our subconscious so that the most well-meaning men may be shocked and startled to find that they are perceived as "sexist" or "chauvinistic" in what they say or do.

Women may be cast into a number of stereotypic roles by the men with whom they work. Frequently men aren't even aware that they are relating to women as representative females rather than as colleagues. A woman may be asked to play the role of mother—the safe figure on whose shoulder men cry, in whom they confide. Or she may be considered cute—a harmless pet who cheers up her colleagues. Seductresses are asked to play a more openly sexual game, beginning with flirtation. These women are viewed as sex objects. Sometimes male sponsors play the role of the protector of an attractive woman, thus disguising their own sexual interest in her. If a woman resists behaving in such traditional ways, she may be labeled "tough," "feminist" (meaning "aggressive"). She is then isolated and cast in the role of another stereotype, that of "the iron maiden."

Secular books indicate that a woman working in a predominantly male environment must make clear from the beginning that she will not play games, whether they are overtly sexual or sexist role-playing. Hennig and Jardim point out that quality relationships are a key to a good atmosphere in the workplace and that a woman must have a sense of her own style as she relates to people singly and in groups. Style results from knowing who we are and how we can best communicate who we are, our perceptions, and our goals. An effective style, however, de-emphasizes personal involvements with colleagues that rob us of our objectivity. Again, there is a constant tension for the Christian who wishes to balance competence with empathy in her relationships at work. If women constantly encounter situations in which behavior from male colleagues isolates them as female, they must learn to anticipate this behavior and figure out a strategy for developing a positive response and handling their emotions. (It may be useful to keep a journal with notes on what action works and what doesn't, on what our emotions have been and how we have learned to handle them. Beginning to handle our emotional responses can involve such a simple thing as deciding to cry in the rest room rather than at our desk.)

One woman explained what being a woman meant when she entered a post which had previously been held only by men. "If you're in a situation where people are not used to a woman in leadership positions, then you are cast immediately in a role of 'woman administrator.' Everything you do is seen as, 'Oh, that's the way women are' instead of, 'that's the way you are as an individual.' I decided early on in my first administrative post that I would try to ignore reactions to me that conceivably could have been reactions to me as a woman and as a female administrator. After a few years of trying to do this, I realized that some responses were so clearly and blatantly sexist that I just had to recognize it or be a fool if I didn't. You get more opposition to certain ideas, to your authority. You're thrown in the role of token. You speak up in a meeting, and you're the only woman there. They turn to you and say, 'What do the women think?' as though you represented all women. I'm sure it's the same for the minority person. I say everybody ought to have the experience of being a minority person. It gives you a sensitivity."

The issue of sexuality is related so directly to the power of men that some women to whom we talked refused to say much about sexual harassment. The instances of sexual advances or harassment which we heard about represented a range of experiences typical within the workforce as a whole. Sexual harassment is so prevalent that in November, 1980, the Equal Employment Opportunity Commission issued interpretive guidelines forbidding it under Title VII of the Civil Rights Act of 1964. The Commission defines it as "unwelcome sexual advances, requests for sexual favors, and other verbal or physical conduct" of a sexual nature that create "an intimidating, hostile, or offensive working environment" or affect employment decisions. A survey made in 1976 by *Redbook* estimated that nine out of ten working women experience some form of sexual harassment. In the past, when women have been seriously harassed, the majority have quit their jobs because that was the only recourse open to them. Now more women may be developing assertive behavior or reporting such actions, but sexual harassment is difficult to prove, especially if one is in a powerless position. We did not encounter anyone who had filed a formal complaint of any sort.

Sylvia is a Mexican American who, in her early twenties, worked at a radio station where she put radio logs together and produced commercials. She described her male bosses as "lecherous old men" who used "terrible language" and had no respect for women. "You Mexican girls are so pretty," was a typical comment. During the annual Christmas party, "the quietest men became big bad wolves" and then would not remember later the sexual advances they had made. On her first job as a professor, another woman found that one of her university colleagues remarked constantly about her beautiful legs, leered at her during department meetings, or else asked to sit beside her. When she asked him to "treat me as a colleague," he said, 'You're a woman; you're beautiful, and I'm never going to let you forget it.'" On her next job, when she had been at the university a relatively short time, she was invited to a party where one of her male colleagues sat down beside her and told her very crudely how much he wanted to go to bed with her.

One woman, a secretary, refused to go into detail about the sexual harassment she had experienced, but it shocked and frightened her. "I was astonished. I don't rate myself 'a ten.' Why me? It seemed so ludicrous. Then I was frightened. And you *are* frightened. You don't have a lot of power and you fear losing your job, and you need that paycheck. You can go to Affirmative Action, but you better have documentation. It's such an emotional thing. It was hard to believe that it was happening, and it was harder to believe that it was happening to me. I was frightened to be alone in his part of the building. I was frightened to take work there. I was afraid that if I went to my boss he wouldn't believe me. It was a very difficult time." She finally talked to another secretary about what type of action she could take to thwart the harassment; this woman served as a one-person support group.

Another person, who did not wish the interview to be taped, had worked closely for years in a laboratory with the same male boss. They worked as colleagues and friends as they cooperated on their research. The issue of sexuality "is bound to arise when men and women work together," we were told. The boss's marriage was unhappy, and he fell in love with his female researcher. She enjoyed her work and did not wish to change jobs. Although the boss labeled her "a puritan," she "stuck to Scripture" and refused to become involved with him. She avoided all compromising situations and never attended the same professional conferences that he did. That status quo arrangement prevailed, but the researcher admitted such might not be the case for other women whose bosses might not respect their Christian principles in refusing to be involved in an affair. "It can be very difficult for a woman whose job or future recommendations depend on her boss."

While we were writing this book, one of us happened to be seated next to a management consultant on an airplane. His first comment when he heard about the book was that the workplace is difficult for women because they have no network, no informal support and communication system comparable to that of men. Although such networks are beginning to appear through caucuses of women in professional associations and through informal contacts, the issue of sexual harassment highlights the need each working woman has for a support group. Only co-workers, banding together, investigating a grievance, gathering evidence, and filing a complaint, can have enough power to counteract a higher-ranking male manager. The individual woman seeking ways to develop assertive behavior in a situation of harassment needs emotional support from a group with whom she can discuss strategies of action.

Inequities and Grievances The Equal Pay Act of 1963 and its 1972 amendment legislate the principles of equality with respect to pay and fringe benefits. Title VII of the 1964 Civil Rights Act, as amended by the Equal Employment Opportunity Act of 1972, bans job discrimination based on race, color, religion, sex, or national origin. Despite such legal guarantees, inequities still exist. Because women are clustered in low-skilled jobs, they earn about fifty-nine cents for every dollar a man earns. They still meet with misunders.anding. And they still have to sneak into certain occupations through "loopholes or back-doors."

Since our study does not constitute a scientific sample, we can make no generalizations about work within Christian organizations. However, we found insensitivity and inequity within the Christian world which paralleled the situation in secular organizations. All the following examples are from the experiences of women working within Christian organizations.

One of the most prevalent practices is to place women in low-paying, non-titled jobs but to give them the responsibilities of a higher salaried position. Faith worked as a copywriter for a Christian company and found that she soon was given added responsibilities, but no change of title or salary. She confronted her boss about it but nothing was done. Then a man was hired to take over these responsibilities at a higher salary and with an appropriate title. He was warned by the boss that Faith would cause him trouble, and he actually repeated the warning so that Faith heard about it. Eventually, there were changes in the company, and the boss offered Faith a higher salary and a more responsible position. Unexpectedly, however, she received an excellent offer for a better position from another company, so she resigned. "I told him I was leaving, which just shattered him. He couldn't believe it. Here he'd finally given me everything I'd wanted. He looked at me and said, 'Well, you've had a lot of problems, haven't you?' I said, 'What do you mean?' He said, 'I guess it would be good for you; you'd meet more people.' Within an hour after I submitted my resignation, the word had gotten out that I was leaving because I wanted to meet men, which was to me the biggest defamation of character and the greatest insult he could ever make. It was his way of coping with his failure to hold me."

Women often have to prove themselves before they can obtain a position that would be readily available to a man with the same qualifications. For instance, Susan, a Presbyterian minister, began her pastoral ministry in a rural area. Although she had completed seminary, she was not yet ordained. Her husband, Bob, was ordained, but he had a teaching position in the area. The two of them began a joint ministry in a small parish, with Bob doing the preaching and the duties requiring ordination. The conservative parish would never have hired a woman pastor had not Susan proved herself first. She "moved in the back door. I was doing some work with youth and Bible study and counseling on a part-time basis. They liked me, and after three years in the position, I told them that my contract would run out in another year and I would like to be free to look for a position in which I might seek ordination. They hemmed and hawed and said, 'Why not us?' They eventually ordained me." Susan then became the pastor of the congregation. As is the case with other ordained women ministers and priests, Susan found that men did not like to come to her for counseling. "I can't do anything if people don't want to be ministered to by a woman. God can't work through me then."

Because so many Christians are not accustomed to seeing women in a leadership role, they are sometimes insensitive to the pressures upon the token woman. Christian special interest groups can even be antagonistic. The director for men's and women's athletics at a church-related college commented, "I think I'm pretty much accepted in the state colleges and outside of our own church circle. I think our church people are the hardest to sell on a woman being in the profession—and our alumni, particularly. I can sense—not antagonism, but the feeling that they would prefer to have a man. Some alumni have put pressure on to have a man.

"Going into the Christian college basketball tournament last year, I felt almost outright antagonism from the church people toward me as a woman athletic director. I think they expected me to go with the wives to the luncheons rather than to the athletic directors' meetings with the men." Not long after our conversation with this person, the title of athletic director was given to another staff member, a man. We could not determine all the reasons for the shift of title, but it appeared that our interviewee would still carry out some of the duties of an athletic director, but for women's sports only.

Discriminatory practices can still be found in the salary scales of some Christian organizations. The issue of equal pay for equal work is a sensitive one within Christian circles, particularly in non-profit organizations. When funds are scarce, the policy has been to pay according to need. Married men, for example, who are the sole supporters of families have been paid higher salaries than single women doing similar work. Then, too, women tend to work in the lower ranking jobs so that their benefits, as well as their incomes, are necessarily lower than those of men. A young professional told us that a different pay scale for men and women had been a widespread problem in her area of Christian work. "I talked to somebody once in the Chicago area about a job. He was talking a certain salary, and I said, 'That's not enough.' Without thinking, he came back with, 'Well, that's all a woman can expect.' I hit the ceiling and said, 'Being a woman has absolutely nothing to do with this.' Immediately he backed down and said, 'Oh, well, we hired a man this week, and that's what we paid him.' But he'd said it."

A faculty member at a Christian college spoke of the relation of a decent salary to her sense of self-worth, even though monetary reward is not her prime motive for working. "In our committee meeting the other day we were talking about increased salaries. I said, 'I know there are people on the faculty who really need it. I don't need it. After all, we're making two salaries, and our house is paid for, and our kids are grown up. I don't really need it.' Someone else spoke up and said, 'I don't need it, either—but, yes I do!' I said, 'Yes, I know how you feel.' I would like to feel that I'm worth as much as anybody else on the faculty, but how much should I fight for that?

"Our pastor said yesterday that when you tithe 10 percent of your income, you tithe 10 percent of your work. I thought, 'Maybe that would be so of somebody in a secular teaching position, but I consider my whole work as my service to God. It's not a 10 percent offering; it's the whole thing."

What should a woman do when she experiences inequity or injustice either in the secular or Christian workplace? How much should she fight for justice? One person described the prevailing attitudes of women within her organization this way: "There's a kind of martyr complex, a submissiveness, a meekness, which tends to perpetuate itself. We're not as aggressive as we might be." What is the balance between a meek acceptance of injustice in which we stifle our feelings and an aggressive pursuit of justice, come what may? Should a Christian pursue grievance procedures or even file a formal complaint?

Today, the pursuit of one's rights by means of individual lawsuits or class-action suits is commonplace. The legal system is the safeguard of our liberties, so the opportunity to redress wrongs is a precious gift at our disposal. On the other hand, the Christian is aware that her model is Christ who never put personal "rights" first in a selfish grasping after "justice." Paul enjoined the Romans to submit to governing authorities in civil affairs, to pay taxes, and to be good citizens (Rom. 13:1–7). The household tables in the New Testament advised slaves to be obedient to their masters. These scriptural models, when coupled with the image in Peter of the submissive wife whose beauty is that of "a gentle and quiet spirit" (1 Peter 3:1–6), are often interpreted to mean that Christians, especially women, are to be doormats. Of course we are to bear testings and injustice with a patient spirit and a trust in the providence of God. Yet, Jesus and the early Christians defied authority on occasion. Jesus overthrew the tables of the money-changers in the temple and denounced hypocrisy. Peter and John announced to the Sanhedrin that they would keep on speaking of the risen Christ. "Judge for yourselves," they told the Sanhedrin, "whether it is right in God's sight to obey you rather than God. For we cannot help speaking about what we have seen and heard" (Acts 4:19–20).

Two friends, to whom we talked on the same day, had just experienced what they felt were unjust decisions by superiors at work. Both were well-established in jobs in which they felt comfortable and would find a change of jobs a difficult experience. Yet they responded in very different ways to injustice.

Louise is fifty-four, single, and had worked for years in a laboratory for a drug concern. She loved her job and felt the Lord had led her to it. When her boss was about to retire, the company decided to transfer everyone elsewhere and close the lab. One day, at 4:00 P.M., all fifty lab employees were called in, and the decision was announced without warning. For Louise, it was "traumatic." She felt the decision was arbitrary and unwise, given the type of work the lab had been doing, and she felt worse when she had to take "a routine job" for a temporary period until she was transferred to a new research position. Louise still didn't know what that position would be when she talked to us, but she felt strongly that the Lord had a purpose in what had happened and that he would take care of her if she would be patient and let him work. Even though Louise felt she had a grievance, she maintained as a Christian that she should make no official complaint but should accept the situation and see what would work out.

Her friend Marilyn, also single, is in her early forties and is an elementary schoolteacher who had excelled as a teacher in the middle grades. Her superiors told her that she was to switch to another school and teach younger children in the fourth grade. She, too, thought the decision was unfair and arbitrary. She cried, experienced utter frustration, and went to speak to the school superintendent, who said, "We think you're the best person for this job, and we want you there. We know you'll do a good job." Marilyn said, "Well, I don't want it." The superintendent answered, "Well, you can fight it through the grievance procedure." So she did. Marilyn followed the official grievance procedure for teachers in her school district, but she did not win a reversal of the decision. "I wondered, as a Christian, should I question what my superiors had told me to do? But I still felt that I had to express my feelings."

Once Marilyn started her new job, she realized the change would be good for her, but she still felt that it had been important for her to be assertive and to pursue the grievance procedures. What advice would she give to others who feel they have experienced injustice and should take legal action of some sort? "Go with your feelings and express your feelings. Then pray about it and find out what the Lord would have you do. Then accept the decision when it comes. I accepted the final decision verbally, then I accepted it within, and finally I was able to go into the new job wholeheartedly. I knew that I had to do the best job that I could." Each of these women experienced injustice and perceived it as such, but each chose to deal with it in a different way.

Serious cases of illegal discrimination cannot be ignored. When such inequity is part of a long-term pattern of injustice which affects a class of working people, action of a political or legal nature may well be required. The motive for the Christian who acts in such cases should be a desire for social justice, not just personal rights. Here the wisdom of the body of believers is an important factor in whether or not to pursue a legal or political course of action. Seek the advice and counsel of other Christians to find the most constructive way of achieving redress of an illegal act. The Sojourners Fellowship in the District of Columbia deals with social injustice in several ways. For instance, Sojourners operates a day-care center for a deprived community where most of the mothers work and need child-care. This is one type of constructive action which is the result of the consensus of the body. But members of the Sojourners community also undertake boycotts, protests, and legal complaints. Again, any action is decided upon by the entire community. (Section 14 of the Appendix lists legal resources available to women who have suffered discrimination and are wondering how to deal with it.)

The View from Below and Above The joys and sorrows of the woman working within an organization are well-illustrated by two final examples.

Eleanor is forty-seven. She is separated from her husband who is an alcoholic. After her marriage, she worked for the telephone company, but during her third pregnancy she quit. When her oldest child was in the first grade, however, she started to work again, this time in a garment factory. She found it boring and could not always keep up with the piece rate, so she quit. Then, five years ago when she separated from her husband, she had to support herself and her children, so she returned to factory work. Again she found piecework hard, and she switched jobs several times. At the yarn factory where she now works, she began by running nine machines doing "doubling." Her boss told her that she had to turn out a thousand pounds of work a day or she would be fired. Since she could not make her quota, she was intrigued by a new job she saw posted for floor help in the twisting department.

Eleanor applied for this job, but she had difficulty getting it. "Are you sure you don't want to wait for an easier job?" the boss asked. It turned out that the work was physically demanding, and the boss thought a man should probably do it. "I had to sign a paper that if I wasn't satisfactory I could be fired in two weeks,"

Eleanor told us; but she added, "I'm sure glad to be out of the factory," meaning, out of piecework. Eleanor works the 11:00 P.M. to 7:00 A.M. shift, walking about eleven miles a night. She pushes carts of yarn up to a thousand pounds in weight, supplying work to the individual machine operators and taking their output to a holding area. "I'm so used to it that the work doesn't tire me," she said. Her boss commented that he was surprised that she could do such hard work.

Every night is different so that Eleanor experiences none of the boredom that she felt in her previous factory jobs. She would prefer to work the day shift, but that would mean a twenty-cent cut in her wage of $3.75 per hour. She also receives an incentive which is a percentage of the pounds produced on her floor. The working conditions are good, she thinks, although a few of the women would like to have a union. Eleanor has concluded that having a union would not significantly increase her wages or benefits. She does admit that there is discrimination by job category at the factory. All her bosses are men. Eleanor has thought of becoming a machine fixer. "I work harder than the machine fixers, but they get more pay." When she inquired, the boss told her to apply, but she is deterred by the fact that she would have to buy her own tools, a considerable expense.

For about ten years prior to her separation, Eleanor experienced mental and physical abuse because of her husband's alcoholism. "If I hadn't been a Christian, I would have shot myself." She never mentioned her circumstances at church—"I was ashamed to speak of it," ashamed for the repossessions of their house and car, the lost jobs, the moves, the abusive treatment. When she couldn't stand it any longer, she went to the legal aid society for assistance. Since her situation has become known, Eleanor has received help from many Christian friends. Tears welled up in her eyes as she spoke of receiving anonymous gifts of money in the mail, Christmas gifts, food boxes from the Salvation Army. A friend paid her rent once when she was behind in her payments. Eleanor commented that her teen-age children earn money to pay for their own clothes and expenses and that she is satisfied, now that she earns enough to support herself.

For Eleanor, the questions of authority and organizational structure relate to practical ways of bettering her lot within the factory. ("The boss tells us we're lucky we're working.") Her livelihood depends on the authority of the boss and the quotas for production.

Betsy Ancker-Johnson's world is quite different. When she talked to us, she had been serving as a vice-president of General Motors for less than a year. (A second woman was appointed as a vice-president shortly after her.) Her career has been a series of "firsts," although she happily admits that the "firsts" are now beginning to disappear for women as they enter new areas of work. Dr. Ancker-Johnson is in charge of all the environmental programs at General Motors, ranging from industrial air and water pollution control to automotive emission control, automotive safety engineering, and product noise control. "My responsibilities cut across the whole corporation," she explained, and she participates in ten of the twenty committees which meet on a monthly basis, overseeing the huge corporation.

As a Christian, she believes she has "to seek the kind of balance that our Lord had," and she fondly recalls studies on "the balanced life" given by Stacey Woods from the Book of Philippians during her days in Inter-Varsity Christian Fellowship. (She participated in the founding of the I-V chapter at Wellesley College when she was an undergraduate, and she later served two years as an I-V staff member.) From that Christian perspective, she sees her responsibility as a balancer, working for better relations between the public and private sectors, reducing the adversary relationship between the two, coordinating the environmental activities of the many sections within General Motors itself.

Now fifty-two, Dr. Ancker-Johnson says that few women in her age bracket worked their way up the government or corporate ladders. They either moved up the managerial ranks very quickly or were brought in at the first or second levels once affirmative action became a reality. "Now the pipelines are beginning to fill with women." There has been a big change in industry within the past ten years, and "there is real commitment" toward equality of opportunity. "It's eerie to be the first woman," she commented, adding that she sensed goodwill from the other executives at General Motors, although they were obviously on their good behavior at first. She smiled and said she could "plot a graph" as the men gradually forgot she was a woman and resumed their normal ways of interacting.

Betsy Ancker-Johnson has always been competitive. Her mother, a homemaker, was "a real driver," and both her parents were college educated. She went into physics when almost no women were in the field, especially in Germany where she did her doctoral work. She has experienced almost every conceivable obstacle that a woman working within a male-dominated organization could anticipate. As an undergraduate at Wellesley she had been encouraged to follow her interests wherever they might lead. She experienced a tremendous shock when she left the idyllic world of an American women's college and began graduate study in Germany.

"During my first year of graduate school, what seemed to me like an infinite number of professors, teaching assistants, and colleagues, none of whom were women, told me that women can't think analytically and that I must therefore be husband-hunting. Consequently, I was never involved in the informal study groups that graduate students form and find so very helpful in the learning process. By the time I had made friends with fellow students who accepted me for what I was—another student—I was past that stage. The resultant discouragement was as great or greater than any I've known since; hence the solid determination with which I emerged with my Ph.D. to go on in research. It needed to be solid, because it seems that a woman in physics must be at least twice as determined as a man with the same competence in order to achieve as much as he does." Had she not had drive, Ancker-Johnson would have been swallowed up by the obstacles that lay ahead.

These obstacles ranged from the concrete (lack of bathroom facilities for women when she was in graduate school) to the relational (the inability of men to accept her as female, a physicist, and a success). Once in the field, she found that she had difficulty even obtaining job interviews because women were supposed to be poor risks, quitting to marry and have children. When she did marry, she decided to keep the name Ancker, adding Johnson to it. On the Friday before her wedding she was rushed because she had to pick up her wedding dress and finish correcting the proofs for an article reporting some research she had done. She added the hyphen and her husband's name to her own as she hurriedly finished correcting the proofs and then rushed off to get her dress.

When she was pregnant with her first child, she was laid off from her job as a research physicist. "My private life was delved into by half-a-dozen executives in interviews that no one should have to endure. Finally, I was told, perhaps in jest, that the decision to lay me off over my protest went all the way to the Board of Directors of this large corporation. Nothing is so conducive to success in research as having a group of people pry into your personal affairs. I wasn't even allowed to enter the laboratory building for three months before the birth to hear a talk or get a book out of my private collection without special permission of the laboratory director. In order to understand something of how I felt, a member of the majority would have to have an advanced case of leprosy."

Other struggles followed. She solved the problem of child-care by having Christian friends in Germany send five different young women as "little sisters" to look after her children and to improve their English at the same time as they lived with the Johnson family. She and her husband took turns in determining what professional move should be made, and when she served in the federal government, he bore the brunt of the family burdens. As Assistant Secretary for Science and Technology in the U.S. Department of Commerce, Dr. Ancker-Johnson could not eat evening meals at home during the week for four years. People don't realize, she told us, "the unreal sacrifices" demanded by government service.

The juggling of concerns which she has faced is unique to being a woman, she thinks. Dr. Ancker-Johnson realizes that "my career has been consuming," but she and her husband spent extensive time with their children on weekends when they were growing up. "Independence came with our lifestyle." She smiled and joked that one time she returned from a trip when her children were older and no one had even noticed that she had been gone!

An internationally known physicist-engineer with several

patents to her credit, Betsy Ancker-Johnson has had to be extraordinarily strong to achieve a position of eminence. One feels that merely surviving has been an achievement, but she has survived with excellence and distinction, a testimony to her strength of mind and will. And to her "sense of being in God's will."

OLD AND NEW CHOICES

Recurring Choices   This survey of Christian women at work has been anecdotal, and it has touched on a variety of topics. Yet a single thread weaves its diversity into a common pattern—decision-making. In a changing world, women can no longer live out the passive fantasies and dreams of the past. Whether thrown into the hurly-burly of the factory or cast in a managerial role, women can take responsibility for their own lives. The difference between Christian and non-Christian women lies in the area of motivation. For the Christian, empowerment to choose is not anchored in a secular doctrine of individual rights or in sisterhood for its own sake. Instead, empowerment derives from the redemptive process which affirms the individual's worth and calling in Christ. His unqualified acceptance of all—male and female, slave and free, Gentile and Jew—binds humans together as persons. The presence of the Holy Spirit energizes them to take risks and to make choices. This experiential and theological basis for decision-making does not free Christians from the need and responsibility to affirm their sisterhood with all women or their personal need of emotional support from other women; it merely enlarges the context in which they view issues facing contemporary women. All women, Christian and non-Christian, must make rational choices about their increasingly complex lifestyles: about career and job planning, retraining, time, priorities, child-care, conflicts, values, and goals. Again, there is a difference in how the Christian approaches such decisions: she sees no conflict between rational choices and her reliance on prayer and the leading of the Holy Spirit.

There are work-related choices which occur again and again for Christian women; some of the most important deal with money and with ethical values. What constitutes good stewardship? How do we spend what we earn, no matter how small or how large our salary? What should be the attitude of the woman with a large income to the needs about her and to money itself? We saw little opulence among the women to whom we talked; at the same time, we observed few decisions to limit lifestyles drastically or to share the savings. There was, however, a strong sense that one should share out of one's abundance. A wife in a two-career couple called her husband the "big breadwinner." "With my money I do things for the children; we take trips, do extra things, send money to people. My husband and I always tithe our money and give extra, too. We always have done that, whether we've made little or much. We support missionaries in various parts of the world, and it gives us great pleasure to do that. A client said, 'I like dealing with you because I know the money you make will go to the Lord's work.' My husband and I talk about things we want to do, special things we would like to give to."

Joan, in business with her husband, explained that she did not equate money with success. Their business doubled in one-and-a-half years and tripled in three. The freedom to do whatever they would like gave them a new kind of security and responsibility. "We realized that we could maintain the business at that level and be pretty comfortable. We were just socking away money. But we realized it wouldn't be good for the business. So we took another enormous step and built a warehouse and put $50,000 in just one piece of equipment." Feeling that the success of their business was a gift from God, Joan saw the ability to take a financial risk to expand the business as stewardship. The eventual increase in profit would express itself in still another form of stewardship. "Everything that we have has been given; to give back financially is only part of it." Stewardship means the sharing of time as well as money. Joan and her husband give a lot of their energy to working with young people within their church. As in so many instances during our interviews, we found that she and her husband felt that other believers really did not understand their work-related goals. "Our goals aren't monetary," Joan explained. "People don't understand what it's like to own your own business; initiatives are often mistaken for greed, when they are really an expression of personal creativity."

Sensitivity to the differences between the haves and have-nots can cause conflicts. We asked Patricia, the attorney, about the fees charged in her large firm. "It's really sad. My firm generally can't represent the average person on the street. My firm's clientele is made up of very large companies. And my firm must support over one hundred people who must be paid from those large fees." She added that she had more conflicts about salary inequities. "I believe it's slightly unethical when the senior partner of a firm makes so much more than my secretary. She cannot support her family on a secretary's salary, and I think that's wrong."

Christians were adamant in their stance that all dealings in the workplace had to be honest. In fact, they find that their ethics often bring joy and delight to others. "God has shown us that our business life and our Christian life are one. We have thoroughly enjoyed being honest with our customers. It's fun to have the freedom to be able to do that, and the customers are startled that there is a company that really runs on trust and honesty."

Elaine, a Realtor, was precise about the type of choices the Christian must never waver in making. "Certain qualities are absolutely necessary, and one of them is honesty. I mean straight down the line, not questionable in any way. I had a gentleman say to me one night when we were preparing a contract, 'Now, Elaine, we're all real estate agents; you just tell us what this person that you're representing will really do.' I looked at him and said, 'No, sir, tonight we're not just real estate agents. I'm a real estate agent who's representing the buyer. You're a real estate agent who's representing the seller, so we're separated in that respect. I cannot tell you what my buyer will do except what he's put in this contract.' They press you, constantly press you, for information they should not press you for. I said to him, 'I've heard the old cliché that every person has their price, but even if it meant a lot of money, I would tell you the same thing. I deal straight down the line. That's how I want you to think of me in all our future dealings.' He couldn't believe it."

The perils of compromise and the cost of maintaining one's honesty were very clear in the story of a woman who refused to carry out the shady policies and practices of other "Christians" for whom she worked. "I was actually being asked by Christians to accept practices that I considered unethical. That's the only time in my life my beliefs have cost me a job. I couldn't do what they asked me to do. I refused to, and I quit. They were both raised in strong Christian homes, but they had been wheeling and dealing in the business world for so many years and they had compromised so subtly for so long that they no longer recognized black and white. Most of the world was gray. I've struggled very hard to make most of my world black and white."

Women in some jobs and professions have to deal with particularly difficult moral and ethical questions. Martha, a nurse, works in a hospital where she cares for very sick newborn infants. Sometimes they are terribly deformed. "Only three times since I've been there have we deliberately let a baby die. In all three cases, they were so grossly deformed that they were not really going to live anyway. There just didn't seem to be any point in going through heroics to try to save them. Our hospital is very pro-life. We will try to save any baby that has any real possibility of being saved, even when there's a possibility that it will be retarded or brain-damaged."

Abortions also concern Martha. She moved and therefore quit a previous job just before abortion was legalized. Friends working at that hospital later reported to her that women who were too advanced in their pregnancy for simple abortions were induced to abort and then put on the post-partum floor. "I had been working on post-partum, and there was no way I could have condoned that. I would have had to quit. I realize people are going to have abortions whether I'm working there or not, and my working or not working is not going to make much difference, I suppose, except to my own peace of mind. That's really why I chose to work at a Catholic hospital in my new location."

Ethical or moral choices may center on issues that appear unimportant but have broader implications. Peggie Robinson, a designer jeweler in Evanston, Illinois, sets limits as to what she will or will not design. "There are some things that as a Christian craftsman I won't do. I have strong feelings that since my talent is a gift from God, I shouldn't be using it in a manner that doesn't really praise him. If people come in and ask me for zodiacs, I won't do them. Sometimes people come in and want occult things, and I refuse them. I finally put a little fish on the outside of my store, and I haven't had a single occult request since."

The athletic director at a Christian college explained how the pressures on her time and energy limited the extent of her lobbying activities within professional organizations. She saw such activities as vital to maintaining important standards. "Our women's basketball team, I think, would have made the state tournament except that it was played on Sunday. I just didn't let them enter. I was furious about that, and I registered a protest. That should not happen again. I was sports chairperson for the state organization, and I didn't let it happen before. Because I was spreading myself too thin, I'm not involved in anything in the state organization now. Consequently, there were no church people to voice a protest."

Making the right ethical and moral choices is a major way that women witness to their faith through their work. A few of our interviewees described how they shared their faith and influenced other colleagues or clients to become Christians, but the majority felt it was the quality of their acts and relationships which really marked them as Christians. "I communicate my Christianity in the way I associate with my students and, hopefully, with my co-workers. I try to let people know where I'm coming from, without making them feel that if they're not coming from there, they don't have anything to offer. I try to understand their difficulty and their point of view. We really affect people more through living than through what we say."

Choices
Facing
the   Despite the fact that reformers such as
Church   John Wesley were involved with the
plight of workers at the dawn of the industrial age and that today, as in the past, some Christian workers live among the poor of the world and share their poverty, the church as a body remains strangely silent on the issue of work. This portrait has focused on the struggles of individual women, but the issues of inequity, alienation, anxiety, and material want affect classes of people, whole groups of women. Individual Christians react out of the goodness of their hearts to the material needs of working women, but collective action is sadly lacking in most congregations or denominations. More often, para-church structures (Christian communities, societies, magazines) are the means whereby collective witness and change on a small scale occur.

In chapter two, Joanna described Christians as the salt of the earth—mysterious, necessary, but unobtrusive. Christians make a difference in the workplace, but the struggles of Christian working women to be the salt of the earth are rendered difficult by the fact that they are women. Robert K. Greenleaf has described the "growing-edge church" as nurturing leaders and as modeling organizational servanthood. This type of church is innovative and open, healing; it builds bridges of understanding. We, on the other hand, encountered little understanding of the full range of the problems and of the potential of working women within the church. Betsy, an attorney, described her experiences in a local congregation when she was a law student. "There were a couple of male attorneys in that church and, granted, they were older, but they were the people who were being discipled or groomed. They were always on the business committee. The pastor wasn't interested in a discipling program for women at all. He was always choosing men to be trained. In fact, I can remember a time when he referred to a bunch of us as being the 'unclaimed jewels.' I could see that singing in the choir would be the extent of what I could do in that church. I was being trained to make decisions, to almost make decisions *for* people. But when I got into church, I was just supposed to sit back and let somebody else do all the decision-making."

The local church faces the choice of affirming the abilities of the individual Christian woman, of calling forth her gifts, and of providing means whereby she can integrate her life at work and within the church. Working women—single, divorced, or married —need support groups from within the body of believers who will accept and try to understand their lifestyles, conflicts, and problems. The local church needs to give people the room to adopt a variety of roles and lifestyles, all compatible with the Christian faith but also with individual personalities. Christian men and women have much to teach each other about the just uses of power and the nurturing of relationships in the workplace. Finally, pastors and lay persons can aid one another in vocational decisions and ethical choices.

If the church can encourage individuals to do prophetic work—to be the salt of society—it can itself be a prophetic voice. In a more ecumenical way, the church has the choice of taking a stand and providing alternative models on such issues as child-care, flexible working hours, organizational life, and the quality of work. In an article, "Work in a New America," published in 1977, Rosabeth Moss Kanter identified two basic concerns of the current workplace. "One theme can be called cultural or expressive: the concern for work as a source of self-respect and nonmaterial reward—challenge, growth, personal fulfillment, interesting and meaningful work, the opportunity to advance and to accumulate, and the chance to lead a safe, healthy life. The other can be called political: the concern for individual rights and power, for a further extension of principles of equity and justice into the workplace and into the industrial order, for equity and participation both in their general symbolic manifestations and in the form of concrete legal rights."

The church can model organizational patterns which enhance the individual woman's sense of dignity and respect; such patterns can say something to those in charge of factories and corporations. The church may preach justice, but it should act it out on its own ground.

The Touch of Life:
Individual
and   This book is filled with and based on
Group Action   true-life stories. Thus, it is only appropriate to end it with two more which present old and new options,
each valid for today: options for individual servanthood and options for servanthood through ecumenical group action.

Dr. Anna Perkins has been a physician in the hills of rural
upstate New York for over fifty years. Now eighty, she drove up in
her four-wheel-drive Cherokee after making a house call on a Sunday afternoon as we waited for her outside the simple frame house
which serves as her office and home. The only luxury we saw was a
100-pound bag of seed which Dr. Perkins intended to feed to the
birds. Her waiting room and examining room are the center of the
house; the Spartan bedroom and living space indicate the centrality
of her medical practice to her life.

A Catholic, Dr. Perkins grew up in Brookline, Massachusetts,
in a cultivated family. As a girl she heard a missionary speak in
church and decided that she would be one, too, although she does
not consider that determination a mature decision or a call. Originally, she thought she should be a nurse in order to serve abroad.
Later she decided that she might as well go ahead and become a
doctor. After graduating from Radcliffe, she went to medical school
at Columbia University because Harvard would not accept women.
She came to realize that her desire to help people could be fulfilled
as much by staying home as by going abroad, so she decided to go
to rural upstate New York where there was a shortage of physicians. She has served there ever since.

Life was "tough" when Dr. Perkins began her practice in 1928.
Transportation was poor, and antibiotics were non-existent. "In
those days I used to go a hundred miles a day. Sometimes much of
it on foot. There is a part of this world called the West Mountain
which is practically inaccessible. I remember this child was going
to have her first baby. For weeks I had urged her to come down
before it was due, but, of course, she wouldn't. Even the horses
were having a terrible time getting up the last hill to her house. So
we walked for a while until the horses managed to catch up with us.

The baby came just after I got there, and I delivered it while the husband wrung his hands and chided me for not having got to the house sooner!" In dealing with the home remedies of mountain people as well as their ignorance and isolation, Dr. Perkins has seen both tragedy and joy. Her entire career has been spent in the same village.

According to Dr. Perkins, the small town "is the only real democracy where people have a place of their own in society, even if they are disapproved of." She sees nothing unusual about her decision to stay in Westerlo. "I haven't been doing just one thing all along; it's been intellectually satisfying." She still makes house calls for nominal fees, and, like those who live about her, she tries to "take people at their real value." When we asked her about the spiritual element in her work, she was direct and sparing in her words, as in all she said about herself. Her model has been the gospel stories of healing. "I have tried to deal with patients the way our Lord would have dealt with them."

Janelle Goetcheus grew up in the Methodist church and knew from the time she was in junior high school that she would be a physician. Married to a Methodist clergyman, she and her family live in a rehabilitated apartment building in the inner city of Washington, D.C. Janelle and her husband had expected to be missionaries, but an invitation from Mary Cosby of the Church of the Saviour to visit the District of Columbia changed their understanding of their call. "During a three-day stay, I was taken over to the Ritz apartment building and walked into a room where there were a number of people just sitting around sharing what kinds of obstacles they personally had in terms of health care. It was a whole new experience for me just to walk those halls and smell those smells. I felt I was being told something that I needed to listen to." The Goetcheus family moved to the Washington area and then into the city itself.

"D.C. has the highest infant mortality rate in the country. It is comparable to some Third World countries." Health care in the inner city is crisis oriented. People only go to the hospital emergency room when it is too late. "In Washington, the only people who qualify for full coverage Medicaid are single mothers with dependent children, the elderly on Medicare who are very poor, or disabled people who have been declared so by SSI [Supplemental Security Income—a federal disability program]. But we have many, many poor people who do not fit into those categories. When those people try to get help on their own at the public hospital, they just give up on health care. It's a very dehumanizing experience for them."

In a letter received after our interview, Janelle Goetcheus spoke of the pain she feels continually for the poor of her city. "A few weeks ago I lost a friend—a patient—a fifty-two-year-old woman who looked eighty-two. She died in an intensive care unit in a Washington hospital following a seizure related to her alcoholism. One morning several weeks before she died she had three grand mal seizures. We were hesitant to leave her in her apartment alone, so our nurse and a sister who volunteers with us took her to the hospital emergency room where she had been before. I called ahead thinking she would need admission. Two hours later the nurse called to say Mary still had not been seen and that she seemed very tremulous. I called the emergency room doctor who curtly informed me that they were quite aware she was there. Mary was sent home later that day, and the nurse and the sister were told, 'This is no big deal; we see hundreds of patients like this every day.'"

With Karin Granberg Michaelson, a counselor, Janelle had a vision for a new option in health care for the poor—a clinic for holistic care which would restore dignity to the individual needing treatment. The two women received the support and affirmation of the Sojourners Fellowship and the Church of the Saviour in their endeavor. In March, 1979, the Columbia Road Health Services opened in the Adams Morgan section of the District of Columbia. A truly ecumenical endeavor, the clinic staff includes two physicians, a nurse, pastoral counselors, a social worker, and a business manager; the staff members are both Protestant and Catholic. Funds must be raised to make up the difference between actual income and expenses, and the staff members receive sacrificially low salaries.

"I think Columbia Road has two real missions," Janelle explained to us. "One is in terms of holistic health care: the church needs to be involved in healing and for too long we have separated what happens to us physically and what happens to us emotionally and spiritually. The other is our commitment to the poor and to the people here in Washington who do not have alternatives for health care. Our fees are on a sliding scale, and at least half our patients are at the lower end of the scale." Patients sit down with the entire health team and share their stresses, medical history, and potential resources for getting better. A program of health care is worked out which emphasizes healing through spiritual, psychological, and medical means. Wholeness, or integration of the person with herself or himself and with others and with God, is the goal of the program.

Janelle Goetcheus and others connected with the Columbia Road Health Services suffer constant frustration, pain, and conflict. They are forced to take political action and to testify before governmental bodies to try to change the system of health care. They are constantly confronted with the slow-moving bureaucracy of government. Their families also share in the process of serving. The Goetcheuses chose to move into the inner city from the suburbs so that they could integrate their values as a family. Their children (12, 10, and 6) have found the adjustment to the public school system difficult. "I think it will be a good experience for them, but it will take about twenty years to find out."

There are fulfillments, too. The realization that there is a place where people can go for quality care in the District is an ever-growing satisfaction. "I hope we can reach more and more." And then there is the openness of the people of the inner city to share their hurts. "A woman came in to see me, and as she was leaving she said, 'How can you be my doctor?' I said, 'Just by your wanting me to be.'"

To change the public health care system is "going to take the church," Janelle Goetcheus maintains. We would broaden her statement. To alleviate the conflicts of working women caught in a time of change, it's going to take the church, beginning with a commitment to action on the local level.

* * * *

The Christian women in this book have shouted their joy and fulfillment in their work. They have whispered their sorrow and cried out their pain. But they have modeled Christ in the patterns of their lives. They ask of other Christians only that they, too, follow his example and offer working women freedom and acceptance to be what they are called to be—fully themselves.

APPENDIX

The resources listed here have been chosen primarily for their practical value to the working woman. They represent some of the best available books and services. The following headings have been used:

1. Career Choices and Changes
2. Tools and Techniques for Finding Jobs
3. Work and Family: Working Mothers and Two-Career Couples
4. Coping with Work-Related Problems
5. Reentering the Paid Job Market
6. Part-Time and Flex-Time Opportunities
7. Volunteer Work
8. Owning Your Own Business
9. Apprenticeships and Nontraditional Careers
10. Resource Centers and Employment Information
11. Professional and Trade Organizations
12. Educational Opportunities
13. Financial Aid for Education
14. Dealing with Discrimination
15. Vocational Resources of Particular Interest to Christians

Free or inexpensive information about jobs and career-related programs is available at your

local public library
college or university placement office
YWCA
women's resource center
chamber of commerce.

221

Also check

> professional associations
> classified ads in newspapers, professional journals, and trade magazines
> Civil Service announcements
> labor unions.

1. Career Choices and Changes

How-To and Self-Help Books

Bolles, Richard N. *What Color Is Your Parachute? A Practical Manual for Job-Hunters and Career Changers.* Berkeley: Ten Speed Press, revised 1979. One of the best career planning books on the market. Bolles' advice on choosing professional counselors is well worth noting. He offers creative alternatives to traditional job-finding techniques. His approach requires considerable self-motivation.

Bureau of Labor Statistics. *Toward Matching Personal and Job Characteristics.* A do-it-yourself tool available free from the Occupational Outlook Service, Bureau of Labor Statistics, Washington, D.C. 20212. Takes 25 job characteristics and rates 280 jobs in those terms.

Catalyst, a national non-profit organization that provides career information and self-guidance material for women, publishes a *Career Opportunities Series.* Each booklet in the series gives the job outlook in a particular field, describes the education necessary for employment, and provides profiles of women at work in the field. Particularly useful for college women in the exploratory stage. Booklets are available on a range of occupations from accounting to urban planning at approximately $2 each. Write: Catalyst, 14 E. 60 Street, New York, NY 10022, for current titles and prices.

Catalyst. *Planning for Work: Self-Guidance Series G1* is for women with at least some college education who have family responsibilities and would like to enter or reenter the labor force but are not sure what field would be right. Designed as a workbook in self-assessment and self-guidance. Cost: $1.75. Write: Catalyst, 14 E. 60 Street, New York, NY 10022.

Figler, Howard E. *Path.* Cranston, Rhode Island: The Carroll Press, second edition, 1979. A career workbook for liberal arts students.

Mitchell, Joyce Slayton. *I Can Be Anything: Careers and Colleges for Young Women.* College Entrance Examination Board, New York, revised 1978.

This book will help you plan a career while still in school and free to do the most about it. Some 200 careers are described. Cost: hardcover $12.95, paperback $7.95. Orders must be prepaid. Write: College Entrance Examination Board, Box 2815, Princeton, NJ 08540.

Robbins, Paula I. *Successful Midlife Career Change: Self-Understanding and Strategies for Action.* New York: Amacom, 1978.

For further information see 9:
Apprenticeships and Nontraditional Careers

Reference Books Useful in Making Career Choices and Changes

Dictionary of Occupational Titles, fourth edition. An Employment and Training Administration publication which contains comprehensive job descriptions and related information on the 20,000 occupations identified in the United States. Known as the "DOT," the volume can be useful in illustrating the wide range of occupations within a particular field and in suggesting possibilities for further exploration. Available in most libraries.

Gale, Barry and Linda Gale. *The National Career Directory.* New York: ARCO Publishing, Inc., 1979. An occupational information handbook which lists over 2,000 references to free or inexpensive printed materials and information available on hundreds of careers.

Loring, Rosalind K., and Herbert A. Otto. *New Life Options: The Working Woman's Resource Book.* New York: McGraw Hill, 1976. A collection of addresses, essays, and lectures on a wide range of work-related topics including volunteer service, handling sexism, keeping physically and mentally healthy, coping with child care, and retirement. Designed as both a textbook and for use by the general public.

Occupational Outlook Handbook, 1978–79. This Bureau of Labor Statistics biennial publication is a major source of vocational guidance information. It contains information on job duties, educational requirements, employment outlook, earnings, and working conditions for several hundred occupations and 35 industries. Available in most libraries.

Sher, Barbara. *Wishcraft: How to Get What You Really Want.* New York: Viking, 1979. Excellent resource section.

2. Tools and Techniques for Finding Jobs

American Association of University Women. The *Job Hunter's Kit.* Contains excellent material including reprints of top articles that focus on preparing for the job hunt, searching for the right job, writing an effective résumé, and interviewing techniques. The kit also contains a selected bibliography on "Career Development for Women," a guide to Catalyst's national network of resource centers, and AAUW's list of professional women's groups. Cost: $10. Write: Sales Office, American Association of University Women, 2401 Virginia Avenue NW, Washington, D.C. 20037. Orders must be prepaid.

Bolles. *What Color Is Your Parachute?* (See section 1.)

Business and Professional Women's Foundation. *Where the Jobs Are: An Annotated Bibliography.* A resource guide to occupations and employment prospects for women. Cost: $1.35 (postage included). Write: Sales/Order Department, Business and Professional Women's Foundation, 2011 Massachusetts Avenue NW, Washington, D.C. 20036.

Catalyst. *Your Job Campaign, Self Guidance Series G2* is part of a set of self-guidance publications for women who are, have been, or expect to be largely home-based while their children are young and who want to undertake employment before, during, or after that period. Includes sample résumés, overviews of career fields, and suggestions for finding a job. 56 pages. Cost: $1.75. Write: Catalyst, 14 E. 60 Street, New York, NY 10022.

Catalyst. *Résumé Preparation Workbook.* Helpful for those at the résumé point in the job-finding process. Exercise space. Cost: $3.50. Write: Catalyst, 14 E. 60 Street, New York, NY 10022.

Department of Labor. *Merchandising Your Job Talents.* Basic exercises in self-appraisal, résumé preparation, writing letters of application, and the interviewing process. 23 pages. Cost: 25¢. Write: U.S. Department of Labor, U.S. Government Printing Office, Washington, D.C. 20202.

Figler, Howard. *The Complete Job-Search Handbook.* New York: Holt, Rinehart and Winston, 1979. Especially useful for those who are not particularly confident or self-motivated. Includes chapter, "For Shy People."

Friedman, Sande, and Lois Schwartz. *No Experience Necessary: A Guide to Employment for the Female Liberal Arts Graduate.* New York: Dell, 1971. A guide for the female college graduate who is uncertain about what she can or wants to do. Describes fourteen career fields accessible to women with liberal arts degrees. Each chapter lists specific sources of additional information.

Irish, Richard K. *Go Hire Yourself an Employer*. New York: Doubleday, revised 1978. Focus is on giving the individual control over his or her own work situation.

Jackson, Tom and Davidyne Mayleas. *The Hidden Job Market: A System to Beat the System*. New York: Quadrangle, 1977. Enables the reader to tap the hidden market, the 85–90 percent of available jobs which are not in classified ads, in employment agency listings, or in placement offices.

Lathrop, Richard. *Who's Hiring Who*. Berkeley: Ten Speed Press, 1977. Provides guidance in choosing your career field and dealing with job-finding problems.

Women's Work. The best of the growing array of magazines aimed at the working woman. Subscription cost: $6.00 per year. Write: *Women's Work*, 1302 18 Street, NW, Suite 203, Washington, D.C. 20036.

3. Work and Family: Working Mothers and Two-Career Couples

Bird, Caroline. *The Two-Paycheck Marriage*. New York: Rawson, Wade, 1979. A comprehensive report on how two-career couples cope with the housework, spend their money, decide whether or not to have children, etc. Chapters include "Coping With the Dream of the Perfect Home," "The Two Career Collision Course," and "New Ways of Working."

Curtis, Jean. *Working Mothers*. Garden City: Doubleday, 1976.

Greenleaf, Barbara. *Help. A Handbook for Working Mothers*. New York: Thomas Y. Crowell, 1978. Treats a number of practical topics including what to do when children get sick, meal planning, shortcuts to house-keeping and entertaining, and making room for friendships. Includes selected bibliography of books helpful to working mothers.

Hall, Francine S. and Douglas T. Hall. *The Two-Career Couple*. Reading, Mass.: Addison-Wesley, 1979. Stresses dual commitment to marriage and to two careers. Employs a readable case-study approach.

Norris, Gloria and Jo Ann Miller. *The Working Mother's Complete Handbook*. New York: Dutton, 1979. Explores the effects of work on marriage, the special problems of single working mothers, guilt, and practical problems such as childcare and sharing housework.

Rapaport, Robert and Rhona Rapaport, eds. *Working Couples*. New York: Harper and Row, 1978.

4. Coping With Work-Related Problems

Most of the following are self-help books. Not all the values can be adopted by Christians; therefore, they should be used with discretion.

Greiff, Barrie S. and Preston K. Munter. *Tradeoffs: Executive, Family, and Organizational Life.* New York: New American Library, 1980.

Hennig, Margaret and Anne Jardim. *The Managerial Woman.* New York: Pocket Books, 1978.

Jongeward, Dorothy and Philip Seyer. *Choosing Success: Transactional Analysis on the Job.* New York: John Wiley, 1978.

_____ and Dru Scott. *Women as Winners.* Reading, Mass. and Menlo Park, Calif.: Addison-Wesley, 1976.

Machlowitz, Marilyn. *Workaholics: Living With Them, Working With Them.* Reading, Mass. and Menlo Park, Calif.: Addison-Wesley, 1980.

de Rosis, Helen. *Women and Anxiety.* New York: Delacorte Press, 1979.

Scott, Dru. *How to Put More Time in Your Life.* New York: Rawson Wade, 1980.

Seaman, Florence and Anne Lorimer. *Winning at Work: A Book for Women.* Philadelphia: Running Press, 1979.

Smith, M. J. *When I Say No I Feel Guilty.* New York: The Dial Press, 1975.

Welch, Mary Scott. "How to Start a Woman's Network." *Working Woman* (March, 1980).

5. Reentering the Paid Job Market

Abarbanel, Karin and Connie Siegel. *Woman's Work Book.* New York: Praeger, 1977. A job-hunting guide with a directory of professional careers, apprenticeships, and technical jobs. Advice on job hunting when you have small children, on using your experience to the best advantage, and on cracking the hidden job market.

Berman, Eleanor. *Re-Entering: Successful Back-to-Work Strategies for Women Seeking a Fresh Start.* New York: Crown, 1980. Overcoming the fear of returning to work, setting workable goals to acquiring a job, factual information on current employment trends, guidelines for choosing among counseling options, a state-by-state list of re-entry programs, and educational opportunities for mature students. Firsthand accounts from women re-entering the job market. Excellent.

The Displaced Homemakers Network, 755 8th Street, NW, Washington, D.C. 20001. Helps women who are widowed, divorced, or separated and have not worked outside the home in several years. Send a stamped, self-addressed envelope and request the address of the program nearest you.

Mourat, Lucia. *Back to Business: A Woman's Guide to Reentering the Job Market.* New York: Sovereign, 1979. A basic guide; common-sense approach to making career choices and job hunting. 117 pages.

Older Women's League Educational Fund, 3800 Harrison Street, Oakland, CA 94611. Send for the free pamphlet, "You *Can* Make It Happen," which contains tips on getting a job.

Prentice, Barbara. *Five Hundred Back to Work Ideas for Housewives.* New York: Collier Books, 1971.

6. Part-Time and Flex-Time Opportunities

Women's Equity Action League. *A Guide to Alternative Employment Opportunities.* Washington, D.C., 1977. Cost: $1.00. Write: WEAL, 733 15th Street, NW #200, Washington, D.C. 20005.

Flexible Careers. *A Report from Flexible Careers.* Cost: $3.00. Write: Flexible Careers, 37 South Wabash Avenue, Chicago, IL 60603.

Scobey, Joan and Lee P. McGrath. *Creative Careers for Women: A Handbook of Sources and Ideas for Part-Time Jobs.* New York: Simon and Schuster, 1968.

7. Volunteer Work

Cavener, James Neal, editor. *Invest Yourself: A Catalogue of Service Opportunities.* New York: The Commission on Voluntary Service and Action. An annual guide to specific projects and placements, with 26,000 openings, as well as the names and addresses of the 150 private North American voluntary service agencies which individually sponsor projects and constitute The Commission on Voluntary Service and Action. Check your library or write: Invest Yourself, Circulation Department, 418 Peltoma Road, Haddonfield, NJ 08033. Make check for $2.50 (includes postage and handling) payable to Invest Yourself.

Loeser, Herta. *Women, Work, and Volunteering*. Boston: Beacon Press, 1974. A guide to help women decide whether they should do volunteer work and how to get started. Includes chapters on "Feminism and Volunteering," "The Volunteer-to-Career Concept," and "How to Locate a Suitable Volunteer Job." Also lists key private and federal agencies which administer volunteer programs.

8. Owning Your Own Business

The Bank of America publishes a series of profiles on owning and operating a variety of businesses and on establishing professional practices. Each pamphlet is $2.00. For a free list of current publications write: *Small Business Reporter*, Department 3120, PO Box 37000, San Francisco, CA 94137.

Better Business Bureau. "Tips on Work at Home Schemes." Free. Send a stamped, self-addressed envelope to the Council of Better Business Bureaus, 1150 Seventeenth Street, NW, Washington, D.C. 20036.

Jessup, Claudia and Genie Chipps. *The Woman's Guide to Starting a Business*. New York: Holt, Rinehart and Winston, 1976. The first half deals with the practicalities of founding and running a business. In the second half, women who have their own businesses tell about their experiences. Lively and readable. Useful resource section.

Kryszak, Wayne D. *The Small Business Index*. Metuchen, N.Y.: The Scarecrow Press, 1978. An index to American and Canadian books, pamphlets, and periodicals which contain information on starting small businesses of various kinds. Gives an overview of the opportunities available.

U.S. Small Business Administration. Your local office of the SBA can advise you about the economic and business climate in your community, inform you about borrowing money, and direct you to business counselors. To find the address and telephone number of the SBA office nearest you look in the telephone book under U.S. Government.

Small Business Administration Publications. "Free Management Assistance Publications," a list of 60 free pamphlets published by the SBA. Write: U.S. Small Business Administration, 1441 L Street, NW, Washington, D.C. 20416. Ask for SBA 115A.

Another SBA publication, *Starting and Managing a Small Business of Your Own*, is a guide to buying, financing, and managing a business. Cost: $3.50. Write: Consumer Information Center, Pueblo, CO 81009.

Small Business Administration Loans. A new program for women of either direct or guaranteed loans. Intended to encourage women to set up or develop small businesses with less risk than they would take on their own. To find out how to qualify, contact your nearest SBA office, or write: Women in Business, Small Business Administration, 1441 L Street, NW, Washington, D.C. 20416.

9. Apprenticeships and Nontraditional Careers

Department of Labor, Women's Bureau. *A Woman's Guide to Apprenticeship*. Includes an overview of women and apprenticeship, a list of apprenticeable occupations, how to become an apprentice, and addresses of regional and state apprenticeship agencies and information centers. Free. Write: U.S. Department of Labor, Office of the Secretary, Women's Bureau, Washington, D.C. 20213.

Lederer, Muriel. *Blue Collar Jobs for Women*. New York: E. P. Dutton, 1979. Discusses the construction occupations, industrial production, mechanics and repairers, scientific and technical occupations, transportation, and other skilled job opportunities. Tells what training is necessary and how to find it, where to find out more about apprenticeships as well as agencies that will help you.

Mulligan, Kathryn L. *Internship Programs for Women*. Lists over 40 programs designed to help re-entry women, low-income women, and students. Cost: $3.00. Write: The National Society for Internships and Experiential Education, 1735 Eye Street, NW, Washington, D.C. 20006.

Renetzky, Alvin, editor-in-chief. *Directory of Internships, Work Experience Programs, and On-the-Job Training Opportunities*. Thousand Oaks, Calif.: Ready Reference Press, 1976. Includes an alphabetical listing plus appendices on Federal Job Information Centers and sources of apprenticeship information.

Splaver, Sarah. *Nontraditional Careers for Women*. New York: Julian Messner, 1973. Discusses over 500 careers for women, including medicine, mathematics, engineering, creative arts, business, manual trades, and government services. Addresses of professional organizations. Useful in obtaining detailed information about specific careers.

10. Resource Centers and Employment Programs

Catalyst has a national network of local resource centers. A state-by-state list is available free from Catalyst, 14 E. 60 Street, New York, NY 10022.

Federal Job Information Centers. The Office of Personnel Management offers federal employment information through a nationwide network of Federal Job Information centers. For answers to your questions about federal employment, you can visit, write, or call the nearest Federal Job Information Center. Call to request job announcements, application forms, and informational pamphlets. Some centers provide information regarding jobs in other jurisdictions.

Renetzky, Alvin, editor-in-chief. *Directory of Career Resources for Women.* Santa Monica, Calif.: Ready Reference Press, 1979. Covers private, non-profit women's organizations, social and community service agencies, college and university affiliated resource centers, YWCAs, independent consulting services, specialized employment agencies, and business and professional organizations. Also contains a Directory of Federal Job Information Centers. Covers reentry programs, career development seminars, displaced homemakers' programs, community referral services, assertiveness training, and career resource libraries. Useful and comprehensive.

The Women's Work Force of Wider Opportunities for Women, Inc. (WOW) has compiled and published a *National Directory of Women's Employment Programs: Who They Are; What They Do*, 1979. The directory lists the programs and services of 140 organizations and provides the names and addresses of contact persons. Listed by region: Northeast, South, Midwest, West. Cost: $7.50. Check your library or write: Wider Opportunities for Women, 1649 K Street, NW, Washington, D.C. 20006

11. Professional and Trade Organizations

Career Guide to Professional Associations. Cranston, R.I.: The Carroll Press, second edition, 1980. A directory of organizations by occupational field.

Colgate, Craig, and Patricia Broida, editors. *National Trade and Professional Associations of the United States and Canada and Labor Unions.* Washington, D.C.: Columbia Books, Inc., 13th edition, 1978. Lists about 6,000 national trade associations, labor unions, scientific or technical societies, and other national organizations in readable format. A letter or phone call to the appropriate organization executive can save time and laborious research.

"Professional Women's Groups," a list of approximately 100 organizations, and professional caucuses. Cost: 50¢. Write: The American Association of University Women, Sales Office, 2401 Virginia Avenue, NW, Washington, D.C. 20037. Orders must be prepaid.

12. Educational Opportunities

Gray, Eileen. *Everywoman's Guide to College*. Millbrae, Calif.: Les Femmes, 1975. Chapters include "The Difficult Decision to Become a Student," "How to Finance Yourself in School," "The Two-Year College—Its Many Advantages for Returning Women," "Choosing a Four-Year College," "Special Programs for Returning Women," and "Occupational Outlook for Women College Graduates Into the 1980s."

Lederer, Muriel. *The Guide to Career Education: If Not College, What?* New York: New York Times Book Company, revised 1976. For sources of training other than college. Each chapter includes a helpful reference section.

Renetzky, Alvin, editor-in-chief. *Directory of Career Training and Development Programs*. Santa Monica, Calif.: Ready Reference Press, 1980. A guide to career training and development opportunities available through business and industry, government agencies, and professional organizations.

Thompson, Frances Coombs, editor. *The New York Times Guide to Continuing Education in America*. New York: Quadrangle Books, 1972. A comprehensive guide prepared by the College Entrance Examination Board.

13. Financial Aid for Education

Business and Professional Women's Foundation, "Financial Aid: Where to Get It, How to Use It," is available free. Write: BPWF, 2012 Massachusetts Avenue, NW, Washington, D.C. 20036.

Clairol, Incorporated's Loving Care Scholarship Program, 345 Park Avenue, New York, NY 10022, offers a free booklet listing a variety of private and government funding sources for help with education costs.

Jawin, Ann J. *A Woman's Guide to Career Preparations: Scholarships, Grants and Loans*. New York: Anchor Books, 1979. A comprehensive guide to financial aid opportunities. Also includes chapters "For Women Who Have Never Worked" and "Finding a Career."

14. Dealing With Discrimination

Bird, Caroline. *Everything a Woman Needs to Know to Get Paid What She's Worth.* New York: David McKay, 1973. Question-and-answer format. A good handbook for women wishing to know how to deal with job-related inequities.

The Wage and Hour Division, Employment Standards Administration, U.S. Department of Labor, 14th Street and Constitution Avenue, NW, Washington, D.C. 20210, handles complaints involving the Equal Pay Act. Complaints should be taken to the nearest office. Consult the telephone directory under U.S. Government, Labor Department. The complainant's name is not revealed.

The Women's Action Almanac. A quick, up-to-date reference handbook that answers questions on sexual harassment, child support payments, pregnancy benefits and health care, making calls on Title IX complaints, etc. Each entry provides background information on each issue and lists pertinent books, magazines, and organizations. Cost: $9.95 hardcover, $7.95 paperback, plus 10 percent postage and handling. Check your local library or write: The Women's Action Alliance, 370 Lexington Avenue, New York, NY 10017.

Women's Bureau, U.S. Department of Labor. *A Working Woman's Guide to Her Job Rights,* 1978. Topics covered include employment services, minimum wage and overtime pay, union membership, maternity leave, tax credit for child care, pensions, etc. Also lists sources of assistance. Cost: $1.60. Write: Consumer Information Center, Pueblo, CO 81009. For a free list of other publications of the Women's Bureau write Women's Bureau, U.S. Department of Labor, 14th Street and Constitution Avenue, NW, Washington, D.C. 20210.

15. Vocational Resources of Particular Interest to Christians

Alexander, John W. *Managing Our Work.* Downers Grove, Ill.: InterVarsity Press, revised 1975. A practical guide to honoring God through managing our lives and our work wisely as good stewards. Emphasizes setting realistic objectives, goals, and standards, and adjusting our workload to match them. Includes a "Manager's Check List" and bibliography of books on general management, planning, organization, and motivation. Directed toward men.

The Christian College Referral Service. An organization of over forty Christian colleges which have joined in an effort to identify highly qualified candidates who want to teach in Christian colleges. Any Christian teacher who has completed an advanced degree may be listed through the service. Write: Christian College Referral Service, Wheaton College, Wheaton, IL 60187.

The Christian Leadership Letter. A monthly publication of World Vision International. For free subscription, write: 919 W. Huntington Drive, Monrovia, CA 91016. The first three years of *The Christian Leadership Letter* have been published as *The Art of Management for Christian Leaders.* The second three years are incorporated into *The Christian Executive.* Both books are by Ted W. Engstrom and Edward R. Dayton and are published by Word.

Christian Legal Society, PO Box 2069, Oak Park, IL 60603.

Christian Medical Society, 1616 Gateway Blvd., Richardson, TX 75080.

Christian Service Corporation. Trains and places skilled laymen and women in two-year assignments with mission organizations in the United States, Canada, and overseas. Write: 1509 Sixteenth Street, NW, Washington, D.C. 20036.

Dayton, Edward R., editor. *Mission Handbook.* Monrovia, Calif.: MARC, 11th edition, 1976. A guide to North American Protestant ministries overseas. For ordering information, write: MARC, 919 West Huntington Drive, Monrovia, CA 91016.

DeJong, Peter, and Donald R. Wilson. *Husband and Wife.* Grand Rapids, Mich.: Zondervan, 1979. Chapters on "The Social Cost of Traditional Sex Roles," "A Biblical Critique of Traditional Sex Roles," and "Implications of a Christian Sex-Role Structure" are relevant to the lives of married Christian women who work.

The Directory of Christian Work Opportunities. A comprehensive guide published semi-annually. Cost: $25.00 per year; $20.00 per single issue. To order or request information, write: Directory Order Department, Intercristo, PO Box 9323, Seattle, WA 98109.

The Ecumenical Women's Center. Offers programs on the life of women in the church, women in professional ministry, violence against women, and women in prison. For a list of resources, write: 1653 West School Street, Chicago, IL 60657.

Faith at Work's Women's Ministry: Wellspring. Sponsors special workshops to help women discover and nourish their gifts. For information,

write: Marie Moore, Faith at Work's Women's Ministry, 11065 Little
Patuxent Parkway, Columbia, MD 21044.

Field, David. *Taking Sides*. Downers Grove, Ill.: InterVarsity Press, 1976.
Contains a brief chapter on work (pages 82–102) which treats "The Bible
and Work," "Personal Attitudes," "Social Issues," and "Working
Relationships."

Fish, Sharon, and Judith Allen Shelly. *Spiritual Care: The Nurse's Role*.
Downers Grove, Ill.: InterVarsity Press, 1978. Written to help nurses
integrate their faith with their practice of nursing. Includes information on
a number of resources available to Christian nurses. A workbook is available which complements the text.

Hargleroad, Bobbi Wells, editor. *"Women's Work Is . . . "*. Chicago, Ill.:
Institute on the Church in Urban-Industrial Society, 1978. A resource
guide detailing the current status of women's work and women workers. It
illustrates how the church is involved in helping bring about justice for
women locally, internationally, and through congregations and coalitions.
The goal of the guide is to encourage ministries in these areas. Cost: $4.00.
Write: The Institute on the Church in Urban-Industrial Society, 5700 S.
Woodlawn Avenue, Chicago, IL 60637.

The Ligonier Valley Study Center. A resource center for Christian education directed by Dr. R. C. Sproul. The vocational process is central in a
couple of the center's programs, including the ten-week resident Leaping
Ahead Program on how to decide on one's life work and how to develop
one's gifts. The center also offers a pre-professional program in the social
sciences, weekend seminars, and cassette tapes. For information, write:
The Ligonier Valley Study Center, Stahlstown, PA 15687.

Miller, Arthur F., and Ralph T. Mattson. *The Truth About You*. Old Tap-
pan, N.J.: Fleming H. Revell, 1977. Emphasizes choosing your work on
the basis of your gifts and motivations.

Nurses Christian Fellowship. A branch of Intervarsity Christian Fellowship. Helps students and nurses to become aware of their potential as
Christians and to recognize their responsibilities for active participation in
the profession. Sponsors workshops, seminars, and conferences, publishes
Bible study guides for nurses, and publishes an issue-oriented bulletin
called "The Nurses Lamp." For information about NCF's ministries and
local chapters, write: Nurses Christian Fellowship, 233 Langdon Street,
Madison, WI 53703.

Scanzoni, Letha, and Nancy Hardesty. "The World Beyond the Home" in *All We're Meant to Be*. Waco, Texas: Word, 1974. A brief chapter on options available to Christian women and the conflicts faced by those who work outside the home.

Thompson Media, Stahlstown, PA 15687, distributes cassette tapes made during Jubilee 1980, a vocation-related conference sponsored by the Coalition for Christian Outreach in Pittsburgh. Outstanding Christian speakers addressed a number of vocations and work-related issues. A catalogue of these tapes will be sent upon request.

Value of the Person. An organization dedicated to the improvement of work-world relationships through the application of Christian values. Distributes a dramatic documentary film, "Miracle of Pittron," about the reconciliation between labor and management at a strife-torn steel foundry near Pittsburgh. The film is for use by corporations, businesses, colleges, churches, schools, etc. VAP also offers one- and two-day seminars designed to improve work life at all levels and tailored to meet the needs of particular companies and institutions. Write: Value of the Person, 52 Dutch Lane, Pittsburgh, PA 15236.

What Are We Doing With Our Work? The title and focus of the August 1979 issue of *The Other Side*.

White, Jerry and Mary White. *Your Job—Survival or Satisfaction*. Grand Rapids, Mich.: Zondervan, 1977. A schematic guide to work and work-related problems. There are two chapters directed toward women: "The Homemaker" and "The Working Woman."

NOTES

Introduction

Data about the labor force is from"Women in the Labor Force: Some New Data Series," report 575 of the Bureau of Labor Statistics (1979); "The Myth and the Reality" a fact-sheet produced by the Women's Bureau of the U.S. Department of Labor in 1973 and revised in 1974 (Washington: U.S. Government Printing Office, 1974); and *The Subtle Revolution: Women at Work*, ed. Ralph E. Smith (Washington: The Urban Institute, 1979).

1 Struggle and Hope

The material about economic hardship (page 21) is from the U.S. Department of Labor's "The Myth and the Reality" (1974). The reference on page 23 is to Robert Coles and Jane Hallowell Coles, *Women of Crisis: Lives of Struggle and Hope* (New York: Delacorte Press, 1978), especially to pages 233–234. Additional stories of working-class women can be found in Nancy Seifer, ed., *Nobody Speaks for Me! Self-Portraits of American Working Class Women* (New York: Simon and Schuster, 1976).

On the role of women and social factors and change (page 30), see Evelyne Sullerot, *Woman, Society and Change*, tr. Margaret Scotford Archer, World University Library (New York and Toronto: McGraw-Hill, 1971). Betty Friedan's *The Feminine Mystique* (New York: Dell, 1963) is the classic secular statement on the image of the ideal American woman in the post-World War II years.

The quotation on page 30 is from Carolyn Heilbrun, *Reinventing Womanhood* (New York: Norton, 1979), page 124; the quotation on page 31 is from Tom F. Driver, *Patterns of Grace: Human Experience as Word of God* (San

Francisco: Harper and Row, 1977), page 134. Colette Dowling gives a secular interpretation of women's fear of independence in "The Cinderella Syndrome," *The New York Times Magazine* (March 22, 1981), pages 47–50, 54, 56, 58, 60, 62; this article is adapted from her book, *The Cinderella Complex: Women's Hidden Fear of Independence* (New York: Summit Books, 1981).

2 Biblical Perspectives on Work

The reference to Linda Lavin on page 39 is from an interview in *Ms. Magazine*, 8 (May, 1980), page 48. The quotations on page 41 are from Studs Terkel, *Working* (New York: Avon Books, 1975), page xiii, and E. F. Schumacher, *Good Work* (New York: Harper and Row, 1979), page 27. The quotation on page 42 is from Abraham Maslow, *Eupsychian Management*, reprinted in *The Future of Work*, ed. Fred Best (Englewood, New Jersey: Prentice-Hall, 1973), page 26. A standard study of motivation and worker satisfaction (page 42) is *The Motivation to Work*, 2nd ed. (New York: John Wiley, 1959), by Frederick Herzberg, Bernard Mausner, and Barbara Snyderman. The reference on page 44 is to Judith M. Bardwick, *Psychology of Women, A Study of Bio-Cultural Conflicts* (New York: Harper and Row, 1971), particularly pages 190–202.

The material on page 50 is based in part on the following sources: Alan Richardson, *The Biblical Doctrine of Work* (London: SCM Press, 1952); John R. W. Stott, "Reclaiming the Biblical Doctrine of Work," *Christianity Today* (May 4, 1979), pages 36–37; Dorothy L. Sayers, "Why Work?" in *Creed or Chaos* (New York: Harcourt Brace, 1949), pages 46–62, and *Are Women Human?* (Downers Grove, Illinois: InterVarsity Press, 1971); C. S. Lewis, "Good Work and Good Works" in *The World's Last Night* (New York and London: Harcourt Brace Jovanovich, 1973), pages 71–81; Joyce Baldwin, "How to Create a Woman," *His*, 33 (May, 1973), pages 7–9, 18; and Nancy M. Tischler, *Legacy of Eve: Women of the Bible* (Atlanta: John Knox, 1977).

Background for pages 50–52 is found in Daniel-Rops, *Daily Life in Palestine at the Time of Christ*, tr. Patrick O'Brien (London: Weidenfeld and Nicolson, 1962), pages 127–137; the article "gune" in Albrecht Oepke, *Theological Dictionary of the New Testament*, ed. Gerhard Kittel, tr. Geoffrey W. Bromiley, I (Grand Rapids, Michigan: Eerdmans, 1964), pages 776–789; and Simone de Beauvoir, *The Second Sex*, tr. H. M. Parshley (New York: Bantam Books, 1961), pages 56–128.

One of the most authoritative discussions of the issues on pages 52–54 is Krister Stendahl's *The Bible and the Role of Women*, tr. Emilie T. Sander (Philadelphia: Fortress Press, 1966).

3 Vocation

Material on page 60 is from Richardson, *The Biblical Doctrine of Work*, pages 35–39.

Pages 61–62 make use of Leland Ryken's "Puritan Work Ethic: The Dignity of Life's Labors" in *Christianity Today* (October 19, 1979), pages 14–19. Ryken cites the passages from Luther and Calvin.

Donald Dayton discusses some of the denominations which early supported the ordination of women (referred to on pages 63–64) in "The Evangelical Roots of Feminism" in *Discovering an Evangelical Heritage* (New York: Harper and Row, 1976), pages 85–98. The reference to Judith Bardwick on page 65 is to *Psychology of Women: A Study of Biocultural Conflicts* (New York: Harper & Row, 1971), page 18.

Other stories of women like Shirley (pages 63–67) who have struggled with their call to ministry within the church are available in Virginia Hearn's *Our Struggle to Serve* (Waco, Texas: Word Books, 1979).

The quotation from Gordon Cosby on page 68 is cited in Howard A. Snyder, *The Problem of Wine Skins: Church Structure in a Technological Age* (Downers Grove, Illinois: InterVarsity Press, 1975), page 132. Snyder summarizes the views of Ray C. Stedman, David R. Mains, Robert Girard, and Elizabeth O'Connor in his chapter, "The Place of Spiritual Gifts," pages 129–138. Material in the section on gifts is also drawn from Rick Yohn, *Discover Your Spiritual Gift and Use It* (Wheaton, Illinois: Tyndale, 1977)

Patricia Mortenson's article, "The Role of Women in Missions," referred to and cited on pages 72–73, is found in *Gospel in Context*, 2 (April, 1979), pages 28–31.

4 The Touch of Life

Material on pages 88–91 is based on Letty M. Russell, *Human Liberation in a Feminist Perspective—A Theology* (Philadelphia: Westminster Press, 1974); Carolyn W. Sherif, "Dreams and Dilemmas of Being a Woman Today" in *Women in Librarianship*, ed. Margaret Myers and Myra Scarborough (New Brunswick, New Jersey: Bureau of Library and Information Science, Rutgers University Graduate School of Library Science, 1975), pages 23–45; Sandra L. Bem and Daryl J. Bem, *Training the Woman to Know Her Place: The Social Antecedents of Women in the World of Work* (Harrisburg: Pennsylvania Department of Education, 1973); and Dorothy Jongeward and Dru Scott, *Women as Winners* (Reading, Massachusetts, and Menlo Park, California: Addison-Wesley Publishing Company, 1976).

The list of qualities of the traditional woman on pages 89–90 is adapted from Helen de Rosis, *Women and Anxiety* (New York: Delacorte Press, 1979), pages 74–75, and is used by permission.

The information on page 90 regarding pink-collar jobs and patterns of working is from Louise Kapp Howe, *Pink Collar Workers: Inside the World of Women's Work* (New York: G. P. Putnam's Sons, 1977), pages 21–22 and 262–263.

5 Creativity and Work

The following sources were useful in the preparation of this chapter: Abraham H. Maslow, "Creativity in Self-Actualizing People," *Toward a Psychology of Being*, 2nd edition (New York: D. Van Nostrand, 1968); John A. Sanford, *Healing and Wholeness* (New York: Paulist Press, 1977); Elizabeth O'Connor, *Our Many Selves* (New York: Harper and Row, 1971) and *Eighth Day of Creation: Gifts and Creativity* (Waco, Texas: Word Books, 1971); Judith Bardwick, "Women and Creativity," *Psychology of Women;* and *The New Orpheus, Essays Toward a Christian Poetic*, ed. Nathan A. Scott, Jr. (New York: Sheed and Ward, 1964).

6 Facing Change

Material on pages 129–132 is based on Gail Sheehy, *Passages* (New York: Bantam Books, 1977); Erik H. Erikson, *Identity and the Life Cycle* (New York: W. W. Norton, 1980); Paula I. Robbins, *Successful Midlife Career Change: Self-Understanding and Strategies for Action* (New York: Amacom, 1978); and Paul Tournier, *The Seasons of Life*, tr. John S. Gilmour (Atlanta: John Knox Press, 1977).

The quotation on page 145 dealing with the stress of women reentering the work force is from Emily Greenspan, "Work Begins at 35," *The New York Times Magazine* (July 6, 1980), page 22. The entire article runs from pages 21–27.

The material on support groups is drawn, in part, from *Support Systems and Mutual Help: Multidisciplinary Exploration*, ed. Gerald Caplan and Marie Killilea (New York, San Francisco, London: Grune and Stratton, 1976). The definition by Caplan, quoted on page 148, is cited in the book on page 41.

7 Coping

The material on time management (page 156) is adapted from Charles Hummel, "Budgeting Our Time" in *Guidelines for Faculty Ministry:*

InterVarsity Faculty Handbook (Madison, Wisconsin: InterVarsity Christian Fellowship, 1979), section I, 6.

Rosemary Ruether discusses the issues of the workday and workweek in "Working Women and the Male Workday," *Christianity and Crisis*, 37 (February 7, 1977), pages 3–8. The quotes we give on page 160 are found on pages 5 and 6 of this article. A follow-up article, with examples drawn from California by Sydney Thomson Brown, is in *Christianity and Crisis* (February 21, 1977), pages 26–29. Information regarding municipal workers in Los Angeles and San Francisco (pages 160–161) is from an Associated Press wire story by Robert Billott, August 27, 1980.

Material on pages 162–164 is based in part on Helen de Rosis, *Women and Anxiety* (New York: Delacorte Press, 1979); Florence Seaman and Anne Lorimer, *Winning at Work* (Philadelphia: Running Press, 1979); Marilyn Machlowitz, *Workaholics; Living With Them, Working With Them* (Reading, Massachusetts, and Menlo Park, California: Addison-Wesley, 1980); and Josef Pieper, *Leisure, the Basis of Culture*, tr. Alexander Dru (New York: Pantheon Books, 1964).

The report of findings about the effects of maternal employment on children (pages 167–168) is drawn from the chapter "Effects on Child" by Lois Wladis Hoffman in *Working Mothers*, ed. Lois Wladis Hoffman and F. Ivan Nye (San Francisco: Jossey-Bass, 1974), pages 126–166.

Pages 168–169 on child care utilize the chapter "Coping with Child Care: The Working Mother" by Karen Hill Scott in *New Life Options: The Working Woman's Resource Book* (New York: McGraw Hill, 1976), pages 307–324. Scott gives an inventory for rating child-care centers on pages 318–320.

Some of the discussion of working couples (pages 169–171) is from Francine S. Hall and Douglas T. Hall, *The Two-Career Couple* (Reading, Massachusetts, and Menlo Park, California: Addison-Wesley, 1979), pages 28–53.

The section on anxiety (pages 171–175) makes use of de Rosis, as well as Barrie S. Greiff and Preston K. Munter, *Tradeoffs: Executive, Family, and Organizational Life* (New York: New American Library, 1980).

The discussion of assertiveness (pages 175–178) is based in part on John Scanzoni, "Assertiveness for Christian Women," *Christianity Today* (June 4, 1976), pages 16–18; R. E. Alberti and M. L. Emmons, *Your Perfect Right* (San Luis Obispo, California: Impact, 1974); and M. J. Smith, *When I Say No I Feel Guilty* (New York: The Dial Press, 1975).

8   Working Within Organizations

The quotation and material on pages 180–181 is from Rosabeth Moss Kanter, *Men and Women of the Corporation* (New York: Basic Books, 1977), pages 250–253. In *The Managerial Woman* (New York: Pocket Books, 1978), pages 21–54, Hennig and Jardim discuss the varying perceptions of men and women with respect to careers and organizational behavior.

On patrimony and secretaries (page 182) see Kanter, pages 73–77. The quotation on pages 182–183 is cited by Michael Korda in *Male Chauvinism! How It Works* (New York: Random House, 1973), page 19.

Kanter's definition of power quoted on page 183 is found in *Men and Women of the Corporation* (page 166). She has an excellent chapter on power (pages 164–205).

The work by Piaget referred to on page 184 is one of a number of studies relating to women and competition cited by Georgia Sassen in "Success Anxiety in Women: A Constructivist Interpretation of Its Source and Significance" in the *Harvard Educational Review*, 50 (February, 1980), pages 13–24. The citation from Sassen, on page 185, is on page 19 of the article.

The study of Harvard's M.B.A.'s referred to on page 185 is summarized in *The Managerial Woman*, pages 99–100.

The quotation from Sassen on page 187 is taken from page 22 of her article.

The description of how women see themselves (pages 187–188) is taken from *The Managerial Woman*, page 208–210.

The quotation from Kanter on page 190 is found on page 47 of her book. She discusses tokenism in detail on pages 206–242.

Robert K. Greenleaf's *Servant Leadership, A Journey into the Nature of Legitimate Power and Greatness* (New York: Paulist Press, 1977) is an important discussion of leadership from a religious perspective, relating to the material on pages 191–192.

The statistics on page 192 are taken from "Women in the Labor Force: Some New Data Series," U.S. Department of Labor, report 575 (1979) and *The Managerial Woman;* the statistics on page 193 are from Roberta Gunner, "Survey Totals: Employment of Women in Christian Organizations," mimeographed (Minneapolis, Minnesota).

The discussion of the stereotypic roles of women (pages 193–194) is based in part on Kanter, pages 233–237.

Hennig and Jardim discuss style and relationships (page 194) on pages 197–207 of *The Managerial Woman*.

The material on sexual harassment (pages 195–197) is based in part on Lin Farley, *Sexual Shakedown: Sexual Harassment of Women at Work* (New York: McGraw-Hill, 1978); "Title VII Sexual Harassment Guidelines and Educational Employment," a paper published by the Project on the Status and Education of Women of the Association of American Colleges; and "Taking the Risk" in *Kaleidoscope*, newsletter in field and cooperative education of Gordon College, 1, no. 5 (Spring, 1980).

The lengthy quotations from Betsy Ancker-Johnson on pages 206 and 207 are from a paper, "Women in Physics," given in 1971 at a meeting of the American Physical Society and reprinted in the *Annals of the New York Academy of Science*, 208 (March 15, 1973), pages 23–28.

9 Old and New Choices

The reference to Robert K. Greenleaf's view of the church on page 214 is from *Servant Leadership*, pages 79–82, 218–248.

On the matter of career-counseling and the local church (page 215) see Darryl D. Larramore, "Career Counseling as Church Ministry," *Christianity Today* (September 19, 1980), pages 30–31.

Kanter's article quoted on page 215 is "Work in a New America," *Daedalus* (Winter, 1978), pages 47–78. The citation is from pages 53–54.

Some of the information on Dr. Perkins (pages 216–217) is based on an article by Vivian Codden, "For 50 Years in Weather Fair and Foul," *Physician's World* 3 (March, 1975), pages 53–56. The story on pages 216–217 is quoted from page 54 of the article.